English Renaissance Song

Twayne's English Authors Series

Arthur F. Kinney, Editor

University of Massachusetts, Amherst

TEAS 424

English Renaissance Song

By Edward Doughtie

Rice University

Twayne Publishers • Boston

English Renaissance Song

Edward Doughtie

Copyright © 1986 by G. K. Hall & Co.
All Rights Reserved
Published by Twayne Publishers
A Division of G. K. Hall & Co.
70 Lincoln Street
Boston, Massachusetts 02111

Copyediting supervised by Lewis DeSimone
Book production by Elizabeth Todesco
Book design by Barbara Anderson

Typeset in 11 pt. Garamond
by Compset, Inc., Beverly, Massachusetts

Printed on permanent/durable acid-free paper
and bound in the United States of America

Library of Congress Cataloging in Publication Data

Doughtie, Edward, 1935–
    English Renaissance song.

    (Twayne's English authors series; TEAS 424)
    Bibliography: p. 166
    Includes index.
    1. Music and literature.   2. Vocal music—England—
16th century—Texts—History and criticism.   3. Vocal
music—England—17th century—Texts—History and
criticism.   I. Title   II. Series.
ML3849.D7   1986   784.3'00942   85-27238
ISBN 0-8057-6915-3

Contents

Editor's Note

A literary scholar who is also a critic of music possesses a rare combination of talents, but Edward Doughtie, who is equally at home in the fields of poetry and song, is eminently qualified to write on both subjects. The result is a comprehensive and lucid book on the development of English song verse during the Renaissance, that glorious, golden age of English poetry as well as English song. Doughtie's analysis of the difficulties in adjusting the rhythms of English poetry to the rhythms of Western music, his history of how humanism promoted English song verse before subsequent decades separated the two art forms once again, and his summaries of the important poets and composers who contributed to the development of a significant body of songs—from airs to madrigals—is unique: here in one compact study is a work both full in its treatment of issues and ample in its specific illustrations, accessible even to those whose knowledge of poetic meter or music is limited. His discussions of the theories of Gascoigne and the poems of Sidney and Spenser show how they were pioneers in these merging art forms; Doughtie also provides illuminating accounts of the poet-composer Thomas Whythorne, William Byrd and the consort song, Thomas Morley and the English madrigal, John Dowland and the English air, and the work of England's best-known poet-composer Thomas Campion, whose contributions—and whose shortcomings—are here delineated sharply for the first time. This book will stand the test of time as the premier introductory study in a central, if difficult, area of Renaissance achievement.

—Arthur F. Kinney

About the Author

Edward Doughtie, born in 1935, earned degrees from Duke and Harvard universities, and is professor of English at Rice University, where he has taught since 1963. His publications include *Lyrics from English Airs, 1596–1622* (1970), *Liber Lilliati: Elizabethan Verse and Song* (1985), and articles on Renaissance song, the earl of Essex, and James Dickey. He served as editor of *Studies in English Literature 1500–1900* from 1973 to 1978, and began another five-year term in 1985.

Preface

Most students of the English Renaissance are now aware that the period was as rich in music as in literature. Thanks to an abundance of excellent recordings over the last twenty years or so, songs of Morley and Dowland are almost as familiar as poems of Shakespeare and Donne. And since a large body of this music is vocal music that uses English verse, it should have particular interest to literary students. I have chosen to study songs of the period framed by the activities of two poets who wrote music for their own verse, Thomas Whythorne and Thomas Campion. During this time, both verse and music underwent significant changes, both individually and in relation to each other. One of the purposes of this book is to explore the mutual influences of music and poetry on each other during this period. One specific subtopic of this influence is the possible effect of music on the important developments in metrics in the sixteenth century. Much of the book will consist of examinations of specific songs exploring how verse and music interact.

It is difficult to cover every relevant topic in enough detail to satisfy both literary and musical readers, even though the book is aimed primarily at the first group. Discussion of the use of song in the plays and masques of the period is limited to a few references in chapters 4 and 7. For more on song in the drama, interested readers should consult works listed in the bibliography, especially those by Bowden, Cutts, Long, Orgel, Sabol, Seng, Shapiro, and Sternfeld.

In quotations I take the texts as I find them, and give modern spelling or old spelling with modernized *i, j, s, u,* and *v.* Rather than swell the notes with references to the sources of each song cited, I give in the text, in parentheses, the year of its publication and the number it bears in that publication. From this information, an individual song may be found in several sources, from the original to various modern editions, all of which are listed in the bibliography. Unless noted otherwise, the verbal texts are quoted from the original books or from *English Madrigal Verse.* Most musical examples are quoted from the original songbooks. Whenever possible I use the original note values in musical examples, but I silently change all clefs to the modern treble and bass clefs. Most references are given in short form in the notes or parenthetically in the text; full citations may be found in the bibliography.

A number of people have helped me with this project, and they have my sincere thanks. Arthur Kinney suggested that I write a study on this topic for Twayne, and has been patient and supportive. My chairman, Alan Grob, and my dean, Allen Matusow, arranged for a Mellon grant which gave me time to write. Kathlyne Evans helped with the bibliography, and Nancy Bosworth, Rene White, and Nancy Dahlberg helped with the final copy of the text. Monroe Spears read all, Jeffrey Kurtzman most, and Philip Brett and Frank Fabry read parts of the manuscript with attention and good will, and saved me from a number of blunders; those that are still evident are of course my own. I have learned a great deal from the writings and conversation of Mark Booth, Isabelle Ganz, S. K. Heninger, John Hollander, Elise Jorgens, Richard Peterson, Diana Poulton, John Ward, and Seth Weiner. The giant on whose shoulders I am trying to climb is my old mentor, Bruce Pattison, whose pioneering *Music and Poetry of the English Renaissance* (1948) still defines many of the issues and problems of the subject, and remains the best introduction. I regret that Louise Schleiner's *The Living Lyre in English Verse* appeared too late for me to make use of it.

The support of my wife, Andrea, has been essential, and for that and many other things I am grateful as always.

Finally, I should like to thank Stainer and Bell, Ltd., and Galaxy Music Corporation for permission to quote examples 4.1–3 from Philip Brett's edition of *Consort Songs,* and example 4.6 from *The Byrd Edition,* edited by E. H. Fellowes and Philip Brett, vol. 15. Thanks to the Huntington Library for permission to edit the musical examples in chapter 3 from their copy of Thomas Whythorne's *Songes;* to the editors of *Renaissance Quarterly* for permission to quote example 5.1 from Frank Fabry's "Sidney's Verse Adaptations to Two Sixteenth-Century Italian Art Songs"; to Oxford University Press for permission to quote texts from *English Madrigal Verse,* edited by E. H. Fellowes, revised by F. W. Sternfeld and David Greer (1968); to the editors of *Criticism* for permission to use revised portions of my article on Campion in chapter 8; to Breitkopf & Härtel, Wiesbaden, for permission to quote from Luca Marenzio's *Sämtliche Werke,* ed. Alfred Einstein, in chapter 5; and to Gruppo Editoriale Fabbri Bompiani for permission to quote from Alfredo Obertello's *Madrigali Italiani in Inghilterra* in chapter 5.

Edward Doughtie

Rice University

Chronology

1600   Airs by Dowland, Morley, and Jones; madrigals by Weelkes; *England's Helicon.*

1601   Airs by Rosseter, Campion, and Jones; Morley's *Triumphes of Oriana;* songs by Carlton.

1602   *A Poetical Rhapsody.*

1603   Accession of King James I; airs by Dowland; Morley dies.

1606   Airs by Bartlet, Coprario, and Danyel; madrigals by East; songs by Alison.

1607   Airs by Ford and Hume; madrigals by Jones.

1608   Madrigals by Weelkes and Youll.

1609   Airs by Jones and Ferrabosco; madrigals by Wilbye; songs by Ravenscroft; Shakespeare's *Sonnets.*

1610   Robert Dowland's *A Musicall Banquet;* airs by Corkine and Jones; songs and madrigals by East.

1611   Byrd's *Psalmes, Songs and Sonnets;* airs by Maynard; songs by Ravenscroft.

1612   Airs by Corkine and John Dowland, songs by Gibbons.

1613   Airs by Campion and Coprario; madrigals by Lichfild, Pilkington, and Ward.

1617   Airs by Campion.

1620   Martin Peerson's *Private Musicke;* Campion dies.

1622   Airs by Attey, madrigals by Tomkins.

1623   Byrd, Rosseter, and Weelkes die.

1626   John Dowland dies.

1627   John Hilton's *Ayres, Or, Fa Las.*

1630   Peerson's *Mottects.*

1632   Walter Porter's *Madrigals and Ayres.*

Abbreviations

A   alto, altus

B   bass, bassus

C   cantus

Ct   contratenor

EETS   Early English Text Society

ELS   Fellowes, Edmund H., ed. *The English Lute-Songs*. Revised by Thurston Dart et al. 1st ser., 19 vols.; 2nd ser., 20 vols. London: Stainer & Bell, 1920–71.

EM   Fellowes, Edmund H., ed. *The English Madrigalists*. Revised by Thurston Dart et al. 37 vols. London: Stainer & Bell, 1913–24, 1956–76.

EMV Fellowes, Edmund H., ed. *English Madrigal Verse, 1588–1632*. 3d ed., rev. Frederick W. Sternfeld and David Greer. Oxford: Clarendon Press, 1968.

JAMS *Journal of the American Musicological Society.*

LEA Doughtie, Edward, ed. *Lyrics from English Airs 1596–1622*. Cambridge, Mass.: Harvard University Press, 1970.

M   medius

STC Pollard, A. W., and Redgrave, G. R. *A Short-Title Catalogue of Books Printed in England, Scotland, and Ireland 1475-1640*. 1926. 2d. ed., rev. W. A. Jackson, F. S. Ferguson, and Katherine F. Pantzer. Vol. 2, I–Z only. London: Bibliographical Society, 1976.

T   tenor

Tx   triplex (treble)

Chapter One
Music and Poetry

If Musicke and sweet Poetrie agree,
As they must needs (the Sister and the brother)
Then must the love be great twixt thee and me,
Because thou lov'st the one, and I the other.
Dowland to thee is deere, whose heavenly tuch
Upon the Lute, dooth ravish humane sense:
Spenser to me, whose deepe Conceit is such,
As passing all conceit, needs no defence.
Thou lov'st to heare the sweet melodious sound,
That Phoebus Lute (the Queene of Musicke) makes:
And I in deepe Delight am chiefly drownd,
When as himselfe to singing he betakes.
   One God is God of both (as Poets faine)
   One Knight loves Both, and both in thee remaine.

Richard Barnfield's famous sonnet from *The Passionate Pilgrim* (1599) is not the advertisement for Elizabethan song that it is often taken to be. It is almost self-destructing—or self-deconstructing. Although it assumes the close relationship between music and poetry, and uses this relationship to describe a sympathetic closeness between the poet and his addressee, the poem contains some subversive ironies. The opening analogy of brother and sister is conventional, but the conditional syntax may allow the thought that Elizabethan siblings got along no better than modern ones, except under compulsion; there are times when they must needs agree. The poem goes on to describe the speaker's friendship, not in terms of song, but of the lute music of Dowland and the poetry of Spenser. Although Dowland was a great composer of songs, the role in which Barnfield presents him is that of the virtuoso instrumentalist. Spenser was a great master of poetic sound but wrote very little that was actually sung. The reference to Phoebus's singing in line twelve is, like Spenser's oaten pipe, only a conventional expression for poetry.

We are reminded, therefore, that by the end of the sixteenth century music and poetry had mature, separate identities. Paradoxically, it is this separation that helped make possible the Renaissance ideal of their unity. Analysis, or understanding of the component elements, made clear what each art demanded of the other, and made possible the self-conscious, deliberate joining of the two that is found in the most characteristic Renaissance songs. At the same time, the challenge to a revered ancient ideal by the actual independence of the arts may have stimulated both propaganda and practical efforts for their union.

The historical circumstances of the union—or rather reunion—of music and poetry will be explored in the next chapter; for the present, I should like to examine some of the general features of each art that come into play when they are joined in song. Almost every point I will make oversimplifies some knotty issue in aesthetics or literary and musical theory. I will try to hint at what some of these issues are, and mention works which will treat them more thoroughly.[1] Some questions will be raised again in later chapters.

Music and Language

Music and language have long been sources of analogies in describing each other. "Music is heightened speech," says one commonplace. We often hear of the musical qualities of a language, or of a composer's tonal vocabulary. Leonard Bernstein (1976) even proposes a grammar of music based on an analogy with transformational grammar, and George Steiner sees setting words to music as a form of translation (1975, 414–25).[2] There are some genuine parallels that underlie such analogies.

Both music and language share the concepts of the sentence or period, and the phrase. The phrase in both is a unit that is recognizably separate, and the separation is indicated by a pause; but it is not a complete or independent unit, as the sentence is. The sentence or period is grammatically complete; in music, it is closed by a full cadence (a tonic cadence, at least in its immediate context).

Music and poetry are both temporal arts—or rather occurrent or serial arts (Johnson, 1972, 2). A painting or a sculpture may reward time spent in study, but such a work can be experienced on one level in a single moment of perception. A poem or a sonata must be read or heard via a series of perceptions. Both poem and sonata can be read silently by anyone who understands the symbols that record them; they may both be experienced aurally when they are performed or recited by others. But both experiences, silent and audible, are sequential: one part of the experience necessarily follows another in an order determined by the artist (except in some modern experimental works). Both also depend to some degree on memory for their effects. As serial, audible arts, music and poetry both have rhythm. Both sometimes have meter. The distinctions between these two terms are often confused because they are used in both music and poetry. I will first offer definitions that seem to fit both arts. Rhythm refers to the time relationship among sounds in sequence. Any series of words, however stressed, and any series of notes, long or short, must have rhythm. Meter, in the traditional view, is a regular pattern that can be perceived, if it is present, underlying the rhythm. We now have to divide the arts in order to illustrate these definitions. "Four score and seven years ago" has rhythm, but not meter. The rhythm of Shakespeare's "When to the sessions of sweet silent thought" has stressed syllables juxtaposed ("sweet silent"); but the metrical pattern, abstracted from the sonnet as a whole, is the familiar iambic pentameter, with regularly alternating stressed and unstressed syllables. Rhythmic patterns and an established meter do not necessarily coincide. In music, the rhythm of the first line of Thomas Campion's "I care not for these ladies" (Rosseter 1601, pt. 1, no. 3) is as follows (Ex. 1.1):

Example 1.1

♩ ♩ ♩ ♩ ♩ ♩. ♩ ♩

The meter (in modern terms) is ¾, or three quarter notes to a repeated group. In triple time, the grouping of three is indicated by an accent on the first beat.

The term "beat" in the last sentence leads to more definition and to the realization that the further this discussion continues, the more division between music and poetry will be necessary. In music, the beat is a pulse in a metric context. A pulse is "one of a series of regularly recurring, precisely equivalent stimuli. Like the ticks of a metronome or a watch, pulses mark off equal units in the temporal continuum" (Cooper and Meyer, 1960, 6). All pulses are not necessarily audible, but they are felt. When the pulses are grouped in twos or multiples thereof, we have duple meter; in threes, triple meter. Duple meter may be perceived without audible accent, just as we perceive the pulses of a clock to be duple when we refer to its "tick-tock." (To confuse the issue further, one can subdivide the pulses into twos or threes; thus

⁶/₈ time is still duple meter, but is "compounded" into two groups of threes.) In poetry, the pulse is noticeable when accents coincide with it and fall at regular intervals, as in some folk verse ("Pease porridge hot"), or in some uses of meter like poulters' measure or that of "Hiawatha" that encourage singsong performance; in sophisticated poetry obvious regularity of accent is generally considered a flaw.

The reader might have remarked that the symbols used to indicate meter and rhythm in music are capable of great precision. Why not use them to indicate the meter and rhythm of verse? Although musical annotation of verse has been tried many times, it is not successful because it is *too* precise, especially about the pitch and length of sound. English verse, like the language itself, relies on stress more than on pitch or quantity. For that reason, the meter and rhythm of Campion's "I care not for these ladies" cannot be fully represented by Campion's own notes. The following musical rhythms are just as faithful to the verse rhythm as Campion's—more faithful in some respects (Ex. 1.2):

Example 1.2

I   care   not   for   these   la- dies

All have in common the coincidence of verbal stress and downbeat. The last version, by suppressing the stress on "for," elevates a possible speech rhythm over poetic meter. None draws out "ladies" so that the second syllable falls on a strong beat. But none is necessarily better than Campion's.

Although musical scansion of verse has severe limitations, musical analysis can sometimes usefully borrow prosodic terms. Grosvenor Cooper and Leonard Meyer (1960, 6), for instance, differentiate rhythmic groupings in music according to the names of the classical poetic feet: iamb, anapest, trochee, dactyl, and amphibrach. We may recall that ancient music in fact had no indications of time, but took its rhythm from that of the verse; St. Augustine's *De Musica* also assumes this identity.

Form

Much music throughout Western culture has taken its form from poetry. A line of verse frequently determines a musical phrase; cadences fall on rhymes, and a completed melody coincides with a stanza. Many, if not most, extant songs in Western music embody these parallels. In some songs they are maintained more strictly than in others. In strophic songs, the melody is repeated more or less exactly, while the words of the stanza change; but the principle of formal repetition is maintained in the verse as well as the music in that the number and length of lines, as well as the rhyme scheme, remain the same in all stanzas. (Special cases like the Pindaric ode or the French fixed forms need not detain us here.) In the other main song form, the through-composed song *(durchkomponiertes Lied),* each line of the text is set to fresh music. This procedure is more common in complex musical forms, such as the motet and the madrigal, and in solo songs after the sixteenth century. The verse used in these songs may be strophic, or it may be a single stanza in a form that strophic poems use. But often the text is a nonstrophic form such as the sonnet, the verse madrigal, or a stichic series, such as couplets—or prose, as in liturgical music.

Each of these formal possibilities has advantages and disadvantages. In strophic form, the repeated music provides considerable formal security. There is a satisfying incremental quality when the returning melody brings new words, when the new comes wrapped in the familiar. For the composer, a relatively short stanza (four to eight lines) can generate a melody that has a readily perceptible—and memorable— shape. But if the poem is long, and the same music is repeated eight or ten times, all but the very best tunes will begin to pall, and the text must help keep the listener's attention engaged. If the mood of the text shifts drastically, the music may seem inappropriate—though there is a tendency for the music to be felt as more generalized and more independent the more it is repeated. Further problems arise when the verbal syntax does not match the form. If there is enjambment, or a pause in the middle of a line, the composer must chose between form and syntax. If he chooses to make the music follow the syntax in one stanza, the fit may be awkward in later stanzas if the syntax is not the same. If he chooses to follow the form, the distortions in the way the listener perceives the syntax may make him misunderstand the words. John Dowland's "Come heavy sleepe" (1597, no. 20) illustrates several of these difficulties, and another song by Dowland, "The lowest trees

have tops" (1603, no. 19) shows how the consequences may sometimes
be ludicrous. In the first stanza of the latter song, the music follows
the syntax of the line "Seas have their source, and so have shallowe
springs" by pausing after "source." But the corresponding line in the
next stanza reads "True hearts have eyes and eares, no tongues to
speake." When this is sung with the pause after the fourth syllable,
the meaning seems to be that hearts have eyes, but ears do not have
tongues.

In the through-composed form, the composer can match musical
and verbal phrases exactly, and can also respond in more detail to nuances of meaning and feeling in the text. The challenge to the composer of a through-composed song is to give the listener a sense of
musical form, of unity and continuity. The rounded, brief, repeated
melody of strophic song produces this sense of form with almost au-
tomatic ease; through-composed songs depend on several other strategies. In polyphonic forms like the madrigal, points of imitation,
sequential passages, and other kinds of repetition, including formal
repetition of whole sections, help give this sense of form, as can imitative passages linking analogous or contrasting segments. Solo forms,
especially the continuo songs of the seventeenth century, must depend
more on a sense of continuity, of thrusting forward to a climax or series
of climaxes. In "In darknesse let mee dwell" (1610, no. 10), John
Dowland uses an eclectic blend of old and new strategies to create an
example of a highly successful solo song:

> In darknesse let mee dwell, The ground shall sorrow be,
> The roofe Dispaire to barre all cheerfull light from mee,
> The wals of marble blacke that moistned still shall weepe,
> My musicke hellish jarring sounds to banish friendly sleepe.
> Thus wedded to my woes, And bedded to my Tombe,
> O Let me living die, Till death doe come,
> In darknesse let mee dwell.

The song begins with a long, drawn-out, but distinctive phrase. Dowland develops the song with imitation between the voice and instrumental accompaniment, and conveys a growing sense of agitation by
using dissonances and shorter note values, repeating some of the verbal
phrases, until (after a quieter contrasting section) he reaches a climax
in a dramatic outburst on "O Let me living die, Till death doe come."
He then returns to the opening phrase, ingeniously reinforcing the
text's image of despair as a prison, as well as rounding off the form.

But in this song the form of the poem is completely lost in the repetitions of words, and the meter is hidden in the wide range of note values used. In this instance, loss is gain, for the meter of the poem is an awkward mix of clumsy hexameters and poulters' measure. In other songs, the trade-off is not so positive.

It is possible to find mixed forms, especially in later music, as well as balanced ABA forms such as the *aria da capo*. One of the more interesting exceptions to the two main approaches is that of a song that originated as a dance, a pavan. John Dowland's "Lachrymae," like other pavans, consists of three repeated sections. When Dowland or an anonymous poet fitted words to this music ("Flow my tears," 1600, no. 2), the results were unlike any other poem, for the first two stanzas, written to fit the music of the repeated first section, are unlike the next two stanzas for the middle section. The last stanza, also different, is repeated whole. The meter is also oddly irregular in places. No poet at this time would have whimsically written two stanzas in one form, two in another, and one more in yet another form, unless he had to fit some predetermined pattern such as that provided by the music.

The practice of fitting words to a tune, instead of the reverse, has important implications for song form. Most of the time the results are not so striking as they are in "Lachrymae," and most of the songs written in this way are broadside ballads, popular songs only indirectly of concern to this study. But there are some important songs by Sir Philip Sidney composed in this manner, and a few more of the lutenist airs were originally dance tunes. As we shall see in the fifth chapter, the experience of fitting English words to foreign music had some effect on English verse as well as song. Later, Robert Burns and Thomas Moore would compose their poems to preexisting tunes, and we still find these *contrafacta* in popular song, parodies, and commercials. If in ordinary poetry the meter is the pattern against which the poet arranges his rhythms, in *contrafacta* the tune in effect becomes the meter. Some tunes can be more demanding than meter, since they control more details of the rhythm, as well as the syntax.

In most extant folksongs, we do not know whether words or music came first, so we do not know whether or not ballads like "The Twa Sisters" or "The Three Ravens" are *contrafacta*. But they are like the "Lachrymae" song in that the words would not have been as they are if they had not been made to be sung. No poet intending his verse to be read and not sung would have used so much repetition and noncommunicating language (i.e., nonsense):

> There were three ravens sat on a tree,
>   Downe a downe, hay down, hay downe
> There were three ravens sat on a tree,
>   With a downe
> There were three ravens sat on a tree,
> They were as blacke as they might be,
>   With a downe derrie, derrie, derrie, downe, downe.

There are nine more stanzas.[3] Many commentators have pointed out that we have more tolerance for certain kinds of repetition in music than in words, though children have more tolerance for songs like "Ninety-nine Bottles of Beer" than adults. (Exact consecutive repetition, as in a stuck record, is intolerable in both words and music.) But in "The Three Ravens," the repetition in the words is not matched in the music. The music makes the verbal repetition tolerable, and the verbal repetition allows attention to turn to the music. The music may add another level of communication (more on that later) and it certainly adds another dimension to the experience if we consider the repetitions and refrains—the low density of information—as invitations to group participation in the song (Booth, 1981, 8–10).

Even if the poem is not written to fit preexisting music, knowledge that the poem will be set to music can affect the poet's use of form. He might be more inclined to use a refrain or repetition to emphasize an important point (e.g., Dryden's "None but the brave, / None but the brave, / None but the brave deserves the fair" in *Alexander's Feast*). He can be almost certain that the composer will set each verbal repetition to music that is not exactly repeated. The poet may strive for more coincidence between form and syntax in a strophic poem, and he may avoid formal complexity that might prevent the words from being understood when sung.

This discussion of form has so far dealt mainly with practical considerations in comparing poetry and music. But the perception of form raises a larger theoretical problem. When I wrote of melodies having "shape" or being "rounded," I slipped in visual or spatial terms that would seem to be out of place in a discussion of serial art. Paula Johnson, drawing on Kenneth Burke, Leonard Meyer, Susanne Langer, and others, has posited two phases in our perception of literary and musical form. The first mode of apprehension she calls "progressive form," in which the audience responds to a series of aroused expectations, which are then fulfilled or frustrated. The second phase she calls "retrospective form," "the form we apprehend in memory when the work itself is not actually externally present to us" (1972, 14). It is this second phase that seems to call up spatial metaphors in describing form. A strophic song may thus generate an image of a spiral, or a series of connected loops, depicting at once repetition and progression. A through-composed song may call up a graphlike image with sequential terraces and climactic peaks. The pattern of notes on the page, from low to high to low again, may contribute to these images. But we should probably resist too much visualization. For one thing, such images are too subjective. In song especially, when music and poetry are running together, such images might blind one to other aspects of form. For instance, in a strophic song some elements are repeated, as in the spiral, but the form of the narrative or thematic development may be an arch or a peak. The spiral image also gives no indication of how the form produces a sense of closure, which, like the beginning, is important in the form of any serial art.

Musically, final closure in strophic songs goes beyond closure at the end of stanzas through such performance practices as slowing down *(rallentando)*, lengthening the final note, declaiming emphatically, or fading away *(diminuendo, morendo)*. The verse for its part must ordinarily give a sense of closure through logical, narrative, or thematic completeness. Closure in the ballad is fairly easy to perceive, for the story comes to its climactic event or revelation. On the other hand, many strophic lyrics work against a strong sense of closure, because the repeated stanzas and music encourage paratactic structures, such as catalogs, or restatements of the central idea in different words with different images or examples. The manuscript histories of some poems show how they have been continued when they seemed to offer no good reason for ending. "Now what is love," set to music by Robert Jones (1601, no. 9) in five stanzas, has sixteen stanzas in one manuscript version and nineteen in another; most are obvious additions *(LEA, 506–8)*. But as Barbara Herrnstein Smith points out (1968, 57–67), some simple devices can indicate closure: one can repeat the opening stanza, thus establishing a frame for the rest, as in Wyatt's "At most mischief"; or one can announce in the text that the song is over, as in Whythorne's "Buy new broom" or Wyatt's "My lute awake."

Closure is usually easier to indicate in a through-composed song. The same musical means may be used as in strophic songs, but the composer may build in more conclusive elements, such as longer preparation for or more emphatic return to the tonic cadence. If the verse is freed from the paratactic structures encouraged by the strophic form, it can present closure more clearly in terms of a problem solved, a logical end obtained. We have already seen one example of closure in a through-composed song in Dowland's "In darknesse let mee dwell." Another example is in the question and answer of Thomas Bateson's madrigal (1604, no. 14):

> And must I needs depart then?
> Can pity none come nigh her?
> Farewell, alas, desert, then:
> O break asunder, heart, to satisfy her.

The musical form is more fully developed than this miniscule bit of verse. Closure in the music is clearly indicated by several repetitions of the last line by all voices on descending figures; the last few repetitions of the last three words are set to longer note values in several of the voices. Moreover, the entire closing section, containing the last two lines, is repeated; what is sounded exactly twice, we do not expect to be repeated exactly a third time without some intervening material.

Between the beginning and end of a song, we are led forward by the desire to complete the syntax of the language and so apprehend its statement. We are also led by the musical logic toward a resolution in musical terms. We do not "understand" music in the same way as language, but we can see parallels in that music and language both have this forward impetus toward completion. In song, as we shall see, the language often gives direction to the music.

The formal parallels between music and language we have explored so far have been those relevant to song. Other applications of these parallels are possible. I will not discuss, but will mention for the record, the imitation of larger musical forms in literature, as exemplified by works such as De Quincey's "Dream Fugue." Unlike *contrafacta*, these experiments have no bearing on our study, and are mostly later. Literary descriptions of music, or what Steven Scher calls "verbal music," depend on the reader's knowledge of music for their effect, but do not pretend to offer literary equivalents of music. They can serve legitimate literary functions of enhancing theme, setting, or characterization. Thomas Mann's *Doctor Faustus* is perhaps the prime example.

Local sound effects in literature brought about by consonance, alliteration, onomatopoeia, and so on, are also called "musical," but again, only by analogy. But musical imitation of natural sounds, which is sometimes used for "word-painting" in Renaissance song, is also one of the devices used in program music, in which literature impinges on music. Our major concern here is with song; the most famous examples of program music are instrumental works such as Paul Dukas's "Sorcerer's Apprentice," supposedly a purely musical retelling of Goethe's "Der Zauberlehrling," or Berlioz's "Symphonie Fantastique," and the "tone poems" of Liszt or Richard Strauss. There are Renaissance examples as well. Though words are not sung in these pieces, words are important for their interpretation; one at least needs to know the title, or the story being illustrated, or the written program, in order to respond to them as the composer wished. (Or images may substitute for words; Walt Disney's *Fantasia* shows us that Dukas's piece is film music in search of a film.)

Expression

Program music brings us to a crucial theoretical issue that is important for song. Does music, like language, communicate? If so, how and what does it communicate? These questions raise some difficult issues about which there is little general agreement. Music may imitate natural sounds, but it cannot convey abstract concepts or conduct arguments; the meanings of notes cannot be looked up in a dictionary. The analogy between music and language is only an analogy, and one with which many scholars are impatient.

It has been said that music is the language of the emotions.[4] Dryden asked, "What passions cannot Music raise and quell?" When we look at the uses of music in our culture, we can see its links to the emotions: music is used to promote solemnity at funerals, patriotic excitement or solidarity at political rallies, a wide range of emotions in films, and Dionysian frenzy at rock concerts. A large part of such responses can be assumed to have been learned or culturally conditioned. But there have been attempts to find some innate, universal basis for music's affective power. Physiological and psychological explanations have referred to the sympathies between musical rhythms and the rhythms of breathing, heartbeat, and sexual activities. Recent experiments trying to link musical elements and dynamic expressions of emotions the experimenters call "essentic forms" are interesting, especially since these essentic forms seem to be biologically and not culturally determined (Clynes and Nettheim, 1982). But in these studies there appears to be a wide gap between elements isolated in experiments—usually brief patterns of sound—and the large and complex body of music and the range of human responses to it. Moreover, cultural distinctions soon make themselves felt; the musical "languages" of India and Japan need to be learned just as the written and spoken languages need to be learned if true communication is to take place. But there may be something to Leonard Bernstein's speculation, based on an analogy with Noam Chomsky's idea of innate grammatical competence, that man has an innate "musical-grammatical competence." "This competence," says Bernstein, "would be our built-in capacity to construe those naturally serialized overtones [from the harmonic series], and to construe them *in different ways,* just as the various cultures of the world may have construed basic monogenetic materials and constructed out of them thousands of particular grammars or languages, all different from one another" (1976, 29–31).

Music's affective force in Western culture does seem to be related to the way this culture has construed the natural materials of music, especially those deriving from the harmonic series. Briefly, the harmonic or overtone series is naturally present in any uniformly vibrating substance, such as a string or a column of air. If a string sounds a low C as its fundamental tone, it is also sounding the octave above, the fifth above (g), the fourth above that (c^1), the next major third higher (e^1), the minor third above that (g^1), and so on up, in increasingly smaller and less audible intervals. The lower on the harmonic series, the more "stable" the notes when sounded together. In this light it is interesting to see the development of tonal harmony in European music from monodic plain chant through organum (voices singing together at intervals of the fourth and fifth) to full harmony using major and minor thirds by the sixteenth century. With the use of voices singing at intervals of the third, as well as the fifth, it is possible to have *triads* (such as CEG), and with the triad we have the basis of tonal harmony.

The point is that musical material derived from the harmonic series contains built-in relationships with different degrees of tension, and this tension provides the dynamic force of musical grammar as well as a basis for some of its affective power. To keep musical technicalities at a minimum—at least for a while—we may take as an example the "folk" guitar player. The first three chords he learns are the tonic (that based on the fundamental), the dominant (based on the fifth), and the subdominant (based on the fourth). In the key of C, the notes of the tonic chord would be CEG, the subdominant FAC, and the dominant GBD. The vast majority of the songs he learns can be accompanied with only these three chords. Whenever he departs from the tonic chord, he and his audience feel a need to return to it. But a pull can also be felt from the subdominant to the dominant. Tension, and thus affect, can be increased by delaying the expected return to the tonic (by going back and forth between dominant and subdominant), or by destabilizing the dominant by adding a seventh (in C, the chord would be GBDF), which pulls strongly to the third of the tonic triad. There are many versions of the story of a musician being aroused from bed by one who played a series of chords on the piano beginning with the tonic and ending with the dominant seventh. Unable to sleep with the unresolved chord ringing in his ears, the musician had to get up and play the tonic chord himself. More complex and subtle effects are possible with the use of other chords and with the possibility of modulating into other keys. Music in which these tonic-dominant-subdominant relationships can be felt, music that can be said to be in a key (based on what note is chosen for the tonic)—this music is said to be *tonal*. Much of the music of the later sixteenth century is tonal in fact, if not in contemporary theory.

Tonal harmony of course is not the only musical element capable of producing affect. Manipulations of tempo, rhythm, texture, and dynamics can be used for affective purposes. One common end of these manipulations is to produce and relieve tension, as it is in melody and harmony. Tension is the basis of Leonard B. Meyer's theory of musical affect. Meyer begins with the psychological theory of the emotions: "Emotion or affect is aroused when a tendency to respond is arrested or inhibited" (1956, 14). As a basic assumption, this is too limited and simple; but Meyer draws out its implications interestingly. In music, Meyer finds the tendency to respond is *expectation,* expectation aroused by the musical stimulus. The musician in the story expected the dominant seventh chord to be resolved; the frustration at having that expectation thwarted moved him—literally moved him out of bed. Expectation, and therefore tension and affect, can be generated by music in other ways than through harmonic progressions. In any element of music in which a norm can be established, a deviation from that norm can produce affect. For instance, a piece of music may begin in triple time and establish the expectation of continuation in triple time; but the composer may introduce a hemiola rhythm—a temporary shift to duple time—which is resolved when the rhythm returns to the original. In melody, says Meyer, there is a tendency to fill in gaps, the rule being that the greater the leap, the greater the tendency to fill in the gap by contrary motion (1956, 131): if a melody skips up a sixth, it tends to turn down by a second or third rather than to leap upward again. Melodies with frequent leaps are thus disturbing, "agitated"; they also take more effort to perform, especially to sing. Meyer supports these and other observations with evidence gathered by the Gestalt psychologists that show the tendency of the mind to complete patterns, solve ambiguities, stabilize shapes. "The mind when left to operate on its own, as it does in the case of remembered patterns and organizations, will improve those figures which are not as 'good' as they might be" (1956, 87). It is this tendency that composers stimulate, frustrate, and satisfy.

Meyer tends to speak in general terms about affect and emotion, without specifying *what* emotion. But we usually specify our feelings, and we often describe music in such terms. And if any one clue is significant to listeners of Western music, it is whether or not the music is in the major or minor. Meyer seems to resist characterizing the minor as sad or serious. Instead, he speaks of the "affective power" of the minor mode, and goes on to discuss it as being more ambiguous than the major, potentially unstable, potentially chromatic; the tonal relationships produce more tension (for instance, the fifth can be approached from a half-step above in the natural minor scale descending, and the lowered third pulls more strongly toward the tonic). Eventually, Meyer concedes that the "minor mode is not only associated with intense feeling in general but with the delineation of sadness, suffering, and anguish in particular." Meyer explains this "association" by noting that the emotional norm, taken to be calm contentment, is associated with "more normative musical progressions, i.e. the diatonic melodies of the major mode and the regular processions of major harmony" (1956, 222–26). Grief and anguish are deviations from this norm, and are thus associated with the musical deviations of chromaticism and minor modality. Moreover, features of the minor mode— movement by semitones or unusual skips and uncommon harmonic progressions—tended to have been given slower tempi than major diatonic music. The effect of the minor mode, then, seems to be a combination of the natural dynamics of music and cultural conditioning or learned associations.

The reader's own expectations, after reading about nonspecific emotion for several paragraphs, may now begin to be resolved. Music can be considered expressive of particular emotions, partly through natural associations, and partly by means of cultural conventions. Before going into details about how these effects are achieved and how they impinge on song, I should repeat a useful distinction made by Peter Kivy between *expressing* an emotion and *being expressive of* that emotion. We express our feelings by our words, our tone of voice, our facial expressions, our gestures. But a gesture may be expressive of a feeling without necessarily expressing that feeling. Kivy uses the example of a St. Bernard, whose face is expressive of sadness because it resembles the drooping countenance of a melancholy person; but the dog's face does not necessarily express sadness, since the dog may not be sad (1980, 12–17).

Kivy develops a theory of musical expressiveness based on the resemblances between human behavior and music. We find such behavior as a brisk step, an "elevated" expression, and speech at a certain level of pitch and volume expressive of cheerfulness. Consequently, when we hear music of a brisk tempo and a moderately high level of pitch and volume—and in a major key—we might describe it as also expressive of cheerfulness. We associate low volume and pitch with despondency because despondent people do not expend the energy necessary for higher pitch and volume. Kivy insists on the term *resemblance* because he believes that music can be expressive of individual emotions (1980, 46–70). The saving link between music and the emotions is the human tendency to animate all perceptions, to see faces in ambiguous patterns, and to find expression in sounds that resemble human emotional behavior (1980, 57–59).

But this theory does not account for the emotions associated with chromaticism and minor tonality. These effects and others, Kivy believes, were established by convention, a convention largely derived from fitting appropriate music to texts. The text, of course, can label the particular emotion of which music is expressive, or describe more particular circumstances that would imply a particular emotion. According to Kivy, the "musical characteristics conventionally associated with joy and sorrow are as easily identifiable and as consistently applied as halo on saint" (1980, 76). Some of these "musical tags" seem to have carried their associations over into instrumental music.

A large and varied number of examples that could be seen both as resembling emotional behavior and as conventional tags has been collected in Deryck Cooke's *The Language of Music;* it provides an empirical base for much of this discussion. Cooke's examples cover the whole range of tonal music, from the thirteenth through the twentieth centuries. Many of these examples are from vocal music, and, not surprisingly, the words support the emotional characterization of the music. For example, Cooke describes the effect of a motif that falls from the tonic to the dominant in a minor key, "taking in the 'mournful' minor seventh and 'anguished' minor sixth," as clearly expressive of "an incoming painful emotion, an acceptance of, or yielding to grief; passive suffering; and the despair connected with death." Among the examples he cites are Ockeghem's chanson "Fors seulement," the opening phrase of John Dowland's "Lachrymae" ("Flow my teares," 1600, no. 2), and Thomas Weelkes's madrigal "Ay me my wonted joys forsake me" (1597, no. 9) at the words "And deep despair" (Cooke, 1962, 162–65). Cooke presents sixteen such melodic patterns as "some basic terms of musical vocabulary," while granting that there is much music that is affective but does not use these patterns.

One example Cooke does not cite is John Bennet's madrigal "Weep O mine eyes" (1599, no. 13), which begins with the same musical phrase as Dowland's "Flow my teares." In this instance, we almost certainly have an allusion or quotation rather than a convention. Dowland's tune was popular, and Bennet is not the only composer to quote it. Allusion in music and song can also produce affect if the audience recognizes the source and has emotional associations with it. Literature is full of this kind of effect—Eliot's quotation of Spenser's *Prothalamion* in *The Waste Land*, for an obvious instance—and we should not overlook its expressive potential in song. Music and poetry, then, can both be arts of *connotation;* and as long as the associations with certain phrases—verbal or musical—are shared by enough people, communication is enhanced.

Kivy's insistence on the need for both theories, of musical resemblance to emotional behavior and of convention, may help us to see the connection between illustrative and expressive devices in music. They seem different enough in the abstract, and in many specific instances: rapid descending scales on the words "running down amain" are illustrative, "word painting"; a dissonance on the word "woes" is expressive. But are the chromatic notes in John Danyel's song (1606, no. 14; Ex. 1.3) illustrative or expressive? Moreover, the musical wincing of the dissonance can be illustrative in a sense, and the rapid major scales illustrating "running down amain" contribute to the cheerful mood of the whole of Weelkes's madrigal, "As Vesta was from Latmos hill descending" (Morley, 1601, no. 17).

Example 1.3

Chromatique tunes most like my passions sound

One might ask, when music is said to be expressive of a text, if it is not like some sound effects in poetry. Most of the sounds in Tennyson's line from *The Princess* about the "murmuring of innumerable bees," as some waggish critic has noted, are present in the words "the murdering of innumerable beeves." The drowsy effect of Tennyson's line depends on the interplay between the sounds and the meaning of the words. The parallel with song is only partly justified. Words do give more specific significance to the tones, which can in turn add nuance, color, and expressive force to the text. But the sounds in Tennyson's line, the nasals, the voiced *s*, the *b*'s, the schwa and long *e*, if divorced from words—any words—make no sense, have no value. Music has a life and dynamic of its own, and many songs can and do thrive without their words. It is this potential for independence that gives the best songs their strength. The union may be difficult, and may come about only through much wrestling and attempts at mutual understanding between the partners. But when the poet adjusts his language and form to the composer's advantage, and the composer understands the words and empathizes with their content and then causes the dynamic forces of his music to support those of the poem, it is possible to have a synergistic whole that is better than either of its parts.

Divergencies

Such a union would illustrate the positive valences between music and poetry. But recognition of the independence of music, and recollection of some of the problems mentioned earlier, such as the fitting of text and music in strophic songs, hint at some of the negative valences. Before going further we should set them out more fully. To begin with the strophic song: for a poet writing a poem in stanzas, it is usually enough of a challenge to make language fit the form and rhyme scheme without noticeably straining, padding, or reaching for a rhyme word. To make the syntactical breaks uniform from stanza to stanza in order to make the music fit would not only be an extra chore,

it would work against the literary value of variety within the regularity
of the repeated form.

In general, poets have to deny themselves a number of sources of
literary interest in writing songs, just as composers have to deny themselves sources of purely musical interest. A composer could conceivably
write a melody to fit all stanzas of a strophic poem, even though the
syntax made for pauses in different places, and different lines were
enjambed. But to do so, the composer would have to avoid musical
pauses or strong cadences except where a pause occurred in all stanzas.
And if an iamb in one stanza fell where a trochee was in another, the
composer might wish to use notes of equal value and pitch so as to
avoid distorting either. If the mood of the poem varied from stanza to
stanza, the composer might wish to avoid music significantly expressive of one stanza but inappropriate for another, so he must compromise yet again. The result of all these compromises would probably be
a bland, neutral, poorly defined tune. In practice, most composers set
the first stanza and let the others shift for themselves.

Not only are there limits on formal and metrical complexity and
variety in both components of a successful song: poets cannot allow
much complexity of image, metaphor, or argument, and composers
cannot admit some kinds of rhythmic, harmonic, or textural complexity, even in nonstrophic settings. Words presented to the ear, words
passing by in a musical medium, cannot be reread, savored, or puzzled
over. A poem that is rich in its own metrical and verbal sound effects,
or which captures the rhythms and inflections of speech, is not well
served by music. To imagine a setting of Keats's "To Autumn" is to be
reminded of Paul Valéry's observation that setting a poem to music is
like using a stained glass window to light a painting (1943, 83). By
the same token, music, like stained glass, may be so rich in its own
elements as to obscure the poem. The musical images inspired by a
poem, if allowed to proliferate, can bury the very words that stimulated them.

Other negative valences have grown from the independent development of the two arts. Differences in handling climaxes impinge on
song, because poets generally use fewer climaxes than composers, and
do not usually place them in the same way. In a strophic poem, one
might find only one climax, but the strophic melody would provide
one for each stanza. As Calvin Brown says, "musical climaxes are usually more definite—so much that they would appear exaggerated when
imposed on the poem, and the poet usually cannot supply the climax
almost at the end where it is most appropriate in music" (1948, 48).

It should be admitted that poetry is most likely to be treated unfairly in a union with music. Composers sometimes pander to performers by writing settings in which melismatic ornamentation and other vocal pyrotechnics obscure the text. Composers sometimes alter the text, or break up lines and repeat phrases until any sense of verbal coherence is lost. Madrigalists are sometimes guilty of these faults. These alterations of course destroy any sense of the poem's rhythm or meter, though most songs take at least some liberties with this aspect of the text. Musical setting also imposes limits on the interpretation of a poem, because it cannot include all of the poem's potential nuances of meaning and emotion. The text of *King Lear* has in it *in potentia* the reading of Laurence Olivier as well as that of James Earl Jones, but we cannot have both in the same performance. A musical setting is one such interpretive performance of a poem. Just as a bad film of a play may be more unfair to the play than a bad stage performance, a musical setting can be especially unfair to a poem by fixing an inadequate interpretation of it; and if the music is especially attractive, it may perpetuate that interpretation. Jack Stein feels that Schubert's settings of Heine are misreadings of the poems, though it might be better to say that Schubert chose one of the readings possible at that time (1971, 4–5, 80–91). But what is most unfair is nevertheless a natural law: a good poem with weak music cannot be a good song, while a weak poem with good music can be, and frequently is, a good song.

Implicit in these statements is the possibility that a good poem can also be good words for music. But as the previous paragraphs suggest, we must adjust our criteria so as not to expect qualities in a song verse that its relation to music would (and should) preclude. Successful song poems are rarely dense, complex, tightly argued, highly allusive, or highly intellectual. But they can be witty, graceful, poignant, humorous, acerbic, sad, wise, soulful, clear, symmetrical, or any number of other good qualities. They can even have certain kinds of complexity, as John Irwin has shown in his analysis of Campion's "Now winter nights enlarge" (ca. 1618, p. 1, no. 12). Mark Booth observes that the complexity Irwin finds in the song "is good for making a subtle song to the extent that the various layers of meaning tend in the same direction, reinforcing and validating each other" (1981, 80). Complexities are fine if they give us things to discover on rehearing a song, or enrich the song subliminally; but if they prevent a basic minimum of comprehension in an oral performance, they raise an aesthetic problem.

Despite these arguments, we are sometimes forced to concede the success of a musically rich setting of a difficult text. Sometimes the work succeeds because the text is well known to the majority of the audience, as in Benjamin Britten's settings of Donne's Holy Sonnets. It is also possible to imagine a setting of a text that is obscure in all senses of the word, but a setting in which the obvious power and depth of the music convinces the listener of the need to become familiar with the text. On the simplest level, we translate the text of a *lied* or *chanson* that attracts us; we read the text of a madrigal; or we puzzle out a symbolist poem incorporated in a more complex piece, not so much as a song as an imbedded program for a tone poem.

Two Approaches to Setting Poems

Partly as a result of these positive and negative valences of poetry and music, there seem to be certain general trends in the practice of making songs, trends observable in different historical periods and on different cultural levels. We may describe two broadly perceived attitudes toward fitting music to texts. They are not mutually exclusive, but are tendencies, best understood through extreme examples. For heuristic purposes, we may call them "classical" and "romantic." These terms are of course anachronistic when applied to the sixteenth century. But for the moment the anachronistic connotations may be useful.

The composer with the classical attitude takes a formal approach to the text. On the practical level, he matches the form and meter of the music to that of the verse, without necessarily considering the syntax or sense of the text. Musical expression of the words is limited; strophic form predominates. The music is more general and tends to rely on its internal dynamics instead of reference to externals, such as the text. On the affective level, this attitude produces *distance*. Under some circumstances, this distancing can have a powerful aesthetic and emotional effect. Among the best examples of this approach are those provided by the folk ballad. B. H. Bronson's description of the effect of the ballad cannot be bettered: the traditional ballad music

operates against narrative effect and acts to reinforce the level impassivity of the characteristic style. And this is a source of its peculiar power. Although it intensifies the emotional (and lyric) effects of the words as they pass, it de-individualizes and objectifies their stated content. It regularizes and levels out the hills and valleys of narrative interest and reduces the varying speeds of travel to its own constant pace. . . . The dominant impression conveyed by a good folk-song sung in the best traditional style is . . . one of genuinely classic impersonality. To this prevailing tone everything contributes. That is why the most brutal and violent, crude and sordid themes, when passed through the crucible of traditional singing, sometimes become, not tolerable merely, but as starkly powerful in their reserve and understatement as all but the very greatest masterpieces of conscious art, and on their own scale of magnitude incomparable.(1969, 129–31)

A good idea of the effect that Bronson describes can be had from Ewan McColl's recorded performance of "Lord Randal," or Jean Ritchie's of "Lord Thomas and fair Annet."

The romantic attitude toward fitting a text with music is not formal, not distancing, but expressive, intimate, emotional, and dramatic. The composer using the romantic approach focuses on the emotions of the text and brings the expressive resources of music to bear on enhancing them. On the practical level, the form of the text may be ignored, though the syntax may be treated more clearly. Through-composed form predominates. The appeal of this approach is obvious to anyone familiar with nineteenth-century *lieder*.

The almost inevitable examples of these approaches are based on Goethe's "Erlkönig." The poem is clearly an imitation of the folk ballad: except for the opening and closing stanzas, the entire narrative is conveyed through dialogue. Like many memorable ballads, it is the story of a tragic encounter between a mortal and a supernatural creature. Goethe is said to have preferred settings that took the classical approach, like real folk ballads. The character who sings the song in its original context, the *singspiel Die Fischerin* (1782), presents it as a folk ballad. The actress Corona Schröter, who played the character in the first performance, composed her own setting of the poem, a simple, strophic version in a major key and 6/8 time (Stein, 1971, 64). Another early setting by Johann Friedrich Reichardt is basically strophic and classic in approach, but when the Erlking speaks, the voice sings in a low, soft, sinister monotone while the melody stays in the accompaniment. The Reichardt setting, especially, closely parallels the meter of Goethe's poem.

But whatever the virtues of Schröter's or Reichardt's settings, the version everyone knows is the intensely romantic treatment by Franz Schubert. Schubert ignores Goethe's stanzaic form and composes fresh music for each line. Formal unity is provided by the unceasing triplets in the accompaniment, which also suggest the speed of the galloping horse, and during the Erlking's invitation, take on a rocking, lulling sound. The characters in the dialogue are dramatized: the father sings his rational reassurances in a low voice; the son cries in a higher register, with similar sequences on higher pitches as his fear mounts; the Erlking also sings high, but softly and seductively. The increasing tension is supported by key changes and the son's rising sequences, which reach their height at the climax. The triplets in the accompaniment stop when the father and son reach home; the interruption of this norm gives force to the narrator's last words—that the child was dead.

Renaissance songs settle at various points between "Lord Randal" and Schubert's "Erlkönig"; to avoid anachronism, I shall call these poles "formal" and "expressive." There are historical reasons why certain songs gravitate toward one pole or the other, and these historical reasons will be explained in the following chapters.

Chapter Two
Historical Contexts
Humanism and the Reformation

At the end of the fifteenth century most Englishmen's view of the world was basically medieval. The great chain of being linked a vast complex of hierarchies that ordered beasts, men, angels, plants, and minerals. Networks of correspondences joined heaven and earth, land and sea, man and the cosmos. The ordering of creation was seen as a musical ordering, *harmonia mundi*. This music was no mere analogy: the concentric spheres containing the planets and stars that revolved around the earth produced music, though it was inaudible to sublunary creatures. The origin of this notion goes back to Pythagoras, who in the sixth century B.C. had discovered from his experiments with the monochord that musical sounds could be described in terms of numerical ratios or proportions. By isolating the diapason (the octave) from the continuum of pitch from infinitely low to infinitely high, Pythagoras "revealed a dependable relationship between the finite and the infinite, some manageable way of dealing with the infinite through knowledge of the finite. The diapason with its numerical ratios and its harmonies exposed in small to mortal comprehension the divinely proportioned structure of the universe."[1]

The implications of Pythagoras's discoveries were developed by Plato, Cicero (*The Dream of Scipio,* and Macrobius's commentary), and Boethius. Boethius described three kinds of music: *musica mundana, musica humana,* and *musica instrumentalis.* The first concerns the harmony or order of the universe, including the motions of the stars and planets, the combinations of the elements, and the succession of the seasons. The second concerns the ordering of the components of the human being, such as the mind with the body, and the parts of the soul and the elements of the body with each other. *Musica instrumentalis,* as the name suggests, is instrumental music, including vocal music, although Boethius does not specify (Bukofzer, 1942, 167; Strunk, 1950, 84–85). Perhaps vocal music, being higher on the hierarchy, also partakes of *musica humana.* Each kind of music is attuned to the others.

The relationship of the human soul to *musica mundana* is the basis of the correspondence between the microcosm and the macrocosm. And because of this relationship, instrumental or vocal music, which reflects the *musica mundana,* affects the human soul. The resulting power of music is attested to by many examples, from David and Saul to Timotheus and Alexander.

These relationships between *musica mundana* and *musica humana* are the materials of speculative music *(musica speculativa).* When music exercises its power on men, it does so through practical music *(musica practica).* Practical music in the Middle Ages generally reflected the abstract, mathematical, symbolic concerns of speculative music in concrete form. (That is, the ecclesiastical music does; the popular music, only a fraction of which was recorded by the musically literate clergy, seems to do so only indirectly.) The favored rhythmic proportions were those called "perfect," that is, in triple time; in music of more than one part, "perfect" intervals, the octave, fourth, and fifth, were preferred. The music was not "expressive" of the text in any way a modern listener would recognize; but it was assumed that if the proportions of the music were right according to *musica mundana,* they would have their effect on *music humana* (J. Stevens, 1961, 61–64). The text could be safely obscured from the conscious apprehension of the listener by being in Latin, by being stretched out over many notes and interrupted by rests, or by having two voices sing different texts simultaneously, as in motets from the thirteenth through the fifteenth centuries. Musical symbolism could be present, sometimes connecting music and text, but it would be apparent only to a learned cleric reading the manuscript—or, like the finished back parts of cathedral statues, to God (Sanders, 1973, 124–27).

The ideas of *musica speculativa* persisted until the scientific challenges of the seventeenth century. But their relation to practical music changed considerably in the Renaissance (Hollander, 1961). The more humanists delved into the newly available texts from pagan Greece and Rome, the more they learned about ancient music and its legendary powers. They were impressed especially by the ethical effects attributed to music. Music as they knew it could be powerfully affecting, but it could not restrain lust, as Agamemnon's Dorian musician restrained Clytemnestra until he was killed by Aegisthus; nor could it halt drunken violence, as Pythagoras did with a spondaic song (Strunk, 1950, 82, 287, 293). Although the humanists could not decipher the few surviving scraps of actual Greek music, they could read descriptions of it, and find that the Greeks gave great priority to the text. Giovanni Bardi recalled that Plato said that the melody should serve the verse, like sauce to the main dish (Strunk, 1950, 6–7, 295). Emphasis on the text is the connecting thread throughout the various humanist theories about song.

Humanist influences moved north from Italy in waves, and affected the arts in varying degrees at different times. Humanist ideas about music came to England as early as Sir Thomas More's *Utopia* (1516), where the music of the Utopians is described in humanist terms:

> But in one thynge dowteles they goo excedinge farre beyond us. For all theire musicke, both that they playe upon instrumentes, and that they singe with mans voyce doth so resemble and expresse naturall affections, the sownd & tune is so applied and made agreable to the thynge, that whether it bee a prayer, or els a dytty of gladness, of patience, of trouble, of mournynge, or of anger: the fassion of the melodye dothe so represente the meaning of the thing, that it doth wonderfullye move, stire, pearce, and enflame the hearers myndes. (1551 ed., sig. R5)

As John Stevens (1961, 65) has pointed out, what is especially new here is the connection made between emotional effects and emotional expressiveness in the music. Some of the motets of Josquin des Prez might have approached the Utopian ideal for More, but not many other contemporary pieces would have. By the end of the century, however, the Utopian ideals would be widely accepted as the obvious goal of the composer.

The next waves of musical humanism to reach England were rather small ripples from the Continent. In France, Ronsard and the Pléiade group attempted to bring music and poetry closer together in order to produce the effects of ancient music, but they did so mainly by encouraging poets to write regular stanzas to facilitate setting, and by encouraging composers to use a simple homophonic style, as in the settings of Ronsard by Nicholas de la Grotte.[2] Some of de la Grotte's songs in arrangements for solo lute were printed in England in Adrian LeRoy's *A briefe and plaine Introduction to set all Musicke of eight divers tunes in Tableture for the Lute* (1574). Another collection of French *chansons* published in England was *Recuil du Mellange D'Orlande de Lassus*, printed by the Huguenot immigrant Thomas Vautrollier in 1570; Lassus's music was not always simple, but always showed concern for the mood and sense of the text. Other developments in French musical

humanism did not influence English song until later. The Académie
de Poésie et de Musique, founded in 1570 by one of the Pléaide, Jean
de Baïf, developed *musique mesurée,* in which the verse was written in
imitation of classical quantitative meters, and the music was restricted
to two note values (with some melismatic subdivision) to match the
long and short syllables. This music did not circulate until after the
Académie ceased to function; Claude LeJeune published six of his
measured settings of Baïf only in 1583, and Jacques Mauduit's *Chan-
sonettes mesurées* with texts by Baïf were not published until 1586.[3] William Byrd's "Constant *Penelope*" and "Come to mee, griefe, for ever"
(1588, nos. 23, 34), and Thomas Campion's "Come let us sound"
(Rosseter 1601, pt. 1, no. 21) are the only English songs that were
composed on similar principles.

While the French humanists focused on the formal relationships between music and poetry, the Italians tended to focus on representational and expressive relationships. Again, the first wave of humanism was
more moderate, the later more radical. Perhaps the most influential
statement of the earlier position was that of Gioseffe Zarlino in his
Institutioni harmoniche (1558), probably the most widely read treatise
on musical theory of the Renaissance. Zarlino's chapter, "How the Harmonies are Adapted to the Words Placed Beneath Them" (Strunk,
1950, 255-61), was later paraphrased by Thomas Morley as "Rules to
be observed in dittying" in his *Plaine and Easie Introduction to Practical
Musicke* (1597, sig. Aa2). Morley proposes to "shew you how to dispose
your musicke according to the nature of the words which you are therein to expresse. . . . For it will be a great absurditie to use a sad harmonie to a merrie matter, or a merrie harmonie to a sad lamentable or
tragicall dittie." Music expressive of "hardnesse, crueltie, bitternesse"
should proceed in whole steps, the horizontal movement resulting in
major thirds and sixths in vertical relation to the bass; one may use
"Cadences bound with the fourth or seventh, which being in long notes
will exasperat [make harsh] the harmonie." On the other hand, "a lamentable passion" should be expressed in motions proceeding by half
steps, producing harmonies with "flat" or minor thirds and sixths. The
horizontal motions of the parts in the natural key are more "masculine," while those that employ accidentals and chromaticism are more
"effiminate and languishing," more expressive of "griefe, weeping,
sighes, sorrowes, sobbes, and such like." If the subject is light, the
note values should be short, "which carrie with them a celeritie or
quicknesse of time"; if the subject is "lamentable," the note values

must be larger and "goe in slow and heavie motions." "Moreover you must have a care that when your matter signifieth ascending, high heaven, and such like, you make your musicke ascend: and by the contrarie where your dittie speaketh of descending lowenes, depth, hell, and others such, you must make your musicke descend." In applying notes to words, one should avoid the "barbarisme" of causing a short syllable to be "expressed by manie notes or one long note," or the reverse. Morley cites the habit of singing many notes on the penultimate syllables of words like *Dominus* and *Angelus* as "a grosse barbarisme." He calls Dunstable a dunce for placing a rest between the syllables of a single word, and says that "you may set a crotchet or minime rest above a coma or colon, but a longer rest then that of a minime you may not make till the sentence bee perfect." But "when you would expresse sighes, you may use the crotchet or minime rest at the most, but a longer than a minime rest you may not use, because it will rather seeme a breth taking then a sigh." One should not make a close until the sense of the words is complete. If these rules are obeyed, Morley concludes, "you shall have a perfect agreement, and as it were a harmonicall concent betwixt the matter and the musicke, and likewise you shall bee perfectly understoode of the auditor what you sing, which is one of the highest degrees of praise which a musicion in dittying can attaine unto or wish for."

Zarlino's precepts were derived from the practice of madrigalists like his teacher Adrian Willaert, a Netherlander who was for many years the chief musician at St. Mark's in Venice. Willaert's manner of giving musical expression to the text seems to have been derived, in turn, from a literary source, Cardinal Pietro Bembo's analysis of Petrarch's expressive language, *Prose della volgar lingua* (1525), as well as from discussions in Bembo's circle in Venice (Mace, 1969). This specific chain of influences was symptomatic of a general shift toward a more expressive rhetoric in both music and literature brought about by humanists' discoveries, such as the recovery of the texts of Cicero's *De oratore* and Quintilian's *Institutio Oratoria*. The constructive techniques of the previous generation of musicians and rhetoricians were under these new influences given expressive values (Winn, 1981, 122–93).

The Italian madrigalists, who exemplified this new musical-rhetorical approach, were known to a few in England as early as the 1530s (Slim, 1972, 1:16–68). But the great vogue of the madrigal in England did not begin until around 1588, the date of the publication of *Musica Transalpina,* Nicholas Yonge's anthology of Italian madrigals

with English words. Morley and his contemporaries thoroughly natu-
ralized the madrigal shortly thereafter, as we shall see in chapters 5–6.
The next and more radical wave of musical humanism in Italy grew
out of the discussions of the "Camerata," a group of musicians, scholars, and amateurs who met at the house of Giovanni Bardi in Florence
in the 1570s and 1580s. One of this group, Vincenzo Galilei, father
of the astronomer and a former student of Zarlino, wrote to a Greek
scholar, the Roman Girolamo Mei, for information about Greek music.
Galilei learned that Greek music was entirely monodic, and concluded
that music with several voice parts could never produce the ethical
effects. After introducing these ideas to the Camerata, Galilei soon
produced his *Dialogo della musica antica e della moderna* (1581), attack-
ing Zarlino and the madrigalists (Strunk, 1950, 302–22). Although
he rejected polyphony, he did not abandon harmony or counterpoint,
for he realized that they could be expressive, especially dissonances;
but a dominant voice must carry the text, with harmony confined to
the accompaniment. Galilei advocated expressiveness based on dramatic speech, rather than on the illustrative devices of the madrigalists.
Later heirs of the Camerata, the poet Ottavio Rinuccini and the composers Jacopo Peri and Giulio Caccini, in developing these ideas collaborated in devising the first operas, which were intended to produce
the effects of Greek tragedy.[4] The ideas of the Camerata are not reflected in English music much before 1610, when Robert Dowland published Caccini's "Amarilli mia bella" in *A Musical Banquet,* along with
John Dowland's dramatic "In darknesse let mee dwell."

Humanist influences on practical music came to England first and
foremost via the Reformation. The humanist connection with the Reformation has long been recognized. With Erasmus's edition of the
Greek New Testament (1516), to cite one example, humanistic learning provided a tool for challenging papal authority and doctrines based
on what seemed to be errors in the Latin Vulgate translation of the
scriptures; Erasmus's work influenced Luther considerably. For both
humanists and reformers, words were therefore of great importance;
the Word for reformers was supreme. Both groups advocated changes
in the styles of vocal music that reflected their concern that the text
be heard, understood, and felt. The reformers did not say much about
expressive techniques, and compared to later sixteenth-century music,
theirs was not noticeably expressive.[5] The main concerns at first were
that the text be intelligible and audible—in the vernacular and without being obscured by musical complexity.

Church music had provoked ambivalence and controversy from St. Augustine through Pope John XXII and Wycliff, and in a sense the Reformation controversies simply revived old issues (Hollander, 1961, 248–53). On one extreme, some reformers would ban all forms of music from church service as a sensual distraction from the spiritual force of the Word. Paradoxically, this position was advocated in 1523 by Huldrych Zwingli, a humanist who was himself a talented musician and composer, and who enjoyed domestic music all his life (Garside, 1966, 7–75). Calvin, also influenced by humanist learning, cited Plato on the power of music, and saw it as a two-edged sword. Because music "has a secret and almost incredible power to move our hearts in one way or another . . . we must be the more diligent in ruling it in such a manner that it may be useful to us and in no way pernicious." Music carries words directly to the heart, as a funnel directs wine into a cask; so the words should be suitable, and none are more suitable than "the Psalms of David which the Holy Spirit made and uttered through him" (Strunk, 1950, 347–48). Moreover, they should not be sung by trained choirs but by the whole congregation. Since they would be sung by all, and since the music must be subservient to the text, the music would have to be simple. Luther also encouraged psalms and hymns in the vernacular, but would not banish more complex part music, texts in Latin, organs, and other instruments as Calvin did (J. Stevens, 1961, 81; Temperley, 1979, 1:10–11).

In England we find the same tensions and conflicts; but the English church eventually came to resemble the Lutheran model in being more inclusive than exclusive. At first, the official church was "reformed" only at its head; Henry VIII had Miles Coverdale's *Goostly psalmes & spirituall Songes* (ca. 1538), which has Lutheran tunes and translated texts, burned in 1546 as heretical. But Thomas Cranmer, in a letter to the king in 1544, shows the Reformation spirit insinuating itself. Cranmer explains how he has translated some processional texts from Latin to English, and advises that "some devout and solemn note" be set to them so that they "will much excitate and stir the hearts of all men unto devotion and godliness. But in my opinion, the song that should be made thereunto would not be full of notes, but, as near as may be, for every syllable a note, so that it may be sung distinctly and devoutly" (Strunk, 1950, 350–51; Le Huray, 1967, 4–7). Cranmer allowed the Reformation to progress rapidly during the reign of Edward VI, and he paid for it with martyrdom under Queen Mary. Under Edward, we find the Injunctions of 1548 for Lincoln Minster stating

that anthems were to be in English, set to a "plain and distinct note
for every syllable one." The Injunctions for York Minster in 1552 required that "there be none other note sung or used . . . saving square
note plain, so that every syllable may be plainly and distinctly pronounced, and without any reports or repeatings which may induce any
obscureness to the hearers" (Frere and Kennedy, 1910, 2:168; see also
Le Huray, 1967, 9, 24–25). Although composers did not stop writing
polyphonic church music, many continued the trend toward a simpler
style that seems to have begun before the Reformation. The spirit of
these injunctions was also carried out in revisions of liturgical chants
and in such works as John Merbecke's *The boke of Common praier noted*
(1550). But especially significant for this study were the metrical
translations of the Psalms.

Coverdale's psalms and Robert Crowley's *The Psalter of David Newely
Translated into Englyshe Metre* (1549) had little impact, but Thomas
Sternhold's collection of metrical psalms became the basis of some of
the most popular song verse of the period. Sternhold's psalms were first
printed, without music, in 1549; in December of that year another
edition followed with further translations by John Hopkins. Nine more
editions were published before Mary's accession in 1553. According to
Edmund Howes's preface to John Stow's *Annales* (1615), Sternhold and
the courtiers sang the psalms to dance tunes, "galliards and measures"
(Temperley, 1979, 1:36). No tunes were printed with these psalms
until the edition published by the Marian exiles in Geneva in 1557,
which contained further psalms translated by William Whittingham.
These tunes are simple in that they consist mainly of half notes and
whole notes in duple meter, with one note per syllable of text. The
most attractive tunes are those adapted from the French psalter; the
English tunes tend to be austere, with no hint of popular origin and
probably with little popular appeal (Temperley, 1979, 1:33–37). There
is no evidence that the psalms were sung by congregations during Edward's reign. But after the exiles returned from Europe, congregational
psalm-singing became popular. John Jewel reports on its rapid spread
in churches, and tells of six thousand people singing together at St.
Paul's Cross in 1560 (Temperley, 1979, 1:37, 43). The year 1560 also
saw the first of many English printings of the Geneva version of the
psalms, and around 1563 John Day printed an edition with four-part
harmonizations of the tunes, most of which are in a simple chordal
style. Despite the printed music, many apparently sang the psalms to
unofficial, "common" tunes; these did not begin appearing in the

psalm books until 1579, and they seem to have more connections with popular song than the official tunes. These common tunes may have been more like the tunes Sternhold used originally, and may account for the contemptuous reference to the psalm tunes as "Geneva jigs" (Temperley, 1979, 1:65–70).

The verse of most of these psalms was in what came to be known as common meter; it is essentially the same as ballad meter or fourteeners, a quatrain of alternating eight- and six-syllable lines, with rhymes on the second and fourth lines. The lines were also regularly iambic. This last feature is highly significant at this particular moment in history, for English verse was in transition from the irregular meters of the fifteenth-century poets and Wyatt to the highly regular meters of the poets who came immediately after the publication of Tottel's Miscellany, *Songes and Sonnettes,* in 1557. Since the relationship between music and poetical meter will be one of the continuing themes of this book, we need to examine the situation more closely at this point. Chronology is important, so I will give dates whenever possible.

Music and Poetic Meter

Two crucial changes in the concept and practice of English verse took place in the sixteenth century. The first change consisted of ordering the stresses in the line into a regular pattern of alternating stressed and unstressed syllables. This change occurred between the time Sir Thomas Wyatt, in the 1530s, wrote such lines as "There was never file half so well filed," and before 1557, when the compiler of Tottel's Miscellany changed these lines, as in "Was never file yet half so well yfiled" (Rollins, 1928, 1:33, 2:161). The second change occurred in the 1570s and 1580s when poets like Sidney learned to internalize the abstract pattern of regular stresses and play off against it the rhythms of speech or incantation. This second change resulted in the fluid and flexible line that sustained English verse for the next three centuries. We will consider the second change in later chapters; the first change alone raises more questions that we can comfortably handle in the rest of this chapter.

English verse before Tottel has been called a metrical "swamp" (C. S. Lewis, 1954, 237). Indeed, in the verse of Wyatt that appears to be iambic pentameter, the only constant is rhyme. Some lines have four stresses, others six; some have nine syllables, others ten, eleven, or twelve. The same description applies to most such verse before the mid-sixteenth century. Heretical as it seems, I do not believe that even Chaucer wrote what we have been taught to read. To give only a quick guerilla strike in what is a long and complex war, it seems to me that Chaucer's "iambic pentameter" is a combination of the old and very basic four-stress rhythm with French syllable-counting verse. Since English is naturally iambic, many ten-syllable lines will scan; but others will read more naturally as old four-stress lines: "Whan Zéphirus éek . with his swéte bréeth." Furthermore, since reading Chaucer as iambic pentameter depends upon pronouncing final *es*, we should be suspicious when we are told to pronounce *es* that were not inflectional, and which were often not present in the manuscripts, in order to *make* the meter regular.[6]

Returning to the sixteenth century, we must confront the question of why regular stresses came to be valued. How we think of meter, what we assume meter to be, affects how we read the meter of a piece of verse. For much of the sixteenth century, those writers who addressed the matter at all thought that native English verse consisted simply of a certain number of syllables per line, plus rhyme. As Derek Attridge has shown, writers like Roger Ascham, with assumptions about meter derived from Latin, did not think English verse had meter at all. Number and rhyme defined English verse for Ascham, around 1563, and for George Puttenham in the late 1560s or early 1570s. Not until George Gascoigne's "Certayne Notes of Instruction" of 1575 was the principle of alternating stressed and unstressed syllables clearly described.[7] So it is difficult to say just why Tottel's compiler felt the need to revise Wyatt's lines. Tottel's preface to the reader offers some hints: "It resteth nowe (gentle reder) that thou thinke it not evill doon, to publish, to the honor of the Englishe tong, and for profit of the studious of Englishe eloquence, these workes. . . . If parhappes some mislike the statelinesse of stile removed from the rude skill of common eares: I aske help of the learned to defend their learned frendes, the authors of this work." Broad general reasons for reforming English meter, then, may be the desire to dignify the vernacular literature and to distinguish it from verse produced by the vulgar. For, as Ascham said, "rash ignorant heads" could "easely recken up fourten syllables, and easelie stumble on every Rhyme" (Smith, 1904, 1:31). This impulse to make English verse worthy of humanist learning may have led to efforts on the part of poets to make writing verse more of a skill, on the analogy of the fairly complex rules for composing Latin quantitative verse. In a few years, poets would be attempting to imitate classical verse more directly. But at this stage they may have been only trying to refine the native verse. The earl of Surrey's translation of part of Vergil's *Aeneid* is the first example of English blank verse. Book 4 was published before Tottel, in 1554, and its iambics are fairly regular. Like classical hexameters, Surrey's verse eschews rhyme; but Surrey may have felt he needed more than just an equal number of syllables for verse to be viable without rhyme, so perhaps he tried to make a pattern of the stresses.

But music may have had some influence on the process as well, although the evidence is thin and more suggestive than compelling. We may recall that Sternhold's metrical psalms were originally written to be sung to dance tunes, "galliards and measures." We also recall that Sternhold's metrical psalms were first printed eight years before Tottel. Unfortunately the tunes first printed with these psalms in the Geneva edition of 1557 do not noticeably reinforce the iambic movement of the verse; if anything, they reinforce the old perception of verse as being simply a number of syllables plus rhyme. In the following example, which is typical of the English tunes in the Geneva edition, there is no clear musical accent corresponding to verbal stress. Although the music was sung to a breve *tactus,* with a whole note on the downbeat and a whole note on the upbeat, it is not clear that any stress was felt on the downbeat at this time (Ex. 2.1, *One and Fiftie Psalmes,* 1557, sig. F1r–v).

Example 2.1

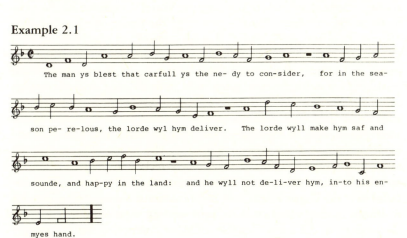

Dance tunes have more regular stress, and the "common" or unofficial tunes are also more regular; but though the latter may have been in earlier use, the only versions we have date from the late 1570s. Perhaps the compilers of the official tunes avoided using popular tunes with vain and worldly associations, even though the French and the Lutherans used such music. From the 1560 edition on, the title pages of many English editions of the psalms specifically state that the psalms were to be used in place of "ungodly songes and ballades, which tende only to the norishing of vice, and corrupting of youth" (Frost, 1953, 5–15). In later editions, however, the tunes were revised so that a regular beat is apparent (Ex. 2.2).

Example 2.2

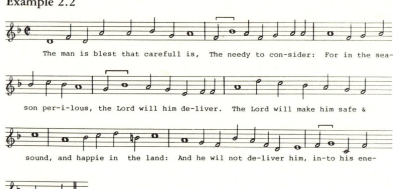

The man is blest that carefull is, The needy to con-sider: For in the sea-son per-i-lous, the Lord will him de-liver. The Lord will make him safe & sound, and happie in the land: And he wil not de-liver him, in-to his ene-mies hand.

This example is from a 1599 collection that contains accompaniments for lute or cittern as well as four-part harmonizations; the passages bracketed are clearly to be felt as syncopations, not metrical shifts.[8] The barring is in the original, but it mainly serves to keep the voice and instruments together; it does not indicate musical accent.

For early evidence bearing on metrical regularity, we must return to the court and those shadowy "galliards and measures." Perhaps the regular accents of some dance tunes encouraged Sternhold to match the stresses of his verse with the beat. Although some dances that could have been heard at court in the 1520s could be adapted for singing psalms, I have not found one that demands verse in regular iambic fourteeners as does a tune like "La Haye" from the French dancing treatise *Orchesography* (1588) by "Thoinot Arbeau" (Jehan Tabourot), or the ballad tune "Chevy Chase." The galliard was a new dance in the 1540s in England, and the typical galliard, with its characteristic five-step rhythm in triple time, in three distinct sections, would not ordinarily suggest common meter quatrains. But some of the galliards printed in Pierre Attaingnant's *Dixhuit basses dances* (Paris, 1529) are in only two sections, each with two four-beat phrases; if played without repeats, they would be structurally like a typical eight-line psalm tune. In the modern transcription, they even begin with an upbeat or pickup note, which would make adaptation to iambic verse especially easy (Attaingnant, 1966, 37, 44). "Measures" is a loosely used term that could indicate several dances, but which in some instances referred to the pavan. The pavan was a stately dance in duple time that was frequently paired with the galliard. Some of the pavans in Attaingnant's collection, though they do not correspond structurally to one or two common meter quatrains, could nevertheless be adapted to them.

The earliest galliards and pavans known to have been in England are in keyboard arrangements found in a manuscript dating from around 1551. But Sir Thomas Elyot mentions "pavions" in 1531, so that dance may have been known by then. Again the galliards and pavans in the keyboard manuscript do not display rhythms that would demand regular iambic fourteeners, but one of the galliards could easily be adapted to fit two common meter quatrains, for it is in triple time, begins with an upbeat, and has eight four-beat phrases.[9]

We may also consider the possible influence on metrical regularity of music that was not written down. Pursuit of such music might seem especially futile, but there is some indirect evidence. Sir Thomas Wyatt returned from a trip to Italy around 1527, and was soon translating not only poems by Petrarch and Alamanni but also *strambotti* by Serafino dall' Aquila (d. 1500). Serafino was famous as an *improvvisatore,* one who sang his own verses to improvised melody and lute accompaniment. The music of Serafino and others was based on formulas consisting of a bass and its implied harmony; these ground basses, the *romanesca,* the *folia,* the *passamezzo antico,* and others were frequently used in dance music. ("Greensleeves" is just one of the tunes made on the *romanesca.*) Several of Wyatt's lyrics—which are more metrically regular than his poems in ten-syllable lines—suggest that he sang them to the lute. One of these lyrics, "Blame not my lute," seems to have been sung to music found in a manuscript dating from around 1551, some lute tablature based on the *folia.* Another Wyatt poem, "Heaven and earth," is connected with lute tablature from another mid-sixteenth-century manuscript; this music is said to be related to the *romanesca* and was published in France as a "Pavane d'Angleterre" in 1555. In the same manuscript is music for two poems by the earl of Surrey, "If care do cause men cry" and "In winters just returne." These poems by Surrey were registered separately in the Stationers' Register within a year after they were published in Tottel's Miscellany, and were very probably printed as broadside ballads. A later poem by Thomas Howell indicated that it was to be sung "To the tune of winters just returne."[10] It must be confessed that these early tablatures are crude and unclear, and that it is not easy to derive a tune from them that will fit the words. Moreover, I cannot see the *romanesca* in "Heaven and Earth." But they at least indicate that these poems of Wyatt and Surrey were sung, probably in a popular or improvised manner, like the broadside ballad.

The history of the broadside ballad parallels that of the metrical psalm, and the two were in competition from almost the first. Folk and minstrel ballads, though both come to have complex relationships with the broadside ballad, are another matter. Some folk ballad stories were very old, but the texts, as one might expect in an oral genre, are fairly scarce before the seventeenth century (Fowler, 1968, 3–64). Of the relatively few ballad texts in Child's collection that date from the fifteenth and sixteenth centuries, some are of minstrel ballads ("Robin Hood and the Monk," no. 119), and others have untypical verse forms ("Riddles Wisely Expounded," no. 1A). Although the four-beat pulse is usually evident, regular iambics are not. The ballad stanza is not as common in poetical texts in general before 1550 as it is afterwards; broadsides and psalms may have made the common meter popular, instead of their taking advantage of a popular form for religious or commercial purposes. But similar blending or interplay between popular and learned song was taking place on the Continent at this time, so it is difficult to be sure of priority (*LEA*, 14–17; Brown, 1964, 25, 29, 35). The reformers and humanists, however, do speak of wanting to differentiate their songs from the vulgar. And although the broadside ballad soon became the most vulgar and plebian of literature, sensational stories sold to the newly literate by Autolycuses in streets and country lanes, it began as a more pretentious form, in which poems by the likes of Surrey were not out of place. Broadside ballads also frequently use the same verse form as the psalms. The two Surrey poems, however, use a related form called poulters' measure, a name coined by Gascoigne from the practice of egg sellers who gave fourteen eggs in the second dozen. The first line (or pair of lines) in poulters' measure has twelve syllables, the second fourteen.

Poulters' measure or short meter, ballad or common meter, and octosyllabics or long meter all are variations of a basic four-beat phrase. They all tend to be felt as isochronous, and pauses take up the spaces in the other forms where the long meter form has syllables. For example, this passage from Thomas Campion's "I care not for these ladies" (Rosseter, 1601, pt. 1, no. 3) uses poulters' measure (Ex. 2.3):

Example 2.3

Her when we court & kisse,

she cries for- sooth let go,

but when we come where comfort is

she ne- ver will say no.

The musical pulse continues in four-beat phrases, but the verse pauses after the sixth and twelfth syllables in the first pair of lines, and after the fourteenth in the next. Gascoigne, writing about "certayne pauses or restes in a verse which may be called *Ceasures*," says that "they have bene first devised (as should seeme) by the *Musicians*" (Smith, 1904, 1:54). Because these pauses are felt as part of the meter, it is difficult to read verse in these four-beat meters without falling into singsong, the kind of regularity that overrides sense and syntax (Thompson, 1961, 34–36). In the following poulters' measure couplets from Gascoigne, the punctuation is more relevant to the metrical pause than to the grammar in line three:

> With sweet entising bayte, I fisht for many a dame,
> And warmed me by many a fire, yet felt I not the flame,

But when at last I spied, the face that please me most,
The coales were quicke, the wood was drie, & I began to toste.
(1573, sig. C4)

An important feature of common meter in regular iambics, and especially of poulters' measure, is how easily the pattern can be *abstracted* from the verse. The patterns can be recognized from being tapped out or recited with nonsense syllables (da-dum)—they are like tunes. Therefore it does not seem unreasonable to find them closely associated with tunes.

To summarize our speculations, then: Wyatt may have brought the fashion of improvising to a ground bass to the court from Italy. Sometime in the 1540s, some dances or dance songs, repeated over and over as tunes are when they are played for dancing, may have infected the ear of Sternhold, who transferred the rhythm to his psalms. Hallett Smith writes that this translation, "commanding an audience roughly equivalent to the whole of the English-speaking race, constituted a body of verse that was plain, bare, regular in beat, iambic, strictly measured. It came at a time when English prosody was in confusion, and it offered some kind of order" (1946, 265–66).

Whatever refinements occurred in the 1540s, the correspondence between music and meters based on four-beat rhythm is ancient, widespread, and especially prevalent on the level of popular and traditional song. But what can these meters tell us about the important *five*-beat line, our iambic pentameter? We sense that the ten-syllable or five-beat line is very different from all the varieties of the four-beat line. The five-beat line is rare in folk and popular verse and may have appealed to more literary poets because, as Derek Attridge suggests, "it is the only simple metrical form of manageable length which escapes the elementary four-beat rhythm." In the five-beat line, the rhythmic pulses do not group themselves "consistently—and insistently—into twos and fours. . . . For this reason it strikes the ear as more faithful to the natural rhythms of speech" (1982, 124–26). Moreover, the five-beat line seems hospitable only to the iamb as the basic foot, while the four-beat line can be based on trochees, dactyls, and anapests. But after Tottel, the five-beat line may have been influenced by the regularity of the four-beat forms. Turberville, Googe, and Gascoigne use regular iambics almost exclusively in all forms. These poets (sometimes excluding Gascoigne) also tried to keep even the pentameter remote from speech rhythms. John Thompson has shown how poulters' measure, with its pronounced rhythm and caesuras, separates verse from speech; he also shows how, in the pursuit of regularity, these poets used artificial diction, frequent alliteration, and unnatural word order to make stressed syllables of relatively equal stress and to heighten the contrast with weak syllables, in both four- and five-beat verse (Thompson, 1961, 63–66). Furthermore, when Gascoigne discusses the caesura, he speaks as if it is just as important in five-beat as in four-beat verse: "in mine opinion in a verse of eight sillables, the pause will stand best in the middest, in a verse of tenne it will best be placed at the ende of the first four sillables: in a verse of twelve, in the midst, in verses of twelve, in the firste and fourtene in the second, wee place the pause commonly in the midst of the first, and at the ende of the first eight sillables in the second" (Smith, 1904, 1:54). In Gascoigne's own blank-verse satire, *The Steele Glas* (1576), there is a comma after the fourth syllable in almost every line, whether or not the syntax demands it. Since the poem is without rhyme, Gascoigne may have felt a need to keep the meter especially strict.

Just how strongly the regular metrical pattern had taken hold is strikingly illustrated in this passage from Gascoigne's "Certayne Notes of Instruction": after stipulating that every word be given "his natural *Emphasis* or sound," he advises

that all the wordes in your verse be placed as the first sillable may sound short or be depressed, the second long or elevate, the third shorte, the fourth long, the fifth shorte, etc. For example of my meaning in this point marke these two verses:

> I *understand your meanyng by your eye.*
> *Yoùr méaniǹg Í uǹdèrstàndd bý yoùr éye*

In these two verses there seemeth no difference at all, since the one hath the very selfe same woordes that the other hath, and yet the latter verse is neyther true nor pleasant, and the first verse may passe the musters. The fault of the latter verse is that this worde *understand* is therein so placed as the grave accent falleth upon *der,* and thereby maketh *der,* in this worde *understand* to be elevated: which is contrarie to the naturall or usual pronunciation: for we say *uǹdèrstánd,* and not *uǹdérstàand.* [11]

In other words, the abstract metrical pattern takes precedence over the natural pronunciation. A bad line is not bad because the stresses do not fit the pattern, but because the pattern makes one mispronounce the words. Gascoigne is applying to a five-beat line a principle often encountered in popular four-beat songs and verses: "Fée, fíe, fó, fúm, / I smell the blóod of an Énglishmán," or

> Up ther spak an eldern knight
> Was sittin' at the Kings right knee
> Sir Patrick Spence is the best Sailór,
> That sails upon the Sea.

The tune demands that the second syllable of *Sailor* be stressed (Bronson, 1959–72, 2:30).

One important thing about Gascoigne's statement is that it recognizes a separation between the metrical pattern and the words. The pattern can be expressed in a diagram with no words at all: the visual represents the aural. The effect of this separation, according to John Stevens (1982, 15–16), is "the liberation of English verse from the bondage of speech." Speech is not banished from verse, but when speech rhythm appears in Donne and Jonson, says Stevens, "It comes now sharply characterized as such, and we catch it with the conscious ear; it is a chosen effect, not as it used to be in Dan Chaucer's day the natural, unquestioned condition of all that English verse could do. Tottel's efforts (I use his name symbolically) have alienated speech and 'made it strange'; Tottel doth murder speech." As we shall see, this separation of verse from speech will eventually allow the internalization of the pattern and the interplay between it and other rhythms; this flexible and expressive medium will contribute significantly to the flowering of poetry in the last quarter of the century.

Separation of elements, or analysis, allows for fuller understanding of the parts and the whole. As separation of verse and speech allows them to be reunited with fuller comprehension and awareness of the powers and possibilities of each, so with verse and music. The same forces that pull verse and music apart, the development of the independent resources of each, can also be used to join them in effective union when poets and composers are motivated by an ideal of union such as that of the humanists.

A catalyst in this process of separation and abstraction, as well as in a number of other cultural processes, is printing. It is of course no mere coincidence that the humanist and Reformation movements occurred at the same time as the development of printing. The printed book is a product of and contributor to these movements, and is part of the process of separation and abstraction. Writing is the first step in the visualized abstraction of language from speech. Writing, and then printing, involve analysis, separating bits of speech into their alphabetical symbols. When these become bits of type, assembled in a composing stick and locked in a chase, these fragments of speech become, more and more, visible and manipulatable objects (see Ong, 1958, 307–14). Words become an early preoccupation of the words that soon come pouring off the presses. What are the true words of God? Of the ancients? It is natural that the humanist and Reformist concern with words, powered by the printing and dissemination of these words, eventually affect the relation of music and words.

Music, as a specialist art with fewer practical uses than language, lagged as a subject for printing. Musical literacy usually lags behind verbal literacy. Nevertheless, Petrucci was printing beautiful music books in Italy very early in the sixteenth century, and even in England, a book of *XX Songes* appeared in 1530 (only the bass part-book survives). Apart from the many reprints of the psalms, and arrangements of psalms such as John Cosyn's *Musicke of six, and five partes* (1585), only John Hall's *Court of Vertue* (1565, a collection of pious verse with psalmlike tunes, including moralizations of some of Wyatt's poems), a translation of Adrian LeRoy's instructions for the lute (1568, revised 1574), and the *Recueil du Mellange d'Orlande de Lassus* (1570, printed by Thomas Vautrollier) appeared in England before Thomas Why-thorne's *Songes, for three, fower, and five voyces* in 1571. In 1575, Thomas Tallis and William Byrd received a patent or monopoly for printing music other than the psalms; they published their *Cantiones Sacrae* in that year, and nothing else until 1588. Joseph Kerman (1962, 259–61) thinks that the lack of printed music in these thirteen years was caused not so much by the restrictions of the patent as by the lack of interest on the part of the patentees' printer, Thomas Vautrollier. After Vautrollier died in 1587, music printing resumed and continued steadily, peaking around 1609 and declining after 1612. The number of music books is small compared to books on other subjects, and compared to music publications on the Continent. The two important works that appeared in 1588, Byrd's *Psalmes, Sonets, & songs of sadnes and pietie*, and Nicholas Yonge's anthology of Italian madrigals, *Musica Transalpina*, will get the attention they deserve in later chapters. In the meantime, I should say something about music in England between the *XX Songes* of 1530 and Whythorne's *Songes* of 1571.

Music at Mid-Century

John Stevens's *Music and Poetry in the Early Tudor Court* gives an excellent account of the subject through the 1530s. Stevens also conveniently summarizes the new order that arises afterwards: "The mid-sixteenth century gets its character from the appearance of such 'new-fangilnes' as the consort of viols, the pavane and galliard, the metrical psalm, the art-song for voice and lute, the new polyphonic style, semi-professional musicians as servants, popular instrumental tutors, and increased musical literacy" (1961, 109). We might add the broadside ballad to this list. Stevens also observes that the influence of French culture, especially in its medieval, Burgundian forms, is gradually superseded by Italian influences. One might also note that the practice of composing parts of a song simultaneously instead of adding parts one by one to a *cantus firmus* or complete melody had increased the sense of tonality in most music, though the theory under which the composers worked was still thoroughly modal (Winn, 1981, 132–34). We have already discussed the psalm and mentioned the dance forms. It remains to describe other kinds of song and the implications of their forms and styles for the setting of poetry.

Although our focus is on secular and nonliturgical devotional song, we must say something about church music. Despite the changes in the musical establishments of English churches with the accession of Elizabeth, church music was not reduced to congregational psalm-singing. Even music with Latin texts continued to be composed, for Latin services were continued at the universities, public schools, and the Chapel Royal. Nevertheless, the English service replaced the mass, and the English anthem generally took the place of the Latin motet.[12] Music for the English service, such as Thomas Tallis's "Dorian" service (which may be partly Edwardian), tended to conform to Reformation practices by having the voices move together homophonically and sing one note per syllable of text in most of its movements. But the anthem could be as polyphonic, imitative, and complex as the motet; in some instances, anthems are in fact motets with English words substituted for the Latin. Generally, the anthem avoids melisma and is more syllabic, becoming somewhat simpler than the motet. Some anthems alternate passages of chordal writing with points of imitation, and some are homophonic throughout.

The local Edwardian injunctions cited earlier had demanded simple, syllabic settings without "reports or repeatings"; these injunctions were swept away during Mary's reign, and though Elizabeth brought back the Reformation, the pendulum did not swing all the way back. Composers of services and anthems operated under Elizabeth's injunctions of 1559, which allowed "for the comforting of such that delight in Musick, it may be permitted, that in the beginning, or in the end of Common-prayers, either at Morning or Evening, there may be sung an Hymn, or such like song to the praise of Almighty God in the best sort of melody and musick that may be conveniently devised."[13] The "best" music for the musician would be polyphonic music. But objections to complex music—as well as to any music at all—continued to be voiced. The author of *The Praise of Musicke* (1586), probably the learned John Case, dealt with these objections, and asserted that "artificiall singing is farre better than their plain Musicke, for it striketh deeper, and worketh more effectually in the hearers." To the objection that the "cunning and exquisite musick" of a choir will not allow the words to be understood, "much lesse any edification taken," Case says first that the fault is not in the art, but in the singers, who should pronounce the words more distinctly. Furthermore, the texts that are sung "are very familiar and known unto the people." The repetition of phrases in polyphonic music is not a fault, but a feature that the objectors should favor, for repetition will help the words be understood; nor is it a fault if the text is understood from the first, "because the often ingeminating and sounding the same thing in our eares doth cause the thing repeated to take deepe roote, and worke effectually in our hearts" (sigs. I6v–8). One is reminded that the objectors and Case tend to agree on the humanistic ends, but disagree about the means.

Some of the milder objectors may have been satisfied by the development of the verse anthem by Richard Farrant, William Mundy, and William Byrd in the 1560s (Le Huray, 1967, 216–25). In this form, choral sections alternate with passages sung by a solo voice accompanied by the organ or other instruments. Sometimes the choir merely repeats a phrase that had been sung by the solo, making apprehension of the text especially easy. Yet musical interest can be sustained by the instruments and their interplay with the solo voice. A similar dynamic is at work in the consort song, in which a solo voice is accompanied by instruments, usually a quartet of viols. Both forms seem to have emerged around the same time (*New Grove*, 1980, "Byrd"). Although many of the consort songs have metrical psalms or other devotional verse for texts, many are purely secular. The consort song allows for an especially clear presentation of the text, even though the accompanying viol parts can be elaborately polyphonic. These songs will be discussed more fully in the fourth chapter.

Other secular songs of the period before Whythorne are musically similar to the anthems in that they range from simple four-part homophonic pieces to fairly complex examples of imitative polyphony; even in the latter, however, there is usually some regard for the articulation of the text, and there are very few melismatic passages. Apart from the consort songs, most of these songs survive only in a book of organ transcriptions made by Thomas Mulliner in the 1550s (D. Stevens, 1952 and 1954). Since the texts for many of the pieces are available from other sources, it is possible to reconstruct them as songs. Sir John Hawkins published five such reconstructions as long ago as 1776 in his *General History of the Science and Practice of Music* (2:920–28). Of these, "Defyled is my name" is a four-part polyphonic setting by Robert Johnson of verses attributed to Anne Boleyn; William Hunnis's "Like as the doleful dove" has a homophonic, note-against-note setting in four parts by Thomas Tallis; and three settings attributed to Richard Edwards have texts that (along with Hunnis's) are all found in *The Paradise of Dainty Devises* (1576): "Where griping grief the hart would wound," a homophonic song alluded to in *Romeo and Juliet;* "By painted wordes the silly simple man," a mildly polyphonic setting of a poem by Francis Kinwelmarsh; and, perhaps the most famous, "In going to my naked bedde." This last song has some points of imitation, as well as homophonic passages. Denis Stevens says that the music "has a light transparent counterpoint which does not prevent the words from being heard clearly and easily" (1952, 60). The poem's five sixteen-line common meter stanzas can all be fitted to the music of the first stanza with very little trouble. Other songs in the Mulliner book include two more songs by Tallis, "O ye tender babes" (the music is homophonic, the text lost) and "When shall my sorrowful sighing slack" (polyphonic). Two poems by the earl of Surrey, "My friends, the things that do attain" and "O happy dames," have settings, the first an anonymous polyphonic one; the second, by John Sheperd, is complicated by keyboard decoration, but is basically homophonic. Jasper Heywood's poem, "The bitter sweet," printed in *The Gorgeous Gallery of Gallant Inventions,* is given a contrapuntal setting, and the verse of the anonymous "I smile to see how you devise," which appeared in *A Handful of Pleasant Delights,* has a tuneful homophonic setting in triple time, beginning with an upbeat.

At least one of the songs, "Since thou art false to me," exists in another version for solo voice with lute accompaniment, and it is possible that other songs could have been performed as accompanied solos (D. Stevens, 1952, 62). We do get a glimpse of how a song by Richard Edwards was performed from Claudius Hollybande (Claude Desainliens), *The French Schoolemaister* (1573, sigs, I8v–K3v). A sample conversation dramatizes a domestic scene on a snowy day, when four male members of the household sing a part song they identify as one composed by "the maister of the children of the Queenes chapall," "Maister Edwards."

This passage also points to the growing interest in domestic music. Musical literacy was no doubt enhanced by printed music in the psalm books, some of which had a chapter of elementary musical instruction. Among the members of the wealthier classes, it was increased by resident teachers like Thomas Whythorne. Whythorne seemed never to be without work for very long, so we may infer that there was a demand for his services, and that others were also making a living teaching music to private citizens and their children. Whythorne frequently composed the music he taught. Despite the lack of printed secular music before 1588, there must have been a number of native part songs circulating in manuscript, as the passage in *The French Schoolemaister* implies, and we know that music was imported from the Continent. Nevertheless, in the 1570s the market for music was not so great as to prevent Whythorne from complaining about the slow sales of his 1571 *Songes;* Tallis and Byrd were also disappointed in the sales of their *Cantiones Sacrae* of 1575, though Latin motets may be presumed to have limited appeal to amateur singers (Whythorne, 1961, 220; Buck, 1963, 6:xxiv). At any rate, a native song tradition had by the 1560s grown from the various seeds in the court, the church, the schools, and some homes, so that Whythorne's songs, while a novelty in print, were not without a context.

Chapter Three
Poet-Composer: Thomas Whythorne

To compare the verse and music of Thomas Whythorne with that of the poet-composer of the next generation, Thomas Campion, is to realize the great changes that occurred in poetic style and in the relationship between words and music. Campion and his contemporaries established for most modern audiences what an Elizabethan song should be: tuneful, witty, sensuous, smooth, with words and music carefully tailored for each other, the music often being expressive of the content of the text. Whythorne, on the other hand, is plain, angular, sententious, with words and music meeting mainly on the formal level, and then not always gracefully. Whythorne and Campion exemplify very well C. S. Lewis's dichotomy of sixteenth-century poetic styles, "drab" and "golden" (1954, 64–65). They also exemplify the unfairness of these terms, because Campion is simply more talented and sophisticated than Whythorne, at least as a poet. But despite their differences, they are similar in ways other than being authors of both words and music. They both write music that, compared to the music of contemporaries like Byrd and Dowland, is amateurish: and both have an attitude toward the setting of texts that is nearer the formal end of the continuum ranging from formal to expressive.

Many of Campion's songs are well known, but Whythorne's are not. Until this century, few have taken the trouble to examine them. Dr. Charles Burney, who was generally unsympathetic toward Elizabethan music, branded Whythorne's songs as "truly barbarous," and for years afterward this opinion was repeated, with no indication that the writer made the effort to score any of the songs from the separate part-books. The words alone are certainly not prepossessing. When Canon Fellowes scored some of the songs around 1920, he found them more worthwhile; and when Peter Warlock edited twelve songs a few years later, he was positively enthusiastic. Opinions have moderated in recent years: E. J. Dent and Peter Le Huray give Whythorne short shrift, though Gustave Reese voices mild interest and approval.[1] Whythorne's reputation among his contemporaries is hard to determine. Whereas Byrd's standing was as high then as it is now, Whythorne was practically ignored. His name appears in none of the sixteenth-century lists of famous musicians, and I know of only one instance of any work of Whythorne's appearing in a contemporary manuscript compiled by someone else.[2]

But Whythorne demands special attention because of his place in history. Except for the incomplete *XX Songes* of 1530, Whythorne's *Songes, for three, fower, and five voyces* of 1571 is the first printed collection of English secular music. Ironically, we know more about his life and less about his songs than any other composer of the period. As yet there is no complete modern edition of Whythorne's songs, and the partial ones are not readily available. Only one song, "Buy new broom," has been recorded.[3] But we are fortunate to have Whythorne's autobiography, discovered by James M. Osborn and published by him in 1961.

From Whythorne's text and Osborn's introduction and notes, we learn that Whythorne was born in Iminster, Somerset, in 1528, the son of an established, if not wealthy, gentleman. He learned to read, write, and sing in local schools, and at ten went to the Magdalen College School for choristers at Oxford. After six years there at the school and one at the college, he became a sort of apprentice to the poet John Heywood. In Heywood's service he "learned to play on the virginals, the liut, and to mak english verses."[4] His models for English verse were the poems he copied for Heywood—songs and sonnets by Wyatt, Surrey, "mr Moor the exsellent Harper," and psalms translated by Wyatt and Thomas Sternhold—and probably the poems of Heywood himself. Osborn dates this activity ca. 1545, well before Wyatt and Surrey were printed in Tottel's Miscellany (*Songes and Sonettes*, 1557) and before Sternhold's psalms appeared around 1549.

After 1548, Whythorne was living in London and teaching music. Around 1553, he went to Europe, spending some months in the Netherlands, then moving to Italy, where he spent half a year learning the language. He visited Padua, Venice, Naples, Rome, Florence, Milan, and other cities, and returned to England via France. He is frustratingly reticent about his musical experiences abroad: he mentions Adrian Willaert only to report his income. From 1555 to 1557 he was in the service of Lord Ambrose Dudley. After teaching in various households until early 1560, he agreed to be the private tutor for young William Bromfield at Trinity College, Cambridge. When Bromfield took his B.A. in 1562, his father took on Whythorne as deputy, a responsibility that proved to be especially trying when the elder Bromfield died and the plague struck London in 1563. When the younger Bromfield returned from abroad and relieved him, Whythorne's health was weakened, so he retired to the country for a rest. While there, he determined to stick to music in the future, and in order to improve his standing in this profession, he decided to publish his compositions. He resumed teaching and began preparing his works for the press. In 1571 they were at last ready, and John Day printed his *Songes, for three, fower, and five voyces*. Probably as a result of this publication, Whythorne was appointed master of music for the chapel of Archbishop Matthew Parker. When Parker died in 1575, Whythorne returned to teaching, and the autobiography comes to an end. Osborn has discovered that he married in 1577. Around 1590 he was in the service of Sir Francis Hastings, to whom he dedicated his only other publication, the *Duos*. He died in 1596, aged sixty-seven.

Whythorne's own title for his autobiography is "A book of songs and sonetts," and his stated purpose is to describe the circumstances of his life that gave rise to his poems. Some of Whythorne's most appealing poems were not set to music and appear only in the autobiography. In answer to a love note tucked under his gittern strings, he wrote "Thoz wurdz I have reherst," which has a whiff of the insouciant charm of the anonymous lyrics—some once attributed to Wyatt—in the Devonshire manuscript. Its minimalist value is enhanced by the narrative context, as is the roughly humorous "Testiminiall" for a poor old woman he calls "Sibyl Silus." The ballad written on "an old grownd" (either a ground bass or a popular tune) beginning "Ther waz A frier men kald Robard" is also lively. Whythorne's other verses tend to be sententious and proverbial, and their occasions are frequently more interesting than the poems themselves (Whythorne, 1961, 31, 168–69, 125–29; Shore, 1981). One striking result of these descriptions of their origin is the realization that even the most conventional, abstract, and didactic verse can have its inspiration in deeply emotional and personal events.

This perception may not enhance the value of these poems for the modern reader, for they are very plain. For example, take this text from one of the 1571 *Songes:*

> Though crooked cares do chance,
> to wretched wilfull wills,

> which unwisely advance,
> the reach of many ills:
> to those thus may we glaunce,
> where wilfull will planteth,
> wit with wisedome wanteth.
>
> (Tx, sig. Dd1v)

According to the autobiography (37), Whythorne wrote these lines around 1550 to force his "wyll to yeeld to reson" in accepting a post as a servant after illness had depleted his finances. We recognize the sententious tone and alliteration as characteristic of mid-century verse, but the regular meter of the first two lines stumbles in the third, and again in the last two lines. The irregularities in Wyatt's metrics are well known, but Sternhold's meters were regular, and a degree of regularity would be imposed on Wyatt by 1557 in Tottel's Miscellany. Some sixteen years later, Whythorne writes in much the same style:

> If flattered be the wicked,
> from ill to worse become they than,
> when malice is likewise praised,
> the harme thereof few suffer can.
>
> (Tx, sig. Ii2)

The occasion for this poem, Whythorne tells us (1961, 171), is a quarrel between himself and another guest, after which he versified a relevant passage from a book called *The Ring of Righteousness.* The alliteration is gone, but the metrical ambiguity remains in lines one and three. By this time Barnabe Googe had published his highly regular *Eclogs, Epytaphes, and Sonettes* (1563), and George Turberville's similar *Epitaphes, Epigrams, Songs and Sonets* (1567) would soon appear. Whythorne seems not to have learned the trick of writing regularly stressed iambics; he certainly never goes beyond regularity as Sidney and those who follow him were able to do. Whythorne seems to have remained a syllable-counter. It is possible nevertheless to find long stretches of regular meter in his verse. In the verse "preface" to the autobiography (1961, 2), after nineteen lines of regular—if not smooth—iambic pentameter, Whythorne writes, "From beginning, unto the very end." If "beginning" takes its usual stress, the line is irregular; to make it regular, one would have to say *bĕgínnĭng.* Presumably Gascoigne in such an instance would have read this line with the latter pronunciation, though he would also have objected to it (see above, chapter 2). The number of syllables remains the same in either reading.

These metrical irregularities frustrated the linguist Rupert Palmer in his study of Whythorne's speech through the phonetic spelling used in the autobiography. Palmer found he could not use the meter of Whythorne's verse as a guide to his stress (1969, 148). Would consideration of Whythorne's music have helped Palmer? Can the music tell us if Whythorne anticipated Gascoigne, and wished his readers to mispronounce words so that the meter would be regular? It is hard to generalize, because Whythorne's music varies in its connections with his texts. Let us begin with a suggestive example. Taking into account all the differences between modern and sixteenth-century stress that scholars like Kökeritz and Dobson can account for, lines like these still seem irregular:

> For to reclaim to frend a froward foe,
> or bring to passe affaires waighty & great,
> if patience cheefly doth work it so. . . .
>   (TxMB, sig. Bb3v; Ct sig. AAa2v)

The normal stress on "waighty," "patience," and "cheefly," which makes these lines irregular, is not supported by the music; or rather, the music supports stresses that would make regular iambics, but would distort pronunciation (Ex. 3.1).

Example 3.1

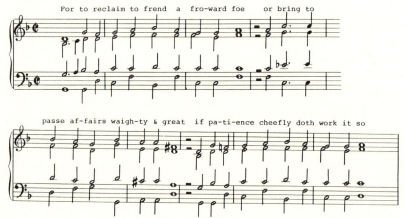

I have added bar lines in this example, as sixteenth-century musicians did when they used scores (Lowinsky, 1960, 156–71). Peter Warlock (1925, 9) writes that "this music must be sung with utmost freedom and flexibility of rhythm, and phrased in strict accordance with the melodic line of the music, without stress accents, and, above all, in complete oblivion of the fact that a bar line ever suggested a strong accent to a singer." Nevertheless, given the *alla breve* mensuration and a simple *tactus* of downbeat on one whole note, upbeat on the second, the normal stresses on the first syllables of "waighty" and "cheefly" fall after the beat, with the second syllable of "waighty" on a downbeat. "Patience" is set to three half notes, with a downbeat on the last syllable.

But what if one shifted to triple time in performance (Ex. 3.2)?

Example 3.2

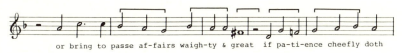

The upward leap of three voices to the first syllable of "waighty" might support the shift in the second line, but the harmony does not change; and in the third line, the last syllable of "patience" would still be stressed, and melodic and harmonic movement work against the normal stress on "cheefly." A shift from duple to triple seems unlikely when the music is not monodic (like the psalm) and the parts are moving together in notes that are for the most part coincidental with the pulse. A similar song presents a similar situation (Ex. 3.3; TxM, sig. Hh3; B, H3; Ct, GGg3; T, BB2v–3):

Example 3.3

A triple grouping would avoid distortions of "court'ous" and "gesture," but the harmonic movement works against such a shift. One might argue that these words still had their romance accentuation at this time, but Levins, in *Manipulus Vocabulorum* (1570), marks accents on the first syllables of "gesture" and "courtiouse" (1867, cols. 192, 225). Though there is nothing in these examples to prompt a metrical shift to save the pronunciation, it is common to find throughout sixteenth-century music passages that vary the rhythm while supporting the iambic meter (Ex. 3.4; TxMB, sig. Bb4; Ct, AAa3). Since Whythorne

Example 3.4

does not hesitate to change the time signature when he wishes to change the meter, it seems we should consider such examples as syncopation, and resist changing the meter for the sake of pronunciation.

The treatment of the irregular lines in the poems quoted earlier, "Though crooked cares do chance" and "If flattered be the wicked," is similar. In the first instance, the last line, "wit with wisdom wanteth," is repeated twice, and the last two words yet again in the triplex; in all three instances, the first syllable of "wanteth" falls on an upbeat, and the second syllable on a whole note or longer. In the second song, the line "when malice is likewise praised" is repeated several times, with different beats on "likewise praised" each time. The piece is polyphonic, so each part has more rhythmic independence than in the homophonic songs. The possibilities suggested by this sample from the triplex are multiplied by the four other voices (Ex. 3.5). It seems that while Whythorne sometimes distorts pronunciation and occasionally at the same time gets metrical regularity, it is not clear that there is a causal connection. In the polyphonic songs especially, he seems merely to be distributing the syllables over the notes without much regard for verse form or stress. A possible reason for this circumstance will appear later.

Example 3.5

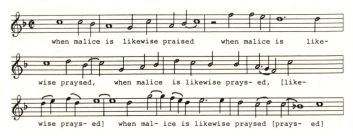

when malice is likewise praised   when malice is   like-

wise praysed,   when malice is likewise prays- ed,   [like-

wise prays- ed]   when mal- ice is likewise praysed [prays-   ed]

So far, most of the examples given of Whythorne's music have been
fairly simple homophonic songs that set one note to one syllable of
text. In these songs, the music and text have a close formal relationship
in that the musical phrase coincides with the line of text, and cadences
parallel rhymes. Usually the last two lines of music and verse are repeated, with no significant change. Many songs of the period fit this
description, from harmonized settings of the psalms to some of the
simpler French *chansons* and Italian *frottole* and *canzonetti*. Contemporary
native songs of this sort are Richard Edwards's "Where griping grief
the heart would wound" and Thomas Tallis's setting of William Hunnis's "Like as the doleful dove" (Hawkins, 1963, 2:924-27). A few
more such songs by Whythorne are "Like as the smoke outwardly seen"
(Tx, sig. Cc2), "Now that the truth is tride" (Tx, sig. Bb4), "Take
heed of words" (Tx, sig. Cc2), "It is a world some sots to see" (Tx,
sig. Cc2r), and a particularly tuneful triple-time psalm, "I will yeld
thankes to thee" (Tx, sig. Ee3v). This last is based on Whythorne's
own metrical version of Psalm 138; the verse is an eight-line stanza
rhyming *aaabaaab*. His version of Psalm 103, "My soule and all that
in me is" (Tx, sig. Ee3v), is in common meter, and the setting is also
in triple time, tuneful and homophonic. Gustave Reese (1959, 816),
picking up on Whythorne's mention of the *villanella alla napolitana* in
the preface to his songbook, says that "The doubtful state that I pos-
sess" (Tx, sig. Ee1v) is an adaptation of this form. It is homophonic,
with a repeated rhythmic pattern (Ex. 3.6),

Example 3.6

♩♩♩ ₒ. ♩♩♩ ₒ

but unlike most *villanelle* it has a sober, almost despairing text, and a suitable minor tonality. Even Whythorne characterizes the Italian form as "a pretty merry one" (1961, 179–80). The virtues of this simple, homophonic kind of music as a vehicle for poetry are that the text can be clearly heard and understood. The limitations are that there is not much variety in the music, nor much opportunity for the music to add an expressive or interpretive dimension to the text. For Whythorne's largely abstract and didactic verses, however, clarity of statement seems more appropriate than emotional expressiveness.

Nevertheless, not all of Whythorne's songs are simple and homophonic, and the rest deserve some description at this point. In the 1571 *Songes,* there are fourteen three-part songs, forty-two in four parts (including five settings of prose texts of the psalms), and twenty in five parts. Some are thoroughly contrapuntal, with independent voices and frequent points of imitation, as in "Thou shalt soon see in ech estate" (Tx, sig. Bb1v), "Beware how sorowes thee oppres" (Tx, sig. Bb2v), and "Nothing is sharper then low thinges" (Tx, sig. Hh4). In these and other songs, the formal parallel between text and music is loosened: different voices sing different words at any given point; individual voice parts repeat words or phrases; a single syllable is set to more than one note, especially at the end of a phrase. One result is a loss in clarity for a listener trying to understand the text; and though the repetitions may help, they break up the verse line. If we consider the songs to be chamber music, aimed as much at the performers as the audience, audibility of text is a lesser consideration. In any event, there is greater purely musical interest in these contrapuntal songs than in most of the homophonic songs.

Most of Whythorne's other songs might be described as basically homophonic, but with a somewhat greater degree of independence in the voices than in the first group. In "Give not thy mind to heaviness" (Tx, sig. Ii4), for instance, an abundance of passing notes and brief melismas does not prevent the different parts from moving more or less together and from sounding the words together at the same time. "It doth belong more of good right" (Tx, sig. Ii1v), "When fliering fortune favoureth" (Tx, sig. Aa3), "The haughtiness of some but base" (Tx, sig. Ee3v), and his paraphrase of Psalm 51, "O Good Lord have mercy on me," in long meter or octosyllabic quatrains, are similar examples.

Some of the most interesting of Whythorne's songs mix homophonic and contrapuntal passages. One of Whythorne's six settings of prose texts of the psalms, "O be joyful in the Lord" (Psalm 100; Tx, sig. Ff3v), alternates free homophonic declamation with imitative passages. In "Who that for truth decrees" (Tx, sig. Bb1), for instance, the song begins homophonically, plainly stating the proposition:

> Who that for truth decrees (as judge most sage)
> true noblenes of right onely to stand,
> in dignitie, or auncient linage,
> or great ritches, or revenues of land.

Then a series of rising imitative sequences on "If therwithall he do not link in band" raises expectation, pointing to the conclusion set homo-phonically:"wisedome, knowledge, and other vertues rare, / his judge-ment then of reason is but bare." The last line is repeated, with brief melismas before the final note. This example suggests that even with abstract sententious verse, music can be used to enhance the *rhetorical* effect of the verse. Whythorne himself testifies both to the rhetorical effect of song and to the "classical" distancing effect, separating the song from the singer: sometimes his poetry "shiuld bee the better hard bekawz that the miuzik joined therwith did sumtyms draw the mynd of the hearer to bee the more attentyv to the song. also if it wer not to bee well taken, yet in asmuch az it waz sung ther kowld not somuch hurt be found as had been in the kas of my wryting being delivered to her to read, for singing of such songs & dittiez waz A thing kommen in thoz daies" (1961, 51). But when the text permits, Whythorne can sometimes use music to support the emotional expression as well, as we can see in one of the most impressive of Whythorne's songs, "Since I embrace the heav'nly grace" (Tx, sig. Ee4–F1; Warlock, 1927, no. 357), which also contains both homophonic and polyphonic passages.

In his autobiography, Whythorne describes the composition of this text following a long passage of religious meditations inspired by the plague of 1563. After quoting James 5.13 on the exhortation to "rejois and be meri in God the lord," he tells how he made the poem from "A vain konseit" he had written earlier, a love song in the same verse form beginning "Sins I embras mi ladies gras" (1961, 157). In other in-stances when poets have written sacred parodies of secular texts, music seems to have been at least an indirect catalyst. It is possible that a germ of the tune for Whythorne's earlier poem (though he does not say he made one) is in the later composition; but it is almost certainly not a contrafact, for the song he published is a through-composed setting of considerable scope.

The song begins in the free homophonic style, with several syllables getting more than one note. After the first cadence, three of the four voices enter in staggered imitative leaps of a fourth from the dominant to the tonic note on "rejoyce." Near the end of the song, an extended contrapuntal passage employs only this one word, "rejoyce," and in many entrances the word is set to this same upward leap, especially in the upper voices. This setting of the word is almost inevitable: in an anthem by John Redford, "Rejoyce in the Lorde alway" (Hawkins, 1963, 2:929), each of the four voices begins with this interval, as does the chorus of Byrd's "Carowle for Christmas day," "From Virgin's Womb" (1589, 24, 35), on "Rejoice, rejoice, with heart and voice." We may also recall the soprano aria in Handel's *Messiah,* "Rejoice great-ly." When this figure continues up the scale, it becomes one of Deryck Cooke's "basic terms of the musical vocabulary" for joy (1962, 119–20). The frequency of ascending scales in this contrapuntal ending, some of them ornamented, also reinforces the feelings labeled by the text. These features, plus the rapid melismata and rhythmic exuber-ance, clearly show Whythorne's capacity for expressive writing; but compared to the later composers, he does not exploit this capacity. Earlier in the piece, he does not allow the line "do yeld my corpse to grave" to lead him away from the major tonality or to introduce any noticeably pathetic effects. On "sigh" in the next line, some minor intervals occur in the moving inner parts, but the effect is fleeting, and the D-minor chord on "dispaire" in the line after is also not very striking in context. There are a few instances in other songs of simple word-painting, such as the ascending figures on the words "when they by groth on hye be brought" in "Nothing is sharper then low thinges" (Tx, sig. Hh4). But on the whole, the relationship between words and music is formal, and such instances of word-painting are best consid-ered decorous or rhetorical rather than expressive.

Even on the formal level, Whythorne is not totally consistent. He frequently ignores the principle of one note per syllable. In almost all the songs except the simplest homophonic ones, Whythorne reveals some habits of declamation and text-setting that seem odd or awkward to modern singers. As Warlock says,

Whythorne's method of phrasing by syllabic distribution is even more radi-cally different from modern procedure in this respect than are the methods of

Byrd and the later Elizabethans. One is inclined to suspect that it is this fact, rather than any purely musical qualitites, that has brought about his almost universal condemnation by the musical historians. If intelligently studied, however, his methods of declamation will be found to yield surprisingly novel and effective results in performance. (1925, 9)

The most common of these habits—and one that can be found in later composers—is that of setting a syllable to a short note tied to one or two longer notes (Ex. 3.7; Tx, sig. Ee4v):

Example 3.7

Sometimes this feature can add to the tunefulness, as in this song, which Warlock (1925, 8) says "has a lilt that sets one thinking of 'Sumer is icumen in'" (Ex. 3.8; Tx, sig. Ii1):

Example 3.8

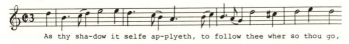

At other times it seems clumsy (Ex. 3.9; Tx, sig. Ii4v):

Example 3.9

And again, combined with rising pitch, it can give a misdirected emphasis (Ex. 3.10; Tx, sig. Ff2v; Warlock, 1927, no. 359).

Example 3.10a

Example 3.10b

Some songs carry this stretching of syllables over several notes to such an extent that it might seem that the words and music were composed independently and joined only by Procrustean force. We know from the verse preface to Whythorne's proposed but apparently unpublished book of song texts that some of his songs were originally composed to fit the verses of others.

> To whoz sonets I miuzik mad to pleaz them now and than
> To pleaz them now and then, that lyk my simpul trad
> I meeterz of myn own devyzd, in plas of thoz erst mad.
>
> (1961, 221)

This statement seems consistent with this manner of describing his project: "I purpozed to put with evry song a Sonett of myn own invension for A ditti therto, most of the which I hav written into this book alredy" (1961, 174). Examples of songs that seem to be the result of the forced marriage of separate, preexisting words and music are the previously cited "If flattered be the wicked" (Tx, sig. Ii2), "As many heads have many wits" (Tx, sig. Aa2v), "The happy life" (Tx, sig. Bb1v), and "If I had not foreseen" (Tx, sig. Dd3v). Other songs, such as "Though frends be frail" (Tx, sig. Aa4), which are not contrapuntal but repeat phrases frequently, may have been assembled in this manner, as may some of the simpler homophonic songs which would fit any verse with the right number of syllables. In some instances, Whythorne may have composed his text with the music in mind, resulting in a contrafact in which the union sounds natural.

All but one of the songs in the 1571 collection were published with all the parts underlaid with text, and so must be considered part-songs. But just as the songs vary in character and texture, it is likely that they could be performed in various ways. As Whythorne himself says in his autobiography (1961, 51), "In thes daies I yuzed to sing my songs and sonets sumtym to the liut and sumtyms the virginals, wher-by I miht tell my tal with my vois aswell az by woord or wryting." Later, in wooing a maiden, he wrote two or three "prety ditties mad of loov, the which bekawz I durst not delyver to her in writing for fear of afterklaps I would sing them often tyms unto her on the virginals or liut" (1961, 177). Around 1564, during Whythorne's vacation in the country, he taught his host's daughter to sing to the lute. "And emong the songs that I tawht her shee learned that I mad my self" (1961, 165–66) was "If thou that hast a trusty frend" (Tx, sig. Ii2v), which was printed among the five-part songs in 1571.

This song is a rather elaborate through-composed setting of a poem in five octosyllabic quatrains. It begins with points of imitation, and maintains a more or less contrapuntal texture until it reaches a section in triple time near the end. But even in the opening, the imitation is not very strict, and the upper voice seems a bit more melodic than the others. In this upper voice, phrases are often separated by rests, and are not frequently repeated; in other words, the relationship of the top voice to the others is very much like that of solo to accompaniment as found in the consort song and in the later lutenist air.

Other songs are similar in that they have a melodic upper voice that would make them suitable for singing as accompanied solos. Warlock (1925, 8) says of the five-part songs he transcribed that they are "virtually ayres." Most of the simpler homophonic songs could be performed as accompanied solos, as well as those in somewhat mixed styles such as "Is there no choice for me." Besides having tuneful upper voices, songs like these tend to avoid breaking up lines into repeated phrases and to keep mostly one note per syllable, except near cadences.

One of Whythorne's songs seems almost certainly to be intended as a consort song. "Buy new broom" (Tx, sig. Ii3v) is printed with text under the upper voice only. The four other parts have only the first phrase for identification. Except for the fact that the solo voice does not repeat phrases and that it has rests between phrases, it is not typical of most other consort songs. The opening notes, which are repeated throughout the song, may be based on the actual cry of the broom seller. There are Continental examples of songs based on street-vendors' cries, such as some the *villote* published by Filippo Azzaiolo in the 1550s and 1560s. Later English consort-song settings of street cries were composed by Richard Dering, Thomas Weelkes, and others.[5] Whythorne's song opens with the voice beginning a point of imitation, followed by the soprano, tenor, alto, and bass parts. Most other consort songs that begin with imitation bring in the solo later. The form is also unusual: the verse is in three quatrains rhyming *a a b b,* with the first three lines containing ten syllables and the last fourteen. The music for the upper voice repeats the opening phrase for every other line of verse, thus: ABACABACABAC. But the four other voices never repeat, maintaining a constantly shifting polyphonic texture. Whythorne probably did not provide words for the lower parts because a totally vocal performance of this particular song would not be practical.

This song is a good example of the rather formal and abstract conception Whythorne has of the relationship between words and music. The verse is syllabic, with no regular iambics:

> By new broom, by new broom, ye may be sure
> store is good, for they will not long endure.
> The new broom sweepeth cleane, a proverb old,
> that applyed is to such as heerafter shall be told.

The musical sections fit each line formally, for there is a note for each syllable. One small adjustment is made in a repeated section; the A section usually begins as in Ex. 3.11.

Example 3.11

Buy new broom,   buy new broom

But the third instance begins thus (Ex. 3.12):

Example 3.12

The double   diligent

The text, a not completely coherent mix of proverbs, applications thereof, and filler (as in line 4 quoted above), does not invite expressive treatment. The broom seller's cry is representational in a sense, a kind of rhetorical trope; but the main effect the musical setting has on the poem is to lighten it somewhat. The jauntiness of the music gives the poem a tone that is not immediately evident in the words, but which suits the circumstances of their composition, the end of the joking relationship between Whythorne and the older Mistress Elsabeth, who would call him her "day huzband" (1961, 89–91).

Whythorne, in sum, sees the relationship between words and music as formal. Music can give a generalizing distance to the substance of the poem, sometimes tone, sometimes rhetorical point, but rarely emotional expressiveness. Musically, Whythorne's songs perpetuate some native part-song traditions, admit only a trace of Italian influence, possibly look ahead to the air, and participate somewhat idiosyncratically in the fashion for consort songs.

Chapter Four

William Byrd and
the Consort Song

"Consort song" is the modern term for a kind of song that was usually performed with one voice accompanied by a "consort" of three, four, or five viols.[1] As an accompanied solo, it is a relative (or ancestor) of the lute song or air and the verse anthem. No doubt part-songs conceived for voices were performed with mixed voices and instruments, or on instruments alone, as many later madrigal publications claimed to be "apt for viols and voices." Conversely, some consort songs were sung as part-songs: William Byrd underlaid the viol parts of his consort songs with words when he published them in 1588 and 1589. Given this fluidity, the consort song probably arose out of part-song sessions to which some performers brought their viols. Some have suggested that it derived from the German *tenorlied* or the French *chanson rustique,* but evidence for such origins is slim, and purely native development is just as likely (*New Grove*).

Some of the early consort songs appear to be homophonic part-songs in which the melodious upper voice becomes the solo and the lower voices are taken by viols (e.g., "How can the tree").[2] Others seem to be more idiomatic in that the solo is quite distinct from the accompaniment, but the accompaniment moves chordally and could be easily played on the lute or keyboard instruments ("In terrors trapp'd," "Mistrust misdeems amiss"). More characteristic are the songs in which the viols maintain a contrapuntal texture, often with the treble viol acting as obbligato to the voice, anticipating its phrases (*vorimitation*) or imitating them ("Mistrust not truth," "Enforced by love and fear"). The master of the form, William Byrd, at first made the accompaniment more strictly polyphonic, with all the voices engaged in points of imitation; in his expressive later songs, he loosened the structure of the polyphonic web. Byrd realized that the advantage of the consort song was that it allowed the composer to exercise his skill in polyphony and thus maintain a high level of musical interest, while the solo voice carried the text clearly on a shaped melody.

Songs for Plays

Although almost any combination of instruments and voices could conceivably have been used in performing these songs, almost all demand a high voice for the solo, and the favorite medium seems to have been a boy singer accompanied by four viols. The widely reproduced portrait of Sir Henry Unton shows such a combination.[3] The form seems to have solidified in songs written for plays performed by the choristers of St. Paul's and the Chapel Royal. Some of the earliest songs, dating from the 1560s, come from such plays or were composed by men associated with the choirboy players. Since the boys were trained singers, their plays were designed so that their talents should not be wasted. And dramatic performances would be especially congenial to solo forms, because they can convey a text clearly to an audience, and because a solo singer can remain in character. The songs from the plays become a heightened form of the set speech, which in the plays of this period is the staple element of the drama (Brett, 1961–62, 79). The particular kind of set speech transformed into song in these plays seems to have been almost exclusively the lament.

For example, Richard Edwards, composer, poet, and master of the children of the Chapel Royal, wrote a tragicomedy, *Damon and Pythias,* that was probably performed in 1564. When Pythias learns that Damon has been betrayed and condemned to die, he soliloquizes:

> What way shall I first beginne to make my mone:
> What wordes shall I finde apt for my complaynte.
> But oh Musicke, as in joyfull tunes, thy mery notes I did borow,
> So now lend mee thy yernfull tunes, to utter my sorow.

The stage direction says, "Here PITHIAS singes, and the Regalles play." The words of the song, beginning "Awake ye wofull Wightes," follow (sigs. C4v–D1v). The music for the song survives in an arrangement for voice and lute (Long, 1967). Although the text specifies regals for the accompaniment and the extant music is not in a consort song arrangement, in most other respects the song is like other consort song laments. I begin with this example because for the other laments no plays survive, at least not in versions that indicate use of the songs.

The song "Guichardo" or "Come tread the paths" comes from a play about Tancred and Gismond. A play called *Gismond of Salerne,* by Robert Wilmot and others, was given at the Inner Temple in 1566 or

1568, and published in a revised version as *Tancred and Gismond* in
1591. Since the original is lost, we do not know whether the song was
used in the Inner Temple version, whether the song was written for a
choirboy adaptation, or whether the boy players used an entirely different play on the same story. In any event, the song must have been
sung by Gismond after Tancred has killed her lover Guichardo. The
words begin in common measure:

> Come tread the paths of pensive pangs
>   with me, ye lovers true.
> Bewail with me your luckless lots,
>   with tears your eyes bedew.

Later the verse switches to poulters' measure:

> Farewell, my lords and friends;
>   farewell all princely state:
> Let father rue his rigour, shown
>   in slaying of my mate.

The verse is in regular iambics, with some reinforcing alliteration. The
musical setting is through-composed; the melody moves in stately
whole and half notes in triple time, and in some passages, reinforces
the meter while smoothing it out (Ex. 4.1).

Example 4.1

Aid me, you ghosts who loathed life, your lovers be- ing slain,

   In other passages, the anonymous composer avoids monotony by
breaking up the pattern of whole note for stressed syllable, half note
for unstressed. In the setting of the opening lines he breaks the flow
by having the voice rest after "paths," "pangs," "me," "true," and "Be-
wail." This passage could be seen as imitative of the broken speech of
the distraught Gismond gathering energy for her farewell; but compared to the later dramatic declamations of Italian and Italian-influenced song, it has a cool, stylized quality; it is more rhetorical than
dramatic. The end of the song was probably conceived by the poet as
a continuation of the common meter:

> Guichardo, if thy sprite do walk,
> come draw thy lover nigh:
> Behold, I yield to thee my ghost;
> Ah, see! I die, I die.

But the song in the musical source is different. By repeating words and inserting exclamations, the composer approaches a more dramatic expressiveness. "Ah! Guichardo" is repeated, as is "Behold," and the last line is full of repeated words (Ex. 4.2).

Example 4.2

Ah, see! I die, I die, I die, ah, see! I die, I die, I die

ah, ah, ah, a-las, I die, I die, I die, I die.

"Farewell the bliss that once I had," "Pour down, you pow'rs divine" ("Pandolpho"), Nicholas Strogers's "A doleful deadly pang," "Ah, alas, you salt sea gods" ("Abradad"), by Richard Farrant (a later master of the children of the Chapel Royal), and several other songs are similar. Many begin with fairly straightforward settings of poulters' measure or fourteener texts, and end with repetitions of "I die." Bottom's Pyramus in *A Midsummer Night's Dream* offers a close parody of these laments.

Except for the dramatic repetitions and exclamations, these songs contain a number of elements we might have expected of works from this third quarter of the century. The verse is in regular iambics, often in poulters' measure or fourteeners, and is often alliterative. The rhyming lines are end-stopped and correspond to musical cadences. Musical phrases match metrical units, with rests in the solo part at caesuras and line-ends. Other early consort songs that do not take dramatic license show even more close parallels with the abstract qualities of these verse forms. It is an old practice for music to take its form from verse: psalms, ballads, and other late medieval songs show such correspondences. But while the songs of Cornish and Fayrfax from the early 1500s sometimes employ long melismas, the consort songs generally have a more formal relationship to the text and restrict musical elaboration mainly to the accompanying viol parts. These passages in the accompaniment fill in rests between phrases in the vocal part, separating the lines of text and further removing the form from the sense and syntax of the words. Just as Gascoigne asserts the primacy of the metrical pattern over pronunciation, so is the formal pattern asserted over the syntax of the sentences. Pattern dominates, as in poulters' measure; but even when the text is in poulters' measure, the music keeps the song from having the thumping quality of the verse. In Robert Parsons's "Enforced by love and fear," the phrasing reflects the strong caesuras of poulters' measure, and there is no compunction about breaking up the members of the first periodic sentence and de- laying its completion until the syntax is in danger of evaporating. Nor does the composer hesitate to give a three-beat rest between "A wretched tale a woeful head" and "Beseemeth to indite," separating subject and predicate (Ex. 4.3).

Example 4.3

This last song is not from a play, though the first stanza would seem to be clearer if it were part of a larger narrative. This narrative context is supplied by the full thirty-two-line version printed in *The Paradise of Dainty Devices* (1576), where it is ascribed to "R. L." (Rollins, 1927, 91–92). The poem develops a lover's complaint that his mistress has made him dread and fear by making him hope. Its somewhat confusing progress is enhanced by references to Jason and Medea and Troilus and Cressida. The regularity of the poulters' measure makes fitting subse- quent lines to the music of the first four relatively easy. Even the cu- rious weak or "Simpsonian" rhyme[4] at lines 24–25 ("to me / forget thee") can be accommodated by dividing a whole note into two halves (the note for "send" in bar 10 above). But the music does force an awkward pause in line 28, between "So greate a wealth doeth rise, and for" and "example doeth disclose" (set to measures 6–10); what might have been seen as a welcome break in the monotonous meter of the poem by itself becomes a flaw when it is joined with music.

This poem is one of several in the *Paradise* that was set to music as a consort song. I have explored elsewhere the parallels and overlaps between the songs and songbooks and the poetical miscellanies of the period (*LEA,* 10–30). But the *Paradise* is remarkable in several respects. First it was compiled by Richard Edwards, author of *Damon and Pythias* and of several of the poems, including "In goyng to my naked bedde" (the part-song setting was discussed in chapter 2), and "When May is in his prime," which has an anonymous consort song setting. Among the other contributors is William Hunnis, who succeeded Edwards in 1566 as master of the children of the Chapel Royal, and whose poem "In terrors trapp'd" has a consort song setting. Thomas, Lord Vaux's "How can the tree" and "Mistrust misdemes amisse" also have anonymous settings as consort songs. At least four other poems from the *Paradise* have consort song settings, two of which are by Nicholas Strogers; and three other poems have music in the Mulliner Book (D. Stevens, 1954, 49, 83, 84). William Byrd published a setting of "From Virgins wombe" in 1589 as a verse anthem. Other poems may have inspired settings that have not survived. Henry Disle, the printer, had some inkling of these musical connections, for he noted in the dedicatory epistle that the poems were "aptly made to be set to any song in .5. partes, or song to instrument."

The psalms also received consort song treatment, as we might expect at this time. In 1585 John Cosyn published *Musicke of six, and five partes,* which contains fourteen consort song arrangements of the psalms, the solo voice singing only slightly altered versions of the official tunes and Sternhold-Hopkins-Whittingham texts, while the viols provide a contrapuntal, sometimes partly imitative accompaniment. John Mundy's *Songs and Psalmes* (1594), apparently modeled after Byrd's volumes, contains settings of psalms in prose as well as in meter, and one unmistakable consort song to a pastoral text. Although the psalm settings have words for all voices, some could be performed as consort songs. William Byrd has settings of psalm texts in all three of his secular publications (1588, 1589, and 1611). The last collection uses only prose texts, but the first two contain metrical translations, two of which are by Sternhold and Hopkins. Further psalm settings survive in manuscript (Byrd, 15:1–16). Unlike Cosyns, Byrd uses his own melodies, which are similar to those of the standard psalm tunes in that they are stately, syllabic, and move largely in half and whole notes. But Byrd's melodies are better shaped, have more rhythmic interest, and have greater range. As in his other consort songs, he sometimes allows the voice a brief melisma near the final cadence.

William Byrd

With Byrd we come to the premier composer of consort songs and one of the great masters of the age, "a Father of Musick," as his contemporaries wrote at his death.[5] In addition to composing around a hundred consort songs, Byrd wrote a number of polyphonic part-songs, keyboard pieces, fantasies for viols, about 180 Latin motets, some English anthems and Anglican service music, and Latin masses and Catholic liturgical music. Born in 1543 under Henry VIII, his musical life spanned nearly all of Elizabeth's reign and much of James's. When he died in 1623, he had outlived two important musical fashions, the madrigal and the lute air, both of which he largely ignored. He did write one of the earliest and most expertly Italianate of English madrigals, "This sweet and merry month of May" (Watson, 1590, no. 28) as if to show how easily such trifles could be done, and then returned to his more serious consort songs and Netherlandish polyphony.

Byrd's first secular publication reflects this seriousness in the title, *Psalmes, Sonets, & songs of sadnes and pietie* (1588). The first ten songs are settings of metrical psalms; the next sixteen, called "sonnets and pastorals," are more varied; the "songs of sadnes and pietie" include the next seven songs, plus two "funeral songs" for Sir Philip Sidney. In his preface, Byrd notes that the songs were "originally made for Instruments to expresse the harmonie, and one voyce to pronounce the dittie," though all parts in the printed books are underlaid with words, presumably to appeal to madrigal and part-song buyers. Most have "The first singing part" as a rubric before the part that was originally the solo. But all (except perhaps one) are consort songs, as manuscript versions confirm (Byrd, vol. 16). The next volume, *Songs of sundrie natures, some of gravitie, and others of myrth, fit for all companies and voyces* (1589) includes several consort songs, but also a number of polyphonic part-songs for three, four, and six voices, and some verse anthems (consort songs with choral passages). The last collection, *Psalmes, Songs, and Sonnets: some solemne, others joyfull, framed to the life of the Words: Fit for Voyces or Viols of 3. 4. 5. and 6. Parts* (1611), appeared after many of the major collections of madrigals and lute airs had been published. It contains only two consort songs (this time with five viols) and two verse anthems, the rest being part-songs—some slightly more madrigallike—and two fantasias for viols alone. The phrase "Fit for Voyces or Viols" in the title had been common in madrigal publications since 1600, reflecting the growing interest in purely instrumental music, which is corroborated by the amount of such music surviving in manuscripts (Monson, 1982). Manuscripts also show that Byrd's interest in the consort song had not diminished, despite the evidence of the published collections (Byrd, vol. 15).

Byrd's example reflects the continued interest in the consort song by other composers. The new fashion for viol playing around 1600 also seems to have brought a revival of the consort song, for many seventeenth-century volumes of madrigals and part-songs contain either consort songs or verse anthems.[6] New consort songs and consort-song arrangements of lute airs continue to appear in manuscripts until the middle of the century (Monson, 1982). Indeed, compared to the longevity of this native style and its relative, the lute air, the Italianate madrigal, however brilliant its life in England, seems as ephemeral as a butterfly.

The independence and tenacity shown by Byrd in his cultivation of the consort song and his lack of interest in the madrigal is also evident in Byrd's Roman Catholicism, maintained while he served in the Chapel Royal and wrote Anglican service music, and in his many and protracted lawsuits. It is also evident in the texts he choose to set. Although he did set words by Thomas Watson and Sir Philip Sidney, he seemed to prefer poets from the previous generation like Francis Kinwelmarsh (of *The Paradise of Dainty Devices*), Thomas Churchyard, the translators of the metrical psalms, the emblem poet Geoffrey Whitney, and Byrd's exact contemporary, Sir Edward Dyer. Their poems and those by anonymous poets in Byrd's songs tend to be plain, serious, sententious, and regular in form and meter. This was the style of poetry Byrd encountered when he first began composing consort songs, probably in the 1570s. Despite Byrd's contrapuntal sophistication and greater sense of melodic values, his settings are like Parsons's and Farrant's in that his approach to the text is formal.

In "Word-Setting in the Songs of Byrd," an essay to which this chapter is much indebted, Philip Brett has shown how Byrd "observed the traditional decorum of forms," as did the earlier Tudor composers (1971–72, 53). Byrd's settings are careful to preserve the form of the text, even when they might distort the sense, as Brett demonstrates with "What pleasure have great princes" (1588, no. 19). Another song from this first collection, "My Soule opprest" (1588, no. 3), not only is typical of Byrd's formal approach, but is characteristic in other ways as well. Although the accompaniment is important, I give only the "first singing part" for this stage of the analysis (Ex. 4.4).

Example 4.4

My Soule op-prest with care & grief, doth cleave un-to the dust:

O quicken me af-ter thy word, for therein doe I trust.

My wayes un-to thee have I shew'd, thou aunswerest me a-gaine. Teach

me thy law & so I shall, be eas-ed of my paine. Teach me thy

law & so I shall, be eas-ed of my payne, be eas-ed of my paine.

As in "What pleasure," there is a syntactical gap when the next-to-last line runs over the formal caesura which the music observes with a rest after "shall." The text is a metrical version of Psalm 119, not from Sternhold and Hopkins, but in their form and style, and Byrd faithfully matches each of the eight- and six-syllable lines of common meter with a musical phrase. Cadences coincide with the line ends and rhymes, but though the voice rests at these points, the moving viol parts allow full repose only at the end. Like the old psalm tunes, the melody covers two quatrains; there are eight in all.

The meter of the poem is regularly iambic, except for "after" in line 3 (and in exactly the same position in the fourth stanza); the second and third syllables of "answerest" in line 6 were probably elided; and one line in the seventh stanza seems to lack an initial weak syllable. The music does not reflect this regularity, even though stressed syllables do tend to fall on the beat. (The *alla breve tactus* calls for a beat on each whole note, beats coming at about the speed of a resting human pulse.) Byrd uses a fairly limited range of note values in this and many other songs; but he avoids a strict correspondence between stressed syllable and beat that would limit them even more. To give rhythmic interest to his melody, Byrd sometimes sets unstressed syllables to longer notes than stressed syllables ("My Soule," the melisma on "I trust," and "unto thee" in line five). More typically, he sets a stressed syllable to a note that begins after the beat but is tied to a note on the beat ("care," "unto" in line 2, "have" in line 5; these are whole notes in the unbarred originals). The treatment of "after" is ambiguous; the first syllable is on the beat, but the second syllable is set to a longer and higher note, which is held over the beat. The music could be compatible with a scansion that read "after" as an inverted foot, or with a reading à la Gascoigne that stressed the second syllable. Byrd also gives a note to each syllable of "answerest," showing that he did not elide the last two for the sake of the meter. Perhaps Byrd, like Whythorne, was not too concerned about the details of regular stress meter as long as the integrity of the line is maintained and the form is clear. Or, more likely, as a greater artist he resisted any musical equivalent of the rigidity and monotony of the regular iambics of the poets of the 1560s and 1570s.

In the part-song version of "My Soule opprest," the lower voices repeat words and verbal phrases freely, as in Whythorne's contrapuntal songs and in the madrigal. This kind of repetition reduces the text to prose. In the "first singing part," repetition is severely limited. The last two lines of most songs are repeated formally; in some songs, as in "My Soule opprest," there can be a coda in which one or two lines are repeated once more. In other songs, brief exclamatory phrases like "O Lord" may be repeated, and in the later songs there is a slight increase in repetitions of other phrases. But these repetitions almost never allow the audience to lose sight of the form of the verse.

Since the texts of many of Byrd's songs are made up of general statements about morality and mortality, the composer is under little pressure to set them to emotionally expressive music. Byrd's decorous, formal style gives the texts an atmosphere of dignity and order, which, along with the intrinsic interest of the music, is all they need. As Brett says of "What pleasure have great princes," Byrd's "melodic invention," in "conjuring up a generalised image of the carefree rustic life, is arguably more suited than a detailed madrigalian commentary to the setting of a poem containing so many impersonal moral statements"

(1971–72, 52). Nevertheless, Byrd's restrained, "classical" style does have room for expressiveness. The text of "My Soule opprest" is more openly emotional: the psalmist announces his care and grief, and fervently prays that he may be eased of his pain. The music is in a minor key. The viols begin with points of imitation on the phrase to which the voice, entering last, sings the first line. The first part of the phrase drops from the tonic to the dominant, rises a half step to the sixth, and sinks back to the dominant (Ex. 4.4). Of this figure, Deryck Cooke writes that "The chief and almost only expressive function of the minor sixth is to act as an *appoggiatura* on to the dominant, giving the effect of a burst of anguish. This is the most widely used of all terms of musical language: one can hardly find a page of 'grief' music by any tonal composer of any period without encountering it several times" (1962, 146). The next half of the phrase, on "with care & grief," simply rises from the tonic to the minor third and falls back. Of this, Cooke says that "To base a theme on the tonic, only moving out as far as the minor third, and returning immediately, is to 'look on the darker side of things' in a context of immobility. . . . Composers have frequently used this progression to express brooding, an obsession with gloomy feelings" (1962, 140). Cooke gives empirical evidence for his interpretations by citing dozens of examples from the fifteenth through the twentieth centuries, in both instances including other songs by Byrd. In the third line of the song, when the psalmist turns hopefully to God on "O quicken me," the melody—for the moment in B-flat major—descends stepwise from the tonic to the dominant, a figure Cooke says is expressive of "an incoming emotion of joy, an acceptance or welcoming of comfort, consolation, or fulfilment" (1962, 159). An especially expressive passage comes in the repeated section near the end, on "I shall, / be eased of my paine." The gently descending lines in voice and viols, expressive of incoming feelings of acceptance or resignation (Cooke, 1962, 133, 136–38), set up a chain of suspension dissonances followed by resolutions, of pain being eased (Ex. 4.5).

This last example could be seen as word-painting—illustrative, as well as expressive. Byrd uses more musical illustration than Whythorne, especially in his Latin motets of 1589 and 1591, but much less in his English songs than the madrigalists.

The fact that this song, like many of Byrd's other songs, is strophic suggests some limitations as to how illustrative or expressive the music could or should be. The passage on "be eased of my paine" fortuitously

Example 4.5

be eas-   ed of my   pain.

coincides with "and send mee some reliefe" in the fourth stanza, and in the eighth stanza with "the length of all my dayes"—not a very direct connection, but not in conflict. The fourth stanza, however, begins with "My heart doth melt and pyne away / for very payne and griefe," which is sung to the music for "My wayes unto thee have I shew'd, / thou aunswerest me againe," and is not very expressive of pain. Nevertheless, the generalized melancholy of the melody, occasionally relieved by hope, is not inappropriate for the text as a whole.

Many of Byrd's songs resemble "My Soule opprest" in one way or another. In the 1588 set, several of the texts that are not psalms are nevertheless serious or religious, such as "I joy not in no earthly blisse" (11), which concludes, "no wealth is like the quiet minde"; Dyer's "My minde to me a kingdome is" (14); the penitential "Prostrate O Lord, I lie" (27), and "If that a sinners sighes be Angels food" (30); and moral exempla and lectures, such as "All as a sea, the world no other is" (28), "*Susanna* faire" (29), and "Care for thy soule as thing of greatest price" (31). But a few of the songs are quite different. "Though *Amarillis* daunce in greene" (12) is a light pastoral that was fresh enough to be reprinted in *England's Helicon* (1600). It has a stanza with rhyming long and short lines that breaks free of any of the usual varieties of four-beat verse. Byrd's setting of it is vigorously rhythmical, mixing 6/4 and 3/2 time like the galliard, expressive not only of Amaryllis's dancing, but also of the pleasurable conflict of the speaker's lovesickness. Even more complex rhythmically is "The match that's made for just & true respects" (26).

The famous "Lullaby" carol (32) employs a lot of free repetition, appropriate for a lullaby, in the burden or initial refrain; music for the stanza proper changes from duple to triple time, but maintains its tone of poignant melancholy while the Virgin meditates on the slaughter of the innocents as she rocks the Christ child. Deryck Cooke (1962, 141,

148) cites three passages from this song as expressive of anguish and "inescapable doom." A striking homophonic passage on "A King is borne, they say" underlines the contrast between Herod and the Prince of Peace. The parallel passages in subsequent stanzas do not benefit as much from the musical contrast, but the setting does not distort them. The last lines of the stanzas present more of a problem, for the first three stanzas read "Oh woe, and woful heavie daie, when wretches have their wil," but the last reads "Oh joy, and joyfull happy day, when wretches want their will." As music is repeated and takes on a more independent identity, appropriateness of every detail is less important in stanzas after the first; but here the contrast in the text is so absolute that the music may not be general enough to contain it.

A similar problem might be perceived in "In fields abroad" (22). In this song, the first three stanzas each present a martial scene that is seen as stirring and inspiring of courage: a soldier, a warship, and a mounted knight. The last stanza is quite a contrast:

> By that bedside where sits a gallant Dame,
>   who casteth of hir brave and rich attyre,
> whose petecote sets forth as faire a frame,
>   as mortall men or gods can well desire,
> who sits and sees her petecote unlast,
> I say no more the rest are all disgrast.

But rather than clashing with the text, the music adds to the comic irony by reinforcing the parallels with the first stanzas. The stirring sight in the final stanza also demands courage, and he who sits and does nothing disgraces the heroes of the first stanzas. The few expressive details in the music contribute to this effect: the bugle call on "wher Trumpets shryl do sound" in the first stanza calls the listener to battle on "where sits a gallant Dame." The sudden minor passage introduced in the treble viol before "wher bodies dead" in the first stanza, and to "whose courage stout" in the third, suggests a fearful mystery to be faced in the last, "whose petecote sets forth. . . ."

Some of the consort songs in the collection of 1589, *Songs of sundrie natures,* are unusual in that two (nos. 17–18 and 22) are for a solo with three-part accompaniment—though as in 1588 all parts have words. Others (nos. 35 and 24, 40 and 25) are verse anthems, with a solo or duet plus four viols and a four-part chorus (the first of these, "From

Virgin's womb," has a text from *The Paradise of Dainty Devices*). These songs do not have words under the viol parts, nor does the rustic dialogue "Who made thee, Hob, forsake the plough" (41). "I thought that love had been a boy" is an especially lively song in triple time with cross-rhythms. In the 1611 collection, the two verse anthems (nos. 25, 28) and the two consort songs (nos. 31–32) use a group of five viols, and the parts are not underlaid with words. These last consort songs are serious and resemble "My Soule opprest" in some ways, but in "Ah silly soul" (31) there are more casual repetitions of words and more melismas in the voice part, and the music is not as strictly imitative; it opens with two subjects in counterpoint rather than just one.

Many fine examples of Byrd's consort songs are preserved only in manuscript. The beautiful and moving elegy for Thomas Tallis, "Ye sacred muses"; another lullaby, "Come, pretty babe"; an extended comic song, "My mistress had a little dog," which is full of mock-tragic expressive effects in its second section; and a comment on the fall of the earl of Essex, "Wretched Albinus," are in this group. The last two are anonymous in the sources, but Brett confidently ascribes these and several others to Byrd on the basis of style and bibliographical evidence (Brett, 1964; Byrd, 15:viii–ix; Dart and Brett, 1960). One especially interesting song is "O God: but God, how dare I name that name." It is ascribed to Byrd in the manuscripts, but is unusual in that it is one of only two sonnets set through-composed as a consort song; Byrd's other sonnet settings repeat the music of the first quatrain for the second, and if the sonnet is in Italian form, the two halves of the sestet share roughly the same music (Brett, 1971–72, 53; Kerman, 1962a, 102). In "O God," the whole final couplet is repeated with its music, as in most other songs, but the rest of the setting, while maintaining the formal separation of lines and repeating no word that cannot be seen as repeated in the metrical context of the original sonnet, responds freely to the intensely emotional nature of the poem. The poem is an anonymous penitential plea for salvation, very "Protestant" (or perhaps Counter-Reformation) in its sense of guilt and in its direct, personal appeal to the diety. The most noticeably expressive feature of the setting, besides some melodic passages that correspond to Deryck Cooke's "vocabulary" for various degrees of unhappiness, is the handling of the exclamations and passionate phrasing (Ex. 4.6; Byrd, 15:17–21). This is closer to the choirboy death songs than to Italianate recitative, but is effective within Byrd's melodic context.

Example 4.6

O Lord,   O Fa- ther dear: I, dust,   yet thine,   slave thine,   child

thine, though   lost,   O save!   O help!   no health, no help in   me!

Some of the other manuscript songs mentioned above as being only recently ascribed to Byrd can nevertheless be dated, and they give us a better view of the composer's later style. Brett says, "While his writing for the solo voice barely altered in style, Byrd increasingly found in the instrumental accompaniment another, and more subtle means of making his songs 'framed to the life of the words.'" Brett discusses a song written on the death in 1608 of Lady Magdalen Montague, "With lilies white those virgins fair are crowned," saying that the accompaniment "maintains the mood of exalted contemplation" suggested by the text (1971–72, 56–57).

Further inferences about Byrd's attitude toward musical expressiveness and rhetoric may be drawn from some of his own published words. The phrase from the title of his 1611 set, that the songs are "framed to the life of the Words," suggests a more generalized attempt to capture the spirit of the text than to express its every detail and nuance. This reading seems compatible with the widely quoted dedication to book 1 of the Latin Catholic service music, *Gradualia* (1605).

For even as among artisans it is shameful in a craftsman to make a rude piece of work from some precious material, so indeed to sacred words in which the praises of God and of the Heavenly host are sung, none but some celestial harmony (so far as our powers avail) will be proper. Moreover in these words, as I have learned by trial, there is such a profound and hidden power that to one thinking upon things divine and diligently and earnestly pondering them, all the fittest numbers occur as if of themselves and freely offer themselves to the mind which is not indolent or inert. (Trans. Strunk, 1950, 327–28)

Brett rightly opposes Fellowes's interpretation of the passage as "Byrd's own statement that beautiful words inspired him inevitably with suitable musical ideas." "It is not the words themselves," says Brett, "but the hidden power of the thoughts behind them to which Byrd refers . . . he implies . . . that all his 'fittest numbers' (*aptissimi numeri*) are but echoes of a greater harmony caught from a profound contemplation of the First Composer." Moreover, Byrd's concern is not to express his own perception of this hidden power, but to help reveal it to the listener. As Brett reminds us, music and poetry share some of the same rhetorical aims. "Byrd focuses his art," says Brett, "on the listener's mind. He seeks to project, or to create an easy passage for, the ideas behind the text" (1971–72, 60–61).

Other statements of Byrd's can be related to the rhetorical concerns described here. In the preface to the 1611 set, Byrd tells the reader that he shall find "Musicke to content every humour: either melancholy, merry, or mixt of both." But he voices his concern that his audience be "carefull to heare them well expressed." If it is not well performed, "the best Song that ever was made will seeme harsh and unpleasant, for that the well expressing of them, either by Voyces, or Instruments, is the life of our labours, which is seldome or never well performed at the first singing or playing. Besides a song that is well and artificially made cannot be well perceived nor understood at the first hearing, but the oftener you shall heare it, the better cause of liking you will discover." The "humour" of the song is there to content the listener, but the song must be well performed and carefully attended to. Even the famous "Reasons . . . to perswade every one to learne to sing" from the 1588 set reflect the rhetorical interests of the time; the fourth reason for singing is that "It is a singuler good remedie for a stutting & stamering in the speech," and the fifth is that "It is the best means to procure a perfect pronunciation, & to make a good Orator."

The power of rhetoric and eloquence was a well-known concern of the humanists. Most of Byrd's songs reflect the influence of humanism only in its rather broad and diluted first wave, and in those Reformation influences that affected even Catholics after the Council of Trent (1562; Reese, 1959, 448–51). The results are an increased concern for the audibility of the text, as embodied in syllabic settings and the use of forms like the consort song and verse anthem; and some increase, however restrained, in the development of expressiveness. But two of Byrd's songs show that he was willing to dabble in more radical humanistic experiments, if only to oblige a friend. Thomas Watson, a member of the Sidney circle, who got Byrd to contribute his only Italianate madrigals to *Italian Madrigals Englished* (1590), also collaborated with him on *A gratification unto Master John Case*.[7] As a tireless propagandist for humanist and Italianate literature, he may have been behind Byrd's two settings of poems in imitation classical meters, "Constant *Penelope*" (1588, no. 23) and "Come to mee, griefe, for ever" (1588, no. 34).

The first poem is a translation in hexameters of the opening of the first epistle of Ovid's *Heroides*. The music of the solo voice, except in lines 5 and 8, consists only of half and quarter notes, corresponding to the long and short syllables of quantitative verse.[8] After four lines, Byrd seems to rebel against the two-note metrical straitjacket, and repeats "Oh" on whole notes; the penultimate note in line 8, just before the cadence, is also a whole note. The viol parts contain a greater variety of note values, and do not move in the same rhythm as the voice. The last feature distinguishes Byrd's song from the *musique mesurée* of the French Académie, in which all voices observe the meter. Although it is reasonable to expect French influence in these songs, it may have come only indirectly through Watson or Sidney; or Byrd's model may have been older German settings of Latin poets like those of Petrus Tritonius (1507).[9]

"Come to mee, griefe, for ever" is one of the two "funeral songs" for Sir Philip Sidney. The verse seems to be an imitation of an aeolic meter, the aristophanean or first pherecratic, consisting of a choriamb (- ˇ ˇ -) and a bacchius (ˇ - -). The main classical model is Horace's ode "Lydia dic per omnes" (1.8), and Sidney used it in "When to my deadlie pleasure" (1962, 154, 431). Although it is possible to substitute a long for a short syllable in the bacchius, Byrd seems to err in consistently giving that syllable a long note. There are some awkward lines in the poem ("With the anoynted oned"), but the song as a whole succeeds, especially through Byrd's use of the sequence in structuring the melody and giving it an expressive climax (Ex. 4.7; 1588, no. 34).

Example 4.7

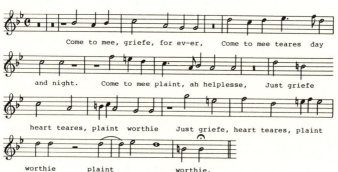

Come to mee, griefe, for ev-er,   Come to mee teares day

and night.   Come to mee plaint, ah helplesse,   Just griefe

heart teares, plaint worthie   Just griefe, heart teares, plaint

worthie   plaint   worthie.

Byrd begins by limiting himself to half and quarter notes, but he introduces slight variations in the third and fourth lines by shifting an eighth note from "teares" to "day" and from "plaint" to "ah." In the next line, in its sequential repetition, and in the coda, the strict quantitative scheme is abandoned, with twice the time given to "plaint" and finally "heart." The metrical scheme, though it is first announced in the accompaniment, begins to vary more radically there after the second line.

Very few of these attempts at writing English verse in classical meters were successful as poems; Campion's came closest, for he recognized the importance of stress in English, and he had learned from Sidney many other valuable lessons, as we shall see. But the experience of trying to write such verse, and observing a composer like Byrd set it to music, may have been valuable to these poets. For just as Byrd would not match his musical rhythms to the strict iambics of the mid-century poets, he resisted limiting his rhythms to those of the classical feet, even when it was arguably more important that he do so to express their quantity, and even when he was free to use other rhythms in the other voices. The musician, then, could show the poet how to achieve variety of rhythm over a constant pulse, to show how rhythm and meter need not be identical. The lesson is repeated in another dimension when a poem is set to music and poetic meter is transformed by musical rhythm.

As we shall see in the next chapter, the experience of writing English verse to foreign music could also be valuable, even if the immediate products were not.

Chapter Five
English Words, Italian Music

In 1588, shortly after William Byrd's *Psalmes, Sonets, and songs* appeared, Nicholas Yonge published *Musica Transalpina,* an anthology of Italian madrigals with English words. Several similar publications followed, along with a number of books of madrigals by English composers and English poets, but in the Italian style. Italian madrigals, *frottole, canzonetti,* and other forms had been known in England for some time. Foreign musicians had been at court since Henry VIII's reign, and manuscript collections, household inventories, and other sources indicate interest in Italian music in some circles for years.[1] *Musica Transalpina* was more of a symptom than a cause of such interest, though printing no doubt broadened the public for these songs and stimulated native composers of madrigals.

The practice of fitting English words to foreign music was also very old. Henry VIII's most famous song, "Pastime with good company," was known earlier on the Continent as "De mon triste desplaisir" (Ward, 1960, 123–24). Some of the tunes used for metrical psalms originally had French or German words. French and Italian poetry had been translated by English poets since Chaucer; but translating to music poses a special set of problems and restrictions. When Chaucer translated a sonnet of Petrarch in *Troilus and Criseyde,* he put it into the rhyme royal of the rest of the poem. When Wyatt tried to follow Italian sonnet form more strictly, the results show evidence of the struggle to come up with equivalent English lines and rhymes. Surrey invented a less demanding sonnet form with a wider choice of rhymes and an easier structure. But Italian music reflects the forms and rhythms of Italian verse, and English words adapted to Italian music must also reflect them.

Sidney

Before the publication of *Musica Transalpina,* Sir Philip Sidney wrote five poems to fit Italian songs; these poems are among the "Certain Sonnets" written before 1581 (1962, 423). Frank Fabry (1970) has discovered the music for three of these poems; "The fire to see my wrongs for anger burneth" and "The nightingale, as soon as April bringeth" were both written "To the tune of *Non credo gia che piu infelice amante,*" and "No, no, no, no, I cannot hate my foe" "*To the tune of a* Neapolitan *song,* which beginneth: *No, no, no, no."* The full incipit of the last song is "No, no, no, no, giammai non cangerò." Fabry found the music in a manuscript of Italian madrigals and *villanelle* at Winchester College. We may recall Whythorne's attraction to the *villanella alla napolitana,* which was a light, often satirical song, usually for three or four voices treated homophonically, with a strophic text. Another poem of Sidney's, "Al my sense thy sweetnesse gained," was written to an as yet unidentified "Neapolitan Villanell."

"Non credo" is an example of the *villanella* as it was refined and made more respectable by northern Italian composers. Each stanza has three sections, the last being a refrain. Sidney also has a refrain in "The Nightingale," but has new material at this point in "The fire to see my wrongs." Sidney follows the Italian in using seven- and eleven-syllable lines and feminine rhymes, but as Fabry points out, Sidney will sometimes use a trochee instead of an iamb (or the reverse) when the notes are of equal value and so neutralize the difference in stresses. This procedure is generally acceptable, but in the third line of "The Nightingale," not only does the first syllable of "proud of" fall after the beat, but the strong beat on "of" is also a fourth higher in the soprano and a third higher in the two middle parts. But even this conflict with pitch stress does not violate strongly the principles Fabry sees Sidney as following: "Sidney never varies the structure of his verses where variation will cause awkwardness," and "Awkwardness in the coupling of words to music occurs when *distinctive* rhythmic combinations stand opposed to natural speech" (1970, 245, 244).

Fabry does find some awkwardness in the soprano part in the eleventh line of both poems; but since the other voices do not move exactly with the soprano at this point, and therefore fit the words more easily, Fabry claims that Sidney was considering all the voice parts and compromised in favor of the lower voices. This may be, but it seems to me that Fabry ignores the universal habit of dividing long notes for better

underlay. Most singers (no doubt including Sidney) would not follow
Fabry's retention of the original note values (Ex. 5.1):

Example 5.1

S'en	va	li-	ber-	e	sol-	e	
My	fall	her	glo-	ry	mak-	eth	("The fire")
Thine	earth	new	springs	mine	fad-	eth	("Nightingale")

Instead, they would change the dotted half note (Ex. 5.2):

Example 5.2

My	fall	her	glo-	ry	mak-	eth
Thine	earth	new	springs	mine	fad-	eth

As we shall see, such changes were made in the madrigal anthologies
of Yonge and Thomas Watson. Occasional divisions of long notes do
not disturb those passages where the rhythms are distinctive, and
which, as Fabry shows, Sidney matches in his verse.

The other Italian song, "No, no, no, no, giammai non cangerò,"
seems to be a *frottola,* consisting of an initial four-line refrain or *ripresa*
and a seven-line strophe. The soprano of the *ripresa* moves more freely
than the other voices and has several melismatic passages; the strophe
is more uniformly homophonic, with a pronounced rhythmic pattern
setting the trochaic verses. The freedom of the soprano in the *ripresa*
allows Sidney to use iambic lines when the Italian is trochaic; but
Sidney has to follow the trochaic strophe quite strictly, resulting in
these lines:

> For so faire a flame embraces
>   All the places,
> Where that heat of all heates springeth,
>   That it bringeth
> To my dying heart some pleasure,
>   Since his treasure
> Burneth bright in fairest light. No, no, no, no.
>   (1962, 155)

The results of writing verse to these foreign musical models, as Fabry says, are "the introduction of trochaics into English poetics and

the reappearance of feminine rhymes after an absence of nearly two centuries" (1973, 234). Later, Sidney used trochaics in the second, fourth, eighth, ninth, tenth, and eleventh songs of *Astrophil and Stella;* feminine rhyme is also a regular feature of five of the songs. Several of these were later set to music.[2] Sidney's contemporaries and followers imitated these features, and seemed to associate them with both music and Italian forms. Around 1598, John Lilliat copied into his commonplace book the words and music of an anonymous English song in trochaics, and noted that it was "In an Italian verse." When he wrote a poem of his own to fit the same music, he noted that it was also "Italiantly versed" (Doughtie, 1985, 99, 103). Thomas Lodge's "Now I see thy lookes were fained" and Samuel Daniel's "Now each creature joyes the other" both use trochaics and feminine rhyme, and both were set to music. A number of other trochaic verses appear in the songbooks (*LEA,* 274, 310; 106, 138, 151, 207, 213, 230, 323, 335, 344, 396).

Sidney's experience in writing words for music, especially Italian music, may have had other and more significant consequences besides introducing trochaics and feminine rhyme to English lyric verse. As was noted in chapter 2, one of the important implications of Gascoigne's description of the pattern of stresses in a line of verse is that it recognized a separation between the metrical pattern and the words, producing, in John Stevens's words, "the liberation of English verse from the bondage of speech." Sidney seems to have been the first poet to exploit this liberation and give verse a new sound. This sound, says Stevens, is "produced by the interplay between *speech* and *metre*—that is, between the sound the words would make if read as prose and the notional metrical pattern that constrains them. . . . The result is a third voice, the voice of performance, which hovers between the two, forsaking neither entirely, committed to neither" (1982, 15–16). We hear this new sound first in the sonnets of *Astrophil and Stella,* in lines like

> Let her go. Soft, but here she comes. Go to,
> Unkind, I love you not: O me, that eye
> Doth make my heart to give my tongue the lie.
> (1962, 188)

Before writing these dramatic lines in *Astrophil,* Sidney had been writing verse for the *Arcadia.* Many of these earlier poems made a virtue of the regularity of mid-century verse; in fulfilling the strict coincidence of language and meter, Sidney capitalized on the resulting formality and artificiality (Rudenstine, 1967, 92–95). In other poems from the *Arcadia,* Sidney engaged in experiments that may have helped him realize the possibilities of separating the metrical pattern from the words, namely writing English verse in classical quantitative meters. John Thompson says that "it was the exercise in classical metres that brought in a new idea of the relation of metrical pattern and language, and consequently a new kind of poetry. In these experiments, Sidney and Spenser must have learned to recognize the possibility that these two elements of verse could be joined without losing their separate identities" (1961, 147). Derek Attridge (1974, 41–77) has since shown us how the Elizabethans read Latin verse, and how intellectual and visual—how abstract—were their principles of scansion. Since long and short vowels in Latin were determined more by spelling than actual sound, attempts to apply these meters to English were hampered by uncertain orthography and the linguistic importance of stress, which was sometimes confused with quantitative length. The complexities of this subject are clarified by Attridge; for our present purposes it is only necessary to see these experiments as demanding that the poets deal with an abstract system separate from, yet relating to, the words of the verse.

Quantitative experiments were frequently associated with music, which, unlike language, is very precise in the designation of quantities. The ancient Greeks were known to have sung their quantitative poetry, and, as we have already seen, humanistic efforts to imitate them, like the French Académie de Poésie et de Musique, touched even composers like William Byrd. Sidney not only tried writing quantitative verse; he had characters in two of the *Arcadia* manuscripts (1962, 388–90) debate the virtues of rhymed and quantitative verse, especially as they relate to music:

Dicus said that since verses had their chefe ornament, if not eand, in musicke, those which were just appropriated to musicke did best obtaine their ende . . . but those must needes most agree with musicke, since musicke standing principally upon the sound and the quantitie, to answere the sound they brought wordes, and to answer the quantity they brought measure. So that for every sembrefe or minam, it had his silable matched unto it with a long foote or a short foote . . . so that eyther by tune a poet should strayt know how every word should be measured unto it, or by the verse as soone find out the full quantity of the musike.

Dicus also links verse form with decorum, some verses being fit for "great matters," while others are only suitable for "amorous conceytes." Rhyming verse is seen only as counting syllables, "saving perchaunce that some have some care of the accent." Music finds rhyming verse "confused," and "is forced somtime to make a quaver of that which is ruffe and heavy in the mouth, and at an other time to hould up in a long that which, being perchaunce but a light vowell, would be gone with a breath." (We recall Zarlino's and Morley's complaints about "barbarisms.")

On the other hand, Lalus defends rhyme, and says that "since musicke brought a measured quantity with it, therfor the wordes lesse needed it." Moreover, "musicke is a servaunt to poetry, for by [the one] the eare only, by the other the mind was pleased. And therfor what doth most adorne woordes, levelled within a proportion of number, to that musicke must bee implied; which if it cannot doe well it is the musitions fault and not the poettes." The poet, as "the popular philosopher," has a duty to appeal to "common eares"; even so, in rhyme "the finest judgment shall have more pleasure, since he that rimes observes something the measure but much the rime, whereas the other attendes only measure without all respect of rime; besides the accent, which the rimer regardeth of which the former hath little or none."

This debate may have been projected from Sidney's own mind. He later summarizes some of the points in *A Defence of Poetry,* and says that the ancient verse is "more fit for music, both words and time observing quantity, and more fit lively to express diverse passions, by the low or lofty sound of the well-weighed syllable" (1973, 119–20). However, Attridge doubts that Sidney did much actual singing of his quantitative verse, for if he had, "he would have come face to face with the inadequacies of his quantitative system as an organisation of the durations of English syllables" (1974, 175–76n.). Sidney concludes evenhandedly that there are virtues in both kinds of verse, and that English is fit for both. As in other areas of Sidney's life and thought, he is drawn to the voice of authority—here the verse of the ancients—and yet resists it (see McCoy, 1979). *Astrophil and Stella* is full of such debates between authority and the rebellious individual: but that work shows Sidney coming down more on the side of Lalus and rhyme, especially after Sidney seems to have discovered how to give rhyming verse some of the qualities of "the well-weighed syllable." He also seems to have stopped making his verse serve other music after his "Certain Sonnets," but rather expected the musicians to serve his verse;

several composers did in fact write settings of the songs from *Astrophil*. But putting his verse to the service of music does seem to have taught Sidney valuable lessons.

Like quantitative verse, and like Gascoigne's diagram of iambic pentameter, poems written to fit a tune also make the poet aware of an external pattern to which he must connect individual words in some sort of significant relationship. Realization of this separation of pattern and words can allow the poet to exploit the possibility of interplay between them. This realization, together with the dramatic decorum Sidney establishes for *Astrophil*, allowed Sidney to give his sonnets a sense of voice, of nuance; he had found a medium "more fit lively to express diverse passions." His verse had achieved that "forcibilness or *energia*" which made it convincing (1973, 117). In "With how sad steps, O Moone, thou climbs't the skies" (1962, 180), Sidney could reinforce the sense of langorous melancholy by using a series of monosyllables that are of almost equal weight. Sidney had found through his ear—and possibly through trying to apply the Latin rules—the natural quantity of these English syllables. The iambic pattern is there, but the contrasts reflected in Gascoigne's jagged diagram have been rounded and flattened. In the passage quoted from the end of Sonnet 47 ("Let her go. Soft, but here she comes"), the rhythms and junctures of speech shatter the diagram, breaking its uniform march to reflect the passion of the speaker. Until the end, that is, when the verse slips back into its mold ("O me, that eye / Doth make my heart to give my tongue the lie"), just as Astrophil's rebellion evaporates and he relapses into submission. Sidney has moved far away from concern with music in these sonnets, and drama, even pre-Marlovian drama, may have helped him do so. But music, I believe, helped him forge the flexible verse that made this drama possible. Ironically, this new voice that Sidney gave to the lyric would encourage developments in poetry that would lead it away from the humanistic revival of the union of poetry and music in song.

The Madrigal

Sidney's poems, like Italian madrigals, had some currency in manuscript before they saw print, but the larger public would experience the new poetry first in the first three books of Spenser's *Faerie Queene* (1590),[3] to be followed in 1591 by an incomplete and not very accurate edition of *Astrophil and Stella*—which contained poems by Samuel Daniel and Thomas Campion as well. A few years earlier, this public might have noticed another aspect of the new poetry in Nicholas Yonge's *Musica Transalpina* (1588). Although readers of *Musica Transalpina* would have been looking mainly for music, and although the English verse there is first and foremost practical translation, a few poems gained currency separated from their music. Two (nos. 16–18 and 42) were reprinted in *England's Helicon,* and nine were reset later by English composers (Kerman, 1962a, 24–25).

Madrigal verses look and sound different from the verses of Gascoigne's generation. For one thing, they are not strophic. Even when strophic poems are used in madrigals, they are through-composed: each stanza becomes, in a sense, a complete madrigal. The madrigal proper is a poem of a dozen lines, more or less, with an unfixed rhyme scheme (though the last two lines almost always rhyme), and an unspecified mixture of seven- and eleven-syllable lines. In Italian, the rhymes are almost always feminine, and the meter is based on syllable count rather than stress, though some attention is given to the relationship of the primary or tonic accent to other accented syllables in the line. In English imitations, the iambic norm is present, but not always regular. For example, here are the words to a sequence of three madrigals as they appear in *England's Helicon:*

> *Thirsis* to die desired,
>> marking her eyes that to his hart was neerest:
> And shee that with his flame no lesse was fiered,
>> sayd to him: Oh hart's love deerest:
>>> Alas, forbeare to die now,
>>> By thee I live, by thee I wish to die too.

> *Thirsis* that heate refrained,
>> wherewith to die poore lover then hee hasted,
> Thinking it death while hee his lookes maintained,
>> full fixed on her eyes, full of pleasure
>> and lovely Nectar sweet from them he tasted.
> His daintie Nimph, that now at hand espyed
>> the harvest of loves treasure,
> Said thus, with eyes all trembling, faint and wasted:
>> I die now,
> The Sheepheard then replyed,
>> and I sweet life doe die too.

> Thus these two Lovers fortunately dyed,
>   Of death so sweet, so happy, and so desired:
>   That to die so againe their life retired.
>
> (1600, sig. Z2v)

The compiler of *England's Helicon* seems to have consulted only the cantus part-book, where rests in the music cause loss of words and a gap in the sense. He appears to have rewritten parts of the second section, which, as the other voice parts make clear, should have read:

> Thirsis that heat refrayned,
> wherwith in hast to dye hee did betake him,
> thinking it death that life would not forsake him,
> and whyle his looke full fixed he retayned,
> on hir eyes full of pleasure,
> ....
> dye now sweet hart, I dye now.
>
> (1588, AT, sig. C1)

The restored version retains the seven- and eleven-syllable lines of the Italian poem by Giambattista Guarini. It should not be surprising to see a monosyllabic line like the fourth in the first section, or the last two lines of the last section, escape strict conformity to the iambic pattern; but it is curious that the rewritten fourth line of the second section should be less regular than the corresponding line in *Musica Transalpina*.

The text in *Musica Transalpina*, however, manages to be both a fairly close translation of the Italian and a fairly close fit to the music by Luca Marenzio (1967, 12–15). In his dedication, Yonge maintains that musicians who tried these versions "affirmed the accent of the words to be well mainteined, the descant not hindred, (though some fewe notes altred) and in everie place the due decorum kept." "Due decorum" may refer to keeping appropriate words with the illustrative or expressive music; the musical and verbal accents are generally compatible; and some of the "fewe notes altred" can be found in "Thirsis." In the quintus and tenor parts, Yonge found it necessary to divide Marenzio's notes in order to fit "that to his hart was nearest" to the music for "di colei ch'adora," and to change the rhythm in all voices from (Ex. 5.3)

Example 5.3

Le ri- spo-   se⏜il Pa-   sto-   re

to (Ex. 5.4):

Example 5.4

The shep-   herd then re- ply- ed

Some of the voices in the second section also required an extra syllable when the composer chose to break the elided Italian "morte et" into three syllables; these voices read "thinking it death *yet*."[4] There are other instances of the more usual kind of padding translation sometimes demands: nothing in the Italian calls for "treasure" or "wasted" (section 2, lines 8 and 9). How Yonge's translator went about his work is suggested by a set of madrigals now in the British Library. In Marenzio's *Madrigali a Sei Voci, in un Corpo Ridotti,* printed by Pierre Phalèse in Antwerp in 1594, an Englishman has written, in a late sixteenth-or early seventeenth-century hand, English words directly over the Italian words underlying the music (Obertello, 1949, 165–78, 383–402).

The music of "Thirsis" provides a subtle and effective expression of the text, which in this instance does not lose much in translation. In a few especially illustrative or expressive passages, the English maintains the effect well, as in the half-step descents on "moro" (Ex. 5.5):

Example 5.5

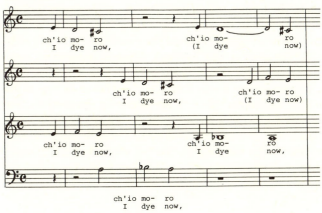

In both languages, "to die" has a sexual meaning that this poem obviously exploits; and it is in representing the sexual drama that this madrigal is especially effective. As Denis Arnold (1965, 8) says, the "short phrases and sudden changes of texture mirror [the] fluctuating intensities" of the erotic episode. By the "construction of motifs which now hurry on the narrative, and now delay it, Marenzio gives a perfect picture of the act of love."

Musica Transalpina contains six other madrigals by Marenzio, and even more by Alfonso Ferrabosco the elder. Ferrabosco was a minor composer by Continental standards, but he had spent at least the years 1562–78 in England, and impressed English musicians with his craftsmanship (Kerman, 1962a, 74–98). (His son, a composer of airs, will be considered in chapter 7.) Other composers Yonge included were Palestrina, Macque, de Monte, Wert, Donato, Ferretti, Conversi, Pordenone, Bertani, Felis, Mel, Pinello, and two rather obscure Flemings, Verdonch and Faignient; Lassus is represented by two *chansons,* and William Byrd by "The fair young virgin." Most of the composers were current, but conservative; the most important for several reasons was Marenzio. That the first Italian madrigals printed in England should include his work is an indication of how fully developed the art of the madrigal was when the English took it up for themselves. Marenzio was the great master of the madrigal in its most characteristic stage, before the mannerist experiments of Gesualdo or the movement into the baroque with Monteverdi.

The madrigal as practiced by Marenzio was a composition for four, five, or six voices, no one of which dominated: there was no "first singing part." The number of voices singing at any one time would vary, as would the texture: some phrases might develop a point of imitation, while others would bring the voices together homophonically. The moving spirit of the music was the text. The ideas, feelings, or images of the text determined the nature of the music. The general mood and atmosphere of the text, or parts of the text, would be reflected in that of the music; and within that context, smaller phrases or individual words would call forth illustration or expression in the music. The formal integrity of the poetic line was less important than the expression of the phrase or word, though major formal divisions—rhymes and cadences—still coincided. In short, Marenzio's treatment of the text, at least in the earlier works reprinted in England, exemplified Morley's "Rules to be observed in dittying." Elsewhere in the *Plaine and Easie Introduction* (1597, sig. Aa3v), Morley speaks specifically of the madrigal in terms that recall Sidney's notion of *energia,* saying that it is, next unto the Motet, the most artificiall and to men of understanding most delightfull. If therefore you will compose in this kind you must possesse your selfe with an amurus humor (for in no composition shal you prove admirable except you put on, and possesse your selfe wholy with that vaine wherein you compose) so that you must in your musicke be wavering like the wind, sometime wanton, sometime drooping, sometime grave and staide, otherwhile effeminat, you may maintaine points and revert them, use triplaes and shew the verie uttermost of your varietie, and the more varietie you shew the better shal you please. In this kind our age excelleth, so that if you would imitate any, I would appoint you these for guides: *Alfonso ferrabosco* for deepe skill, *Luca Marenzo* for good ayre and fine invention. . . .

Marenzio was especially known for his treatment of the text, even by the English. The pamphleteer Thomas Nashe could use him in a simile intended to insult Gabriel Harvey; Harvey's verse, says Nashe, is mere street balladry which, if sung to common tunes like "O man in desperation," "like *Marenzos* Madrigals, the mournefull note naturally [would] have affected the miserable Dittie" (*Strange Newes*, 1592, in Nashe, 1958, 1:265).

Marenzio's means of making the note take on the character of the ditty range from the subtle (as in "Thirsis") to what has seemed to some to be naive or silly. For instance, Marenzio, like his contemporaries, will frequently indulge in "eye music," the effect of which can be appreciated only by those reading the parts, or by musicians knowledgeable enough to visualize the parts on hearing them. Thus *occhi* (eyes) will be set to two whole notes side by side, and words like "night," "dark," and "blind" will be set to *note nere,* black notes. I would also put in a similar category the setting of syllables like *mi fa* (it makes me) to notes corresponding to *mi* and *fa* in solfege (Chater, 1981, 1:62, 2:163; Einstein, 1949, 1:221–45, 2:608–88).

Besides employing those illustrative and expressive devices recommended by Zarlino and Morley, Marenzio uses melismas with words referring to natural phenomena such as flowers, wind, rivers; motion, especially flight and running; certain emotions or emotionally related actions such as joy, laughter, or singing. He also uses brief melismatic turning figures to illustrate turning, returning, or repeated action; to suggest circular objects such as a crown, or a bow or arch; and, in some contexts, to express grace or pleasure. When voices move in contrary motion, they can express coming together if they move toward each other, and separation if they move apart. Imitative passages in quarter or eighth notes when the entrances are close together may suggest flight and pursuit. Wide leaps in the melodic line are sometimes used along with texts expressing anguish, savagery, error, or distance (Chater, 1981, 1:49–54, 2:117–37).

Rhythmic patterns are also associated with certain emotions suggested by the text: a half note followed by two quarters is frequently found with words of heroism or resolution, while changeableness or volatility is given a contrary pattern, especially in diminution (two eighths and a quarter note). Triple time is associated with dancing and celebrating. Shorter note values are expressive of speed, brevity, happiness; long notes, especially when they stand out from their context, can suggest stability or absence of motion; repeated notes can suggest constancy (Chater, 1981, 1:55, 2:137–41).

Marenzio's use of melodic intervals, such as the minor second or third to express pathos, parallels the uses described by Deryck Cooke for most of western tonal music. Other features, such as selection of the mode, distribution of the voices, and use of chromaticism and dissonance are also influenced by the nature of the text (Chater, 1981, 1:55–64, 37–48). Not all these characteristics are evident in the madrigals selected by the English, who avoided examples of adventurous harmony, dissonance, and chromaticism (Kerman, 1962a, 58, 64).

We may see some of these devices at work in a madrigal taken from the next collection after *Musica Transalpina,* Thomas Watson's *Italian Madrigals Englished* (1590). All but five of the twenty-eight madrigals are by Marenzio, and two of the five are Byrd's four- and six-voice versions of "This sweet and merry month of May." Watson is to us a minor poet, but he was respected by his peers in the Sidney circle. His *Hekatompathia* (1582) was a collection of eighteen-line sonnets imitating Italian and classical poets, with didactic notes on sources and arguments for each poem. Watson is of some historical importance because of this work, the earliest lyric sequence in English. We do not know who made the translations for *Musica Transalpina,* but it is clear that Watson wrote the words for his madrigal collection. The title page says that they are "Englished not to the sense of the originall dittie, but after the affection of the Noate." In his Latin verse dedication to the earl of Essex, he says that they are "juncta Italis Anglica verba notis." The point seems to be that, unlike Yonge's translator, he will not try to reproduce the original text, but will concentrate on fitting English words to the disposition or general character ("affection") of the music. Joseph Kerman (1962a, 58) asks, "But is it not the general principle of the madrigal that the 'affection of the note' is designed specifically to reflect the 'sense of the ditty'?" Watson succeeds in the reverse process only intermittently.

"Zephyrus breathing" has a recognizable origin in Petrarch's famous sonnet, "Zefiro torna"; Yonge had a fairly literal translation for Conversi's setting in *Musica Transalpina*, "Zephirus brings the time that sweetly senteth," and a quick comparison reveals the difference in approaches.

> Zephirus brings the time that sweetly senteth,
> With flowres and herbs and winters frost exileth,
> Progne now chirpeth, and Philomele lamenteth,
> Flora the garlands white and red compileth,
> Fields doe rejoice, the frowning skye relenteth.
> Jove to behold his dearest daughter smyleth,
> Th'ayre the water the earth to Joy consenteth,
> Each creature now to love, him reconcileth.
> (Yonge, 1588, no. 52, first part)

> Zephyrus breathing, now calls nymfs from out their
>   bowres,
> to play & wanton, in roobes of sundry flow'rs:
> Progne chirpeth, & sweet Philomele recordeth:
> And Flora seeing what the spring affordeth
> Smyleth so sweetly, that heaven it self inflamed,
> Greatly rejoyceth, to but heare her named:
> The welkin, water, and earth, all are full of pleasure,
> All creaturs joy in love, as Natures treasure.
> (Watson, 1590, no. 4)

Watson manages to make some of his words appropriate for the music: where Marenzio (Virgili, 1952, 3–8) has little melismas on "e i fior e l'erbe" (and flowers and herbs), Watson writes "to play and wanton." But Watson does not match Marenzio's subtlety in changing textures. The third line, "Progne chirpeth, & sweet Philomele recordeth," is close to the original, "e garrir Progne e pianger Filomena," though Marenzio's contrast between chirping and weeping is lost in Watson: descending eighth-note melismas illustrate "garrir" in all parts but the bass, but the voices come together with whole- and half-note chords on "pianger Filomena."

Marenzio sets the sonnet in two sections, with a strong cadence at the end of the octave. Curiously, Watson gives only this first part. The second part in Marenzio begins with musical contrast, following the contrast in the poem between the cheerful images of nature in the octave and the unhappy poet's lament in the sestet. The movement slows to whole and half notes, with suspension dissonances in minor tonality. Kerman thinks that "It is a possibility that Watson found Marenzio's beautiful setting of the sestet of 'Zefiro torna' too 'extreme' for his taste." As Kerman points out (1962a, 58), Watson printed most of the other pieces from Marenzio's first book of five-part madrigals (1580) that Yonge had not already published, but he excluded "Doloroso martir," probably the most harmonically daring of that collection.

Watson's other texts are not always as carefully tuned to the "affection of the note" as "Zephirus," and many are much more remote from the Italian texts. Instead of the fifth stanza of Petrarch's Canzone 127, "Non vidi mai" (Marenzio, 1966, 14–23), Watson has "When first my heedless eyes," a tribute to "Astrophil" (this in the year before the publication of Sidney's sequence). In this madrigal, shivering melismas on "gelo" (ice), become less meaningful on "measure." In the setting of Tasso's "Vezzosi augelli" (Virgili, 1952, 9–12), or "Evry singing bird," the breeze murmurs ("mormora l'aura") to a gently hesitant, descending melismatic pattern (countered by ascent in the tenor); but where the Italian has the voices all on the single syllable "mor-" Watson eliminates the melisma and makes the voices babble "Zephirus, Zephirus, Zephirus, Zephirus," a syllable on each note. In the next phrase Watson does the same thing on "the leaves."

Since Watson frees himself from the obligation to translate the sense of the Italian, one might expect to find better English poetry, or at least verse that does not demand changes in the music. Unfortunately, neither result is evident. The verse is no better than that in *Musica Transalpina,* and does not even have the first anthology's advantage of introducing some of the great Italian poets in faithful, if awkward, guise.

In 1597, Nicholas Yonge published a second book of *Musica Transalpina,* which, besides more Ferrabosco and Marenzio, contained pieces by Vecchi, Croce, Venturi, Palavicino, and others. More light madrigals appear in this collection than in the first. Croce's "Ove tra l'herb'ei fiori," from the Italian anthology commissioned by a Venetian gentleman in praise of his wife, *Il Trionfo di Dori,* ends like the others in that collection with the line "Viva la bella Dori." The translation, "Hard

by a Cristal fountain," is turned into praise of Queen Elizabeth, and
the final line is "Long live faire Oriana." This madrigal became the
seed of Thomas Morley's famous collection of native tributes, *The
Triumphs of Oriana* (1601). Another important madrigal in Yonge's second book is Marenzio's "Doloroso martir," which had not been printed
in Yonge's first book or in Watson. "Doloroso martir" is the most
"advanced" madrigal yet to appear in England, mild though it is by
Continental standards (Kerman, 1962a, 61–64). The translation is
fairly close:

> Dolorous mournefull cares, ruthles tormenting
> Hatefull guyves, cursed bonds, sharpest enduraunce,
> Wherein both nights & days my hart ever renting
> Wretch I beewaile my lost delight & pleasaunce,
> Woefull loud cryes, sadde scriches, howling lamenting,
> Watry teares shedding, & everlasting greivance
> These are my dainties & my daiely feding,
> & my lives comfort, bitter gall exceeding.
> (Obertello, 1949, 296)

Along with black notes on "notte" and "nights," the music abounds in
pathetic effects, especially suspensions. There is one startling chromatic progression on "Misero" and "beewaile" (Ex. 5.6; Marenzio, 1967,
16–18).

Example 5.6

"Catene" (chains) produces a long chain of suspensions; the English
word at this point, "endurance," almost works. "Hore" (hours) is separated from the surrounding context by rests, and set to a half and a
quarter note; the English is quite different, but it could be argued that
it works almost as well. Since all the voices are together on two G
chords at this point, Yonge simply reverses the quarter and half notes,

and sets them to "my hart." The rests suggest the anguished heart skipping a beat.

Although an English version of Giovanni Croce's *Le Sette Sonnetti Penitentiali* (1603) appeared in 1608 as *Musica Sacra,* the last of the Italian madrigal anthologies was published in 1598, the year after Yonge's second book. *Madrigals to five voyces. Celected out of the best approved Italian Authors* was compiled by Thomas Morley, the English composer most responsible for naturalizing the Italian style. Morley included three madrigals by Ferrabosco, but only one by Marenzio; the others, by Feretti, Giovanelli, Vecchi, Venturi, Macque, Orologio, Mosto, Belli, Sabino, and the transplanted Englishman Peter Phillips, were mostly of the lighter sort of madrigal (Kerman, 1962a, 66–67). The translations tend to be paraphrases after the manner of Watson.

Some of the pieces in Morley's collection were not madrigals but canzonets. The year before, Morley had published a whole collection of *Canzonets or Little Short Songs to Foure Voices: Celected out of the best and approved Italian Authors.* In his *Plaine and Easie Introduction* (1597, sig. Aa3v), Morley describes canzonets as being of the "second degree of gravetie" after madrigals, "wherein little arte can be shewed being made in straines, the beginning of which is some point lightlie touched, and everie straine repeated except the middle." That is, for a three-line stanza, the music would take the form AABCC; but not all canzonets have a middle section (Kerman, 1962a, 152–69). Some imitative polyphony and word-painting was possible, but not as much as in the madrigal. In Italy, the *canzonetta* was usually strophic, with an epigrammatic point or *concetto* at the end of the last stanza. But in England, only one stanza of text is given, so that many texts seem even more trivial than they would have if translated in full. Here is all Morley gives of Giovanni Croce's "Mentre la bella Dafne" (a poem obviously modeled after Guarini's "Tirsi morir"):

> *Daphne* the bright when frankly she desired
> with *Thirsis* her sweete hart to have exspired.
> Sweete (thus fell she acrying.)
> Dye for I am adying.
>   (Obertello, 1949, 344)

The original Italian has two more stanzas, ending with both lovers returning to life after their welcome death. The music does not have a middle section, but uses some imitative counterpoint in the second section (Kerman, 1962a, 282). When Morley and other Englishmen wrote their own canzonets, they through-composed only one stanza, often with enough complexity to make many canzonets indistinguishable from the lighter madrigals (Kerman, 1962a, 152–59).

A more distinctive lighter form imported by Morley was the *balletto.* Like his *First Booke of Canzonets to Two Voices* (1595), Morley's *First Booke of Balletts to Five Voices* (1595) is unlike the other collections under discussion in that the music is for the most part Morley's own. But in each case simultaneous English and Italian editions were printed, and the sources of most of the Italian texts are known. The music relies heavily on Italian models, Anerio for the canzonets, and Gastoldi for the ballets. Morley defines ballets in general as "songs, which being song to a dittie may likewise be daunced," and in particular as a "slight kind of musick," "commonlie called *fa las,* the first set of that kind which I have seene was made by *Gastaldi*" (sig. Aa3v). Ballets are strophic (even in English), usually homophonic, and have the characteristic "fa la" refrain after each of two repeated sections. Although there is no evidence that they were ever danced in England, they have dancelike rhythms. Some of Morley's best known songs, "Now is the month of Maying," "My bonny lass she smileth," and "Sing we and chant it," are ballets, and the well-known Christmas song "Deck the halls" is an imitation ballet. Kerman describes how Morley complicates his Italian musical models by making the "fa las" more polyphonic, and by composing the verse sections of some in a more contrapuntal canzonet style. Especially interesting is Kerman's comparison of Morley's English and Italian versions and, on the evidence of the declamation of the texts, his conclusion that Morley wrote "English ballets, not Italian ballets with English words adapted. First he translated poems from Italian *balletti* and *canzonette*; then he set the translations to music—keeping an eye on the Italian compositions, however; then he adapted the Italian poems back for his Italian editions" (1962a, 136–47). Morley's procedure seems curious, but perhaps it enabled him to assimilate the Italian musical style more thoroughly while working toward an English version of it; it is rather like Roger Ascham's technique of having students translate a Latin passage into English, and then back into Latin (Ascham, 1967, 78).

Before turning to the native English madrigal, we need to consider what effect all these translated musical texts might have had on English poetry. They introduced new rhythms and sounds, and they contributed to the vogue for amatory Petrarchan and pastoral subjects, light-

ening the general tone of English verse. The bulk of the poems in this
vein would become as boring as the preachy proverbs of mid-century
verse, but for a while they must have been refreshing. On the other
hand, it seems safe to say that the main concern of the translators was
to provide words for singing Englishmen, and that the focus of attention was on the music. We do not find an epidemic of madrigal verses
with feminine rhymes in the general poetic population; the infection
is largely confined to songs. We may also concede that poems called
"madrigals" which appear outside of musical publications may have
purely literary models. The earliest of these, Basilius' "Madrigall" from
the third book of Sidney's *Old Arcadia* (ca. 1577–80), is a fifteen-line
poem of mixed six- and ten-syllable lines with masculine rhymes
(1962, 80). Barnabe Barnes included twenty-six "madrigalls" in his
Parthenophil and Parthenophe (1593), but these can be defined only as
nonstrophic poems with lines of irregular length. Although they use
some feminine rhyme, they are not serious imitations of the Italian
form; one is forty-two lines long. *England's Helicon* (1600) contains
texts from *Musica Transalpina* and Morley's *Madrigals to Foure Voyces*
(1594), but the four other poems in the book called "madrigals" are
all strophic, with only a smattering of feminine rhyme. A *Poetical
Rhapsody* (1602) contains a number of madrigals; two are from the
second *Musica Transalpina,* but most are by Francis Davison, the compiler. Davison traveled in Italy between 1595 and 1597, and the
models for most of his madrigals can be found in Luigi Groto's *Rime*
(1587). Several of Davison's madrigals were later set to music by English composers. Although some of Davison's verses employ feminine
rhyme and seven- and eleven-syllable lines, many do not, and though
they are not strophic, some are more symmetrically ordered than is
characteristic of Italian madrigals: pairs of rhyming long lines alternate
with pairs of rhyming short lines in "Madrigal XI," for instance (Rollins, 1931, 1:217, 90–91; 2:43–46, 128–29).

The madrigal verse of the musical anthologies is further separated
from these literary madrigals by their style. Michael Smith shows that
the demands of writing English verse to fit the Italian music, especially
the need to find feminine rhymes, produced "extraordinary" results.
Once past such combinations as "pleasure-measure-treasure," the best
sources of feminine rhymes in English are verbs and verbals ending in
-ing or in a pronounced *-ed.* "So many gerunds, present participles and
past participles tend to have a loosening effect on the syntax, and to
secure them a place at the end of the line often involves inversion or

other confusing structural distortion." The resulting style is "disjoint-ed," "histrionic," "exclamatory," and often lacking in the logic or clar-ity of the original; the padding often needed to fill out the lines consists of "conventionally evocative terms" or "trigger-words" (Smith, 1974, 165, 174–75). Some of these qualities may be perceived in ex-amples quoted so far. In "Zephirus brings the time," the *-eth* endings grate on the ear, but the parallel verbs at least make for a firm struc-ture. In Watson's "Zephirus breathing," there seems to be a logical confusion about whether Flora's smiling or the sound of her name caus-es heaven to rejoice. All have examples of "trigger-words" ("sweetly," "dearest," "frowning,""inflamed"). "Dolorous mournefull cares" seems disjointed and exclamatory, though in this instance the Italian is also. But the text Watson provided for Marenzio's setting of Tansillo's "Ne fero sdegno mai Donna si mosse" is quite different from the Italian:

> In chayns of hope & feare, singing & crying,
> I clyme & fall: I live, but ever dying:
> O tyrant Love, ô come at once & slay me,
> That flying hence down, wher Charons boat doth stay me,
> From cruell Armaryllis to convay me,
> Whose prowd aspiring hart doth but delaie me,
> I may dance in Elysium, there resounding
> With joy, the paynes of Love, & the deep wounding.
>
> (1590, no. 22)

Smith quotes this text as an especially significant example in support of his thesis that "the eccentric style of the madrigal was deliberately cultivated," not just an unhappy consequence of translating to music. "The translators were aware of the limitations and dangers of the imi-tative translation style, but they chose to exploit them rather than to overcome them" (1974, 172). Just as the music of the Italian madrigal was distinctive and therefore imitable, so, they wished, should be the texts. Smith suggests that Yonge, Watson, and Morley were interested in starting an artistic fashion for commercial gain. But as he admits, the poetical side of the fashion never seems to have caught on outside the musical world of the madrigalists.

Nevertheless, these translations may have had an indirect or con-tributory effect on the process of developing the flexibility and expres-siveness of English verse. Some of the parallels are at least suggestive. The fashion for the madrigal coincided with the fashion for nonstrophic verse like the sonnet and the epigram. Nonstrophic forms like dramatic

blank verse and narrative couplets were also gaining currency and influence. Madrigals, and canzonets as they were written in England,
were not strophic, and when set to music their lines were often broken
up into shorter phrases, some of which were repeated, and many of
which were illustrated with musical word-painting. This shift of attention from exterior form—from the repeated strophe, the matrix re-
filled—to interior or local effects may parallel the introduction of
speech rhythms and other mimetic effects into the iambic line. In
short, Sidney's "Go to, unkind" has a counterpart in Marenzio's chromatic progression on "Misero." Both artists were trying to achieve *energia* or "forcibleness" (as Sidney defined it) in order to be convincing
and persuasive, and to keep "due decorum."

Chapter Six
The English Madrigal

Original English songs in the Italian style—madrigals, canzonets, and ballets—come to over seven hundred compositions, printed in thirty-six collections or parts thereof. Although these numbers are small by Italian standards—Marenzio alone published twenty-two sets—they are large enough to demand some selectivity in the following discussion. Detailed surveys of the music are available in the studies of E. H. Fellowes and especially Joseph Kerman.[1] I should like to focus on the nature of the verse in these collections, on some of the ways music affected this verse, and on how the music can act as an interpreter of the poetry.

Most critics agree that the finest composers of the English madrigal were Thomas Weelkes and John Wilbye, who wrote some serious madrigals of considerable profundity. Two other fine composers, George Kirbye and John Ward, concentrated on serious texts and serious music in the madrigal style. But the pioneer composer of Italianate songs in England, and the most influential, was Thomas Morley, who specialized in the lighter forms. Besides the two anthologies of Italian *Canzonets* (1597) and *Madrigals* (1598) with English words, Morley published in 1595 the *Balletts* and *Canzonets to Two Voices* in simultaneous English and Italian editions. Earlier he had published the first collections of original English works in the Italian style, the *Canzonets . . . To Three Voices* (1593) and the *Madrigalls to Foure Voices* (1594); in 1597 came his *Canzonets . . . to Five and Sixe Voices,* and in 1601 he edited *The Triumphes of Oriana.* As Kerman (1962a, 159) has shown, some songs in the volumes entitled *Canzonets* are "more properly light madrigals," and some of the *Madrigals* are canzonets. More important than the carelessness about nomenclature is Morley's preference for the lighter style, and his influence on the later English madrigalists. Morley, says Kerman, is "the supreme English composer of canzonets; his ballets and madrigals tend constantly to the canzonet style. The influence of Thomas Morley on the English madrigal is the influence of the Italian canzonet." As we have seen, Morley and the English dropped all but the first stanza of the strophic Italian *canzonetta,* resulting in a number of brief texts that say very little. The music is dominant in these lighter forms. Though the text labels the prevailing mood and occasionally provides material for musical illustration, musical considerations seem to come first. The musical preoccupation of the English was general. As Bruce Pattison (1970, 104) says, "The English copied the musical effects of the Italians; the Italians had their eyes fixed on the poetry." In some ways this musical dominance can be seen as an aspect of the native English style that persists in the new Italianate songs. Morley was a pupil of Byrd, and a comparison of, say, Byrd's three-part songs from his 1589 set with songs from Morley's *Canzonets . . . To Three Voices* (1593) will show, despite significant differences, a similar preference for rather dense, continuously imitative polyphonic texture.[2]

Madrigal Verse

Morley's collections also perpetuated the kind of verse that resulted from writing English words to Italian music (see the previous chapter). Many of Morley's texts were in fact loose translations or paraphrases of Italian texts; four of Morley's original songs are resettings of texts from his own anthology of Italian *Canzonets* (1597). Other composers reset eighteen other poems from the Italian anthologies (one of them twice; Kerman, 1962a, 24–25). Morley's books and those of many other English madrigalists contain texts that look like translations, even when no immediate model can be found. Like this text from his own English *Canzonets . . . to Five and Sixe Voices* (1597), they have feminine rhymes, mixed line lengths, and some of the syntactic and stylistic features of the anthology imitations:

> I follow, lo, the footing
> Still of my lovely cruel,
> Proud of herself that she is beauty's jewel.
> And fast away she flieth,
> Love's sweet delight deriding,
> In woods and groves sweet Nature's treasure hiding.
> Yet cease I not pursuing,
> But since I thus have sought her,
> Will run me out of breath till I have caught her.
>
> (1597, no. 17)

Much of the verse in the madrigal books is like this, mere *poesia per musica,* and is not of much interest apart from its music. In Italy, the madrigal had its origin as part of a literary movement (Mace, 1969), and composers made a point of setting texts of high literary quality, though they also set their share of anonymous trivia. Petrarch's sonnets were set over and over; half a volume would be given over to a setting of a *canzone* of Petrarch, each stanza getting separate treatment. Stanzas from the narrative poems of Ariosto and Tasso were set, as well as verse in madrigal form by Sannazaro, Guarini, Bembo, Alamanni, and others. The English were mainly drawn to the music of the madrigal, and often slighted the texts, as can be seen in the translations and paraphrases. Watson, for instance, dropped the sestet of Marenzio's setting of Petrarch's sonnet "Zefiro torna," and printed the two parts of Luigi Tansillo's sonnet "Ne ferò sdegno," set by Marenzio, in the wrong order, so that the sestet comes before the octave. And as we have seen, some of the words Watson supplied for the music had little connection with the original text.

The English did not set poems by their own literary figures with anything like the same frequency as the Italians. Those who did set stanzas of Spenser's *Faerie Queene,* like Richard Carlton (1601) or Orlando Gibbons (1612), wrote more in the native style of Byrd. The only truly madrigalian setting of Spenser is George Kirbye's "Up then Melpomene" (1597, nos. 22–23), two stanzas from the November eclogue of *The Shepheardes Calender.* Sidney is the most frequently set major poet, but only eight madrigals use his words, and several of these use only distorted fragments of longer poems. "The nightingale, so soon as April bringeth," which Sidney had written to fit Italian music, appears in Thomas Bateson's setting (1604) with only the first seven lines of the first stanza. Ten of Francis Davison's madrigals from *A Poetical Rhapsody* were set by Robert Jones (1607) and John Ward (1613). Ward also adapted rather freely two texts from Michael Drayton's *The Shepherds' Garland* (1593), and another from a poem of Drayton's that was printed in *England's Helicon* (1600). Since Ward also set texts from Sidney, his is one of the more literary sets. Other poets whose verse was chosen by the madrigalists are Barnabe Barnes, Thomas Campion, Henry Constable, Samuel Daniel (one stanza), Sir John Davies, Walter Davison, Robert Greene, Bartholomew Griffin, Thomas Howell, Chidiock Tichborne, George Wither, and Sir Henry Wotton. Ben Jonson's "Slow, slow, fresh fount," which cries out for madrigal treatment, has only a weak three-part setting by Henry Youll (1608, no. 8). Most of these poets are minor, and most have only one or two poems in the madrigal books—some even less than one poem, given the madrigalists' habit of setting only one stanza. The great bulk of the madrigal texts are anonymous *(EMV)*.

A number of the anonymous texts are more interesting as poetry than many of those by known poets. Most of the pathetic laments are completely vapid without their expressive music, but this poem from Morley's 1597 *Canzonets* stands out because of its restraint and the effect of the rhyming long and short lines in reinforcing the sense of loss. The homophonic music, incidentally, preserves the verse structure until the last line.[3]

> O Grief! e'en on the bud that fairly flowered
> The sun hath lowered.
> And, ah, that breast which Love durst never venture,
> Bold Death did enter.
> Pity, O heavens, that have my love in keeping,
> My cries and weeping.
>   (1597, no. 7)

Another poem from the same collection is a conventional *carpe diem* statement, but it is neat and succinct:

> Ladies, you see time flieth,
> And beauty too, it dieth.
> Then take your pleasure,
> While you have leisure.
> Nor be so dainty
> Of that which you have plenty.
>   (1597, no. 20)

This last item was one of several madrigal texts canonized by the late Yvor Winters (1939; in Alpers, 1967, 113, 125). Some of Winters's choices are as puzzling as his autocratic manner is maddening, but his interest in the following poem may have been supported by his love of boxing:

> Damon and Phyllis squared,
> And to point her the place the nymph him dared.
> Her glove she down did cast him,

> And to meet her alone she bade him haste him.
> Alike their weapons were, alike their smiting,
> And little Love came running to the fighting.
> > (Morley, 1597, no. 14)

The monotony of pastoral and amatory conventions in most madrigal verse may perhaps make the reader overvalue the novel, the odd, the quirky. But a welcome change of pace in Morley's collections is provided by the narrative madrigals, which have about them more of the English countryside than the Italian court, though they may be modeled on the Italian *caccia* (Einstein, 1944, 70–71; Fabry, 1964, 74–77). These narratives are more effective with their music, but they are also refreshing to encounter on the page. "Arise, get up my dear" (1593, no. 20) tells of a wedding celebration, with "merry maidens squealing," "Spice-cake, sops in wine," music and dancing. "Whither away" (1593, no. 7) is a monologue of a lover chasing his sweetheart, who allows herself to be overtaken. "Ho! who comes here" (1594, no. 18) celebrates a troop of morris-dancers, and is imitated later by Thomas Weelkes in "Strike it up, Tabor" (1608, no. 18). "Ho! who comes here" as a poem is, however, especially false to its musical embodiment, which uses dialogue and variants between the voices in a way that cannot be resolved easily into a single text.

From these and other examples one might gather that the better madrigal texts share many of the qualities of good light verse: brevity, wit, formal control, linguistic playfulness, technical ingenuity. There is not much of the last quality in madrigal verse, but there is a respectable number of examples of the other qualities. The comic rhyme of the concluding couplet of this item is almost worthy of Byron:

> Lady, when I behold your passions,
> > So divers and so oft constrained
> Upon such slight or no occasions,
> > As though you were with grief sore pained,
> I enter into these persuasions:
> A man might sail from Trent unto Danuby
> And yet not find so strange a piece as you be.
> > (Farnaby, 1598, no. 19)

A similar expression of male frustration is "Ay me, can every rumour" (Wilbye, 1598, no. 3). The following from Wilbye's 1609 collection is also sexist, but is redeemed by its wit, which has more of the flavor of the seventeenth century:

> Love me not for comely grace,
> For my pleasing eye or face,
> Nor for any outward part,
> No nor for my constant heart;
> For those may fail or turn to ill,
>   So thou and I shall sever.
>   Keep therefore a true woman's eye,
>   And love me still, but know not why,
> So hast thou the same reason still
>   To dote upon me ever.
>   (1609, no. 12)

This last example is representative of a new kind of madrigal verse. Although the Italian vein continues through most of the madrigal texts, there does seem to be a gradual decline over the years of the kind of verse found in the translated anthologies and in Morley, and an increase of verse in a more native style. This verse tends to be more normal in syntax, uses less feminine rhyme, and is generally more epigrammatic.

Thomas Weelkes in his last collection, *Ayeres or Phantasticke Spirites* (1608), showed a taste for nonsense. Weelkes's "Ha ha! ha ha! This world doth pass," a satire on flattery, is admired by several aficionados of nonsense, and was chosen by W. H. Auden for inclusion—among several madrigal texts—in his edition of *The Oxford Book of Light Verse* (1938, 117–21). Here is the second stanza:

> Tie hie! tie hie! O sweet delight!
>   He tickles this age that can
> Call Tullia's ape a marmasyte
> And Leda's goose a swan.
>   Fara diddle dyno,
>   This is idle fyno.
>   (1608, no. 19)

But the editor of *The New Oxford Book of English Light Verse,* Kingsley Amis, has some harsh criticisms of this piece and of those who admire it. Some, I think, are justified, especially if it is considered as a poem, not a song text. Of the fourth line, Amis says that "Weelkes presumably meant something like 'Call Audrey's goose Leda's swan,' but that was too hard for him.'' It seems to me that the poet is merely citing another example of flattery, and that what we call Leda's swan was always a goose. Amis claims that "can" at the end of the second line is misleading because of the emphasis it receives in this position. The mostly homophonic music mitigates this emphasis by having "can" set in all voices to a (fast) whole note followed by a half note on "Call," with no rest or break in between; the voices linger just long enough on "can" to register the rhyme, then flow on before the inappropriate meaning crystallizes. The "ha ha" and "Tie hie," Amis says, "are doing the same job as the music-hall comedian's red nose and check trousers: making quite sure the audience knows that the performer is trying to be funny" (1978, x). In the song, these noises work more like an artistically transfigured laugh-track, stimulating laughter by imitating it in infectious three-part counterpoint.

Verse and Music in the Madrigal

Thus it would seem risky to judge these poems apart from their music. It would be more charitable toward most of them if we did not. For in the hands of one of the better madrigalists, a mediocre poem can become part of a much more significant aesthetic experience. This experience is largely musical, and is consequently of less interest to those with more literary concerns. But though these texts do not do well on their own, they are important to the madrigal as a whole; and by understanding why they appealed to the composer we may revise our own expectations about verse found in the madrigals.

We might postulate that the best verse for madrigals is that which facilitates the production of a good madrigal. The most successful madrigals are those in which the text stimulates the composer into making music that is varied but coherent and expressive, music that in reflecting the feelings, actions, and images of the text, uses those musical materials most characteristic of the madrigal: varied textures, polyphony, homophony, flexible rhythms, expressive harmonies. By this standard, the following bit of cheerful idiocy is a good madrigal text because it led Wilbye to compose a good madrigal:

> Flora gave me fairest flowers,
>   None so fair in Flora's treasure.

These I placed on Phyllis' bowers,
  She was pleased, and she my pleasure.
Smiling meadows seem to say:
Come, ye wantons, here to play.
                        (1598, no. 22)

What may have attracted Wilbye to these words is their easy generation of a mood by doing little more than listing pleasant pastoral objects, persons, and actions. The text demands only a musical
reinforcement of the atmosphere of pastoral love, flowers, pleasure,
"smiling meadows," and playing wantons. The idea of playing is illustrated by imitative scale passages in the upper four voices; and there
is a slight reminiscence of Flora's original gift in the music for "These
I placed on Phyllis' bowers." It is not very pictorial, but is very expressive of the lighthearted mood.

On the other hand, the text of Weelkes's contribution to *The
Triumphs of Oriana* demands pictorial treatment in almost every line,
and was probably valued because it did:

As Vesta was from Latmos hill descending,
She spied a maiden Queen the same ascending,
Attended on by all the shepherds' swain,
To whom Diana's darlings came running down amain,
First two by two, then three by three together,
Leaving their goddess all alone, hasted thither;
And mingling with the shepherds of her train,
With mirthful tunes her presence entertain.
  Then sang the shepherds and nymphs of Diana:
    Long live fair Oriana.
                        (Morley, 1601, no. 17)

At least this verse has some coherence: it compliments the Queen by
showing Diana's attendants deserting the goddess to pay homage to
Elizabeth, symbolically endowing her with more than divine chastity
and power. The music ascends to Latmos hill, descends with Diana,
ascends in melismatic scales with the Queen, and comes "running
down amain" in eighth notes with Diana's darlings. This is of course
very naive, but it is carried off with such musical verve that it is difficult to be severe toward it. The numbers of deserters are matched by
the numbers of singers, but repetition distributes the voices so that
"First two by two" is sung by the second soprano and alto and then by

the first soprano and first tenor; two groups of three voices do the same for "three by three," and all join in on "together." One voice sings "all alone." The most notable show of virtuosity comes on the refrain line shared by all the madrigals in the *Triumphs,* "Long live fair Oriana." The bass, after one statement of the rapid phrase (Ex. 6.1a) the other voices will toss about in sequence, sings "Long" to the equivalent in modern notation of four tied whole notes. But this bit of illustration is also a pedal note controlling the harmony of the other voices, and as it turns out, is the first note of an extensively augmented version of the phrase sung by the other voices (Ex. 6.1b).

Example 6.1a   Example 6.1b

The bass repeats a less augmented version of the phrase in a higher register, and finally returns to the original statement near the end. The increasing diminution of this phrase in the bass adds to the sense of approaching climax and conclusion.

The text of "As Vesta" was probably written specifically for musical setting, and offers more opportunities than problems for the composer. But sometimes the text will demand that the composer interpret the words, that he give the poem a reading. Like an actor, the composer, by his choices of emphasis and tone, affects the audience's understanding of the text. One of Morley's most familiar pieces provides a good example:

> April is in my mistress' face,
> And July in her eyes hath place,
> Within her bosom is September,
> But in her heart a cold December.
> (1594, no. 1)

As a poem, this is very slight, but it is neat and coherent. It is not even original: it was translated from a poem by Livio Celiano that was set to music by Horatio Vecchi. The Italian has eight more stanzas (Obertello, 1949, 514–16). Morley's setting offers a distinctive inter-pretation and gives the poem some dramatic immediacy. The first two lines are clear enough: the lady's face is fresh and springlike, and her eyes appear to have a summerlike warmth. The little eighth-note figure on "July in her eyes" may suggest a sparkle. But what are we to make of September in the bosom? In some climes, September would be an extension of summer; in some, it would be autumn, with its ambigu-ous associations of harvest abundance and approaching death. Morley, rather than increasing the positive associations established so far with music suggesting fullness or a ripening toward harvest, treats Septem-ber as the onset of winter. The descending minor scale on "September" is like the fall of leaves. In the poem, the main contrast would seem to be between three months of positive associations and cold December. Morley delays the contrast by setting "But in her heart" with hopeful rising sequences as a possible contrast to the chill of September. This hope is dashed by the revelation that her heart is even colder than her bosom.

Another way of studying how composers interpret the text is to compare different settings of the same poem. In Italy, this would be an especially rich exercise, since there are dozens of different settings of the same poems. Although a number of poems were reset by the English madrigalists, most of these were set only twice. Some, how-ever, involved one of the best composers, John Wilbye, in competition as it were with others and with himself. "Alas, what hope of speeding" was first set by Wilbye's neighbor and probable acquaintance, George Kirbye, in four parts (D. Brown, 1974, 12). The text consists of ten seven-syllable lines with feminine rhymes, which give it an Italian flavor. The suffering lover and perverse mistress are conventional, but despite some awkwardnesses ("flied") and complicated syntax in lines 7–9, the conclusion manages to show some wit:

> Alas, what hope of speeding,
> Where hope beguiled lies bleeding?
> She bade come when she spied me;
> And when I came she flied me.
> Thus when I was beguiled,
> She at my sighing smiled.
> But if you take such pleasure
> Of Hope and Joy, my treasure,

> By deceit to bereave me,
> Love me, and so deceive me.
>   (Kirbye, 1597, no. 2)

Kirbye's setting is a respectable effort, musically quite engaging. He begins by setting "Alas" in the sopranos to parallel minor thirds (Ex. 6.2):

Example 6.2

The tenor joins them in singing the rest of the first line and the second homophonically. The opening "Alas" is repeated in the tenor and bass, with the rest of the first two lines now sung by all four voices. Each of the next four lines is also repeated, with similar variations in the music. Along the way, "flied" and "smiled" are sung to melismas, "smiled" being stretched out over the value of six half notes. As Morley prescribes, there is a rest before "sighing," first in three parts, then twice in all four parts together. When the speaker turns to address the lady after line 6, a new section begins. These last four lines are formally repeated; within this section, only the next-to-last line is repeated in the course of some imitation. As Philip Brett says, Kirbye races to the end "hoping, as it were, not to drop the syntactical egg from the musical spoon" (1979, 5).

When Wilbye published his four-part setting a year later (1598, no. 9), he followed Kirbye in some details, but he radically shifted the proportions. The structural division of the madrigal comes at the same place, after the first six lines, but Wilbye does not repeat the final section. In the first section, only the fifth line and half of the fourth are repeated, though with different music; so Wilbye's first section is only twenty-nine bars or whole notes long while Kirbye's is forty-four whole notes. In this first section Wilbye begins with a suspension dissonance on "Alas"; like Kirbye, he also has melismas for "flied" and "smiled," but they are briefer and not repeated. The rest before "sighs" is in only two voices, and it is also not repeated. As David Brown (1974, 15) observes, "Despite Kirbye's more pointed musical illustration of certain words, it is Wilbye who reveals the greater variety." Other details add to this variety. In the third line, Wilbye has the sopranos repeat a motif on "She bade come" that is first harmonized with an A-minor chord, then with a C-major chord, suggesting growing hope at her summons; but the voices fall back to A minor in the next line. The music for the first part of "Thus when I was beguiled" recalls Kirbye's opening "Alas" (Ex. 6.2); the repetition is different, though still expressive of the speaker's pain.

Wilbye shifts the focus onto the last four lines of the text, onto the witty point. Each line in this section is repeated, line seven in a slower-moving imitative passage, and line eight in almost identical music for each repeat. This part is generally expressive of "pleasure" and "hope and joy," but the shifting between F-natural and F-sharp on "hope" is disturbing. The phrases float free of their syntax in this setting, but they still communicate that the speaker's hope and joy are bereaved by deceit. Line 9 is repeated four times to music "as wayward in harmony, melody, rhythm and texture as the behaviour of the deceiving dame it expresses" (Brett, 1979). Rising sequences and repetitions of phrases within the line lead strongly to the crucial last line. Although Wilbye

Example 6.3a (Kirbye)

Example 6.3b (Wilbye)

follows Kirbye in having the soprano and bass move in parallel thirds, the declamation and repetition make Wilbye's setting more emphatic (Ex. 6.3). The union of the lady's and lover's purposes is realized in the parallel voices.

Kirbye's setting seems to take the poem more at face value: each line is of almost equal importance. Wilbye seems to realize that the posturing in the first lines is mainly to set up the wit of the last line, so he adjusts the rhetoric of his setting accordingly, and keeps the tone of the first part from sounding too seriously pathetic.

Some of the same differences may be found in Wilbye's own two settings of the same text. "Lady, when I behold the roses sprouting" appears twice in the 1598 set, once for four voices (no. 10) and again for six voices (no. 24). The four-voice setting is simpler and more homophonic, and the rhetorical emphasis is distributed fairly evenly throughout the madrigal. The six-voice setting is much more elaborate musically, reflecting more of the courtly artificiality of the text while at the same time making the text less audible to a listener. This version also throws more rhetorical focus on the last line, which contains the epigrammatic point: "Whether the roses be your lips, or your lips the roses." The polyphonic repetitions of this line, above descending whole-note scales, make for exciting music; it has the effect of transforming the line from a pale conceit to a mysterious, almost mythical identity of lips and roses.

The infusion of meaning through music when it is not immediately evident in the text is especially notable in Weelkes's setting of this unpromising verse:

> Care, thou wilt despatch me,
> If music do not match thee. Fa la.
> So deadly dost thou sting me,
> Mirth only help can bring me. Fa la.
>
> Hence, Care, thou art too cruel,
> Come, music, sick man's jewel. Fa la.
> His force had well nigh slain me,
> But thou must now sustain me. Fa la.
> (1600, pt. 1, nos. 4–5)

The form of the verse suggests a light ballet; but the ballet, with its seven-syllable lines, feminine rhymes, and "fa la" refrains, seems at odds with the subject of care. Perhaps another composer might have taken the opportunity to contrast the melancholy of the verse with gaiety in the refrain, acting out the power of music to banish care. Weelkes's interpretation is more daring and more subtle, as well as thoroughly madrigalian. Weelkes's music makes the speaker attempt to use music as an antidote to care, but fail. The "fa las" are integrated into the piece as expressions of the speaker. They come in more rapid figures that attempt to bring cheer, but are defeated by the harmony. Donald Tovey compares the effect to the "la la, la la" sung by Verdi's suffering jester, Rigoletto.[4]

The first line, like the first of each of the couplets, begins in whole and half notes, the voices changing mainly in minor seconds, with many suspension dissonances; when the soprano enters, "Care" falls on an augmented triad of E-flat against G and B-natural, a combination that occurs again on "deadly" and on "slain" in the next-to-last line. The note values shorten to quarters and occasional eighths in the second line, and the main motif continues into the first set of "fa-las;" major tonality attempts to assert itself here, but minor chords persist in retaining the melancholy mood. Slow-moving dissonances return on "So deadly dost thou sting me," culminating on a searing simultaneous false relation (F and F-sharp). The next line (which we might untangle to read "only mirth can bring me help") is again integrated with the "fa-las," but this attempt to bring mirth is more heroic. The main motif has four eighth notes, which are repeated in sequences that strive upward in mostly major harmonies; but just before the closing cadence in this section, the minor returns with a figure in the soprano (D to F-natural to D, Ex. 6.4) which Deryck Cooke (1962, 140) says compos-

Example 6.4

Fa   la la la la la   la   la,   fa la la la la la   la

ers have used over the years to express "an obsession with gloomy feelings, a trapped fear, or a sense of inescapable doom."

The second half returns to music similar to the opening, but the harmonies are much more painful; indeed, this passage is one of the most daring in English music before the nineteenth century in its abrupt modulations to remote keys. Donald Tovey (1937, 5:7) writes that here Weelkes produced a "chain of modulations which Schubert or Brahms would have been proud to sign," adding that "it had far more force against a severly modal background than it can possibly have in the complex luxuries of later music." It begins with a double chromatic progression, slightly cushioned by the rest in the lower voices (Ex. 6.5; Kerman, 1962a, 213–14).

Example 6.5

After this opening, as Kerman (1962a, 219) points out, the passage "consists of five cadential formulas in a row, the first four of which are not allowed to resolve," thus frustrating expectation and heightening affect. Another augmented triad, this time on G, B, and D-sharp, with B in the bass, finds "Care" in some voices, "cruel" in others. The modulations finally resolve in the mediant, on B-flat. The next line is set to descending half-note G-minor scales in imitation, anticipating the faster descending scales in the "fa-la" section. Cooke (1962, 133, 162) finds descending minor scales expressive of "incoming painful emotion, an acceptance of, or yielding to grief," which counters any positive note in the text. The last couplet returns to half- and whole-note movement, swelling on "force" and falling on "slain," and the rhythms of "But thou must now sustain me" return to those of line two, "If music do not match thee," above a sustaining four-bar pedal note. The final "fa-las" attempt one melodic leap and fall back in resignation.

Kerman observes (1962a, 219) that the harmonic adventures in this madrigal are not representative of the great bulk of English madrigals, or even those of Weelkes. Nor should this madrigal be taken as evidence that all writers of song verse deliberately left space in their lyrics, as it were, expecting them to be filled out with music and transformed into masterpieces by a Weelkes or a Dowland. But it does say something about the volatile nature of the relationship between words and music. If music cannot move beasts and stones, it can sometimes move stony and beastly verse into a new dimension. But, by the same token, it can smother eloquent poetry in its own empty rhetoric if the composer is not a match for the poet.

Despite the power of some madrigalists to transcend their texts, to make a poem more meaningful than it first appears, even good madrigals can present problems. The problem with the following madrigal of Weelkes's is one of decorum:

> Thule, the period of cosmography,
>   Doth vaunt of Hecla, whose sulphurious fire
> Doth melt the frozen clime and thaw the sky;
>   Trinacrian Ætna's flames ascend not higher.
> These things seem wondrous, yet more wondrous I,
> Whose heart with fear doth freeze, with love doth fry.
>
> The Andalusian merchant, that returns
>   Laden with cochineal and China dishes,
> Reports in Spain how strangely Fogo burns
>   Amidst an ocean full of flying fishes.
> These things seem wondrous, yet more wondrous I,
> Whose heart with fear doth freeze, with love doth fry.
>   (1600, pt. 2, nos. 7–8)

"Thule" is a "metaphysical" poem in that it yokes heterogeneous images together with some violence, and is interesting largely for their heterogeneity. The poem has also attracted attention because of its reflection of the spirit of exploration, of Drake and Hakluyt's *Voyages*. It is a letdown to have the wonders of the newly opening world brought back to Petrarchan freezing fires. But the concept is not that remote from Donne's "O my America! my new-found-land" (from "To his Mistris Going to Bed"), however more concentrated and suggestive the latter. And like other metaphysical poems, it raises questions of decorum. Philip Brett, recalling Ben Jonson's criticism of Donne's *First Anniversary* (1611) as "profane and full of blasphemies" because it treats the death of a young girl in terms more appropriate for the Virgin Mary, thinks that a composer like Byrd could not have approved "either of the destruction of the poetic form to which the madrigal is prone, or the employment for light matter of a style Morley describes as 'next unto the Motet, the most artificial,'" noting that Byrd's only madrigal was in honor of the queen. Consequently, Brett feels, Byrd would have been "censorious about the towering musical monument erected upon the triviality of 'Thule, the period of cosmography'" (1971–72, 62). This madrigal, like Donne's poems, may point to a larger shift in what was felt to be decorous, from a more balanced "Renaissance" aesthetic to a more extreme "mannerist" one.

If one can swallow the rhetorical expediency of the couplets, realizing that they do at least serve to unify the poem, just as the repetition of the music for these couplets gives structural stability to the musical form, one can then proceed to enjoy the musical monument. It is indeed a monument of wondrous images: the boiling eighth-note melismas on "sulphurious" are followed by stable homophony on "frozen" and rapid polyphony on "thaw"; Ætna's flames ascend, the flying fishes fly on interwoven ascending and descending eighth-note scales, and Fogo burns on strangely descending chromatic scales; and "wondrous" is illustrated by an abrupt chromatic modulation from F to E-flat. The whole is full of testimony to Weelkes's rich musical imagination. But the couplets remain an irritant.

More generally applicable objections to the madrigal have arisen out of reaction to some of the earlier and rosier evaluations of its relation to poetry. E. H. Fellowes had written that "Elizabethan music was indeed 'married to immortal verse' in equal partnership" (*EMV*, xvii), and Bruce Pattison said that "The madrigal was a very satisfactory compromise between the claims of music and poetry" (1970, 98). John Stevens offered a corrective to these views in "The Elizabethan Madrigal: 'Perfect Marriage' or 'Uneasy Flirtation'" (1958). Stevens does a good job of stressing some points that needed making in 1958. He dispels the romantic notion that Renaissance song was part of a continuing tradition of natural union between music and poetry by pointing out the independence of the two arts before humanism and the Reformation aroused new concern for their mutual relationship. He also stresses the rhetorical character of Elizabethan lyrics, disputing romantic assumptions that lyrics should be personal expressions of emotion. Opposing Hallett Smith's speculation about the effect on the poet's ear of "hearing interpretations of verse by music so sensitive, imitative of every suggestion of color or emotion in the words, free and inventive in the matter of rhythm as were the madrigals" (1952, 270), Stevens stresses "the rhythmic insensitiveness; the crude pictorialism; the occasional gross misunderstandings of the madrigal composer" (1958, 27). He cites as an example Orlando Gibbons's setting of Ralegh's "What is our life? a play of passion" (1612, no. 14), where in the line "Our mirth the music of division," "division" is set to a descending eighth-note scale, illustrating the musical meaning of the word as a passage of rapid notes despite the context of the poem demanding that the word refer to music during the intervals of a play. Gibbons's setting may be seen as misleading, but it also can be seen as enriching the poem with a pun that only the music could add.

To be sure, madrigals can furnish examples of crudeness, insensitivity, and misunderstanding. But some of Stevens's arguments are compromised by his reliance on Gibbons for examples. For, as Joseph Kerman (1962a, 122–27) has made clear, most of Gibbons's songs are not madrigals, but adaptations of the native style of Byrd. Hence when Stevens complains that Gibbons divides his two-part setting of a stanza from *The Faerie Queene,* "Fair ladies, that to love captived are" (1612, nos. 10–11), after line 4, in the middle of a sentence, he does not recognize that Gibbons is dividing according to formal considerations: ending the first section after line 5 would have broken the rhyme scheme so that the second section would not have a rhyme for line 7. The more syntactically oriented madrigalists, like Wilbye, would have ignored the form.

Some of Stevens's objections to Gibbons's "Dainty fine bird" (1612, no. 9) must also be seen in the light of the formal priorities of the native style. But one point he raises has more general significance. In this poem, says Stevens, there is "the most delicate play (or 'syncopating') of the speech-rhythm against the metrical pattern," notably in the second line: "Dainty fine bird that art encaged there, / alas, how like thine and my fortunes are." The sense demands some extrametrical emphasis on "thine" and "my," while retaining the metrical stresses on "like" and "fortunes." This is the kind of effect Sidney first made possible, as we have seen in the previous chapter. Stevens admits that we "have to reconcile ourselves to losing, in any musical setting this subtle, ever-shifting tension and resolution" (1958, 29–30). But Gibbons's setting fails to reflect the metrical effect even crudely. Although many madrigalists do take their musical rhythms from those of the text, subtleties of rhythmic and metrical interplay are often lost, especially under the musical demands of polyphony. Except for the structural points of reference offered by rhyme, most madrigal texts might as well be prose.

On the other hand, John Hollander (1975, 30–36) has demonstrated that the rhythmic independence and repetition in the different voices of a polyphonic setting can "possibly get at the richness of rhythmic texture developed in accentual-syllabic English verse." As an example, he takes the last line of Weelkes's "Hark, all ye lovely saints above" (1598, no. 8), "Then cease, fair ladies; why weep ye?" The line can have three different meanings depending on the stresses given the last three syllables. The meter and rhyme point to a stress on "ye," meaning, says Hollander, "'Why *you*, of all people?'" But the music, with its repetition of the line and different rhythms in the different voices, generates all three possible stresses and possible meanings.

While some metrical effects may be lost, the madrigalists generally "made great efforts to follow the verbal rhythm in the individual voices," as Pattison says (1970, 98). Examples of rhythmic insensitivity can of course be found, as well as rhythms that generate irrelevant stresses or misleading rather than enriching ambiguities. But composers like Wilbye usually respect the verbal rhythm so that the texts are not awkward to sing. To get a fair idea of the distance traveled in attitudes toward the text in polyphonic music, the following example from Wilbye's "Draw on, sweet Night" (1609, no. 31; Ex. 6.6) should

Example 6.6

That un- to thee, to thee, I con-se-crate it whol- ly,

[that un-to thee I con-se- crate it whol- ly.]

be compared with a passage from Whythorne cited earlier (Ex. 3.5); this is also a single voice part from a polyphonic passage.

Polyphony brings us to the issue on which the madrigal is most vulnerable to attack from the literary point of view, that of audibility. Frank Kermode has observed that the composer of madrigals "subjects his poem to a process resembling, and perhaps in his mind identified with, the rhetorical device of Amplification. . . . This may help us to see why the madrigalists were so assiduous in *descriptio,* the rhetorical function they could most easily simulate." But because imitative polyphony was one of the most common ways of musical amplification, this meant, says Kermode, "disastrous inaudibility" (1949, 266–67). Samuel Pepys once complained that "singing with many voices is not singing, but a sort of Instrumentall music, the sense of the words being lost by not being heard, and especially as they set them with Fugues of words, one after another" (1974, 8:438; also quoted by Kermode, 1949, 267). This same objection was made against Tudor church music, and Giovanni Bardi made it against the Italian madrigal (Strunk,

1950, 294–95). One defense that has been offered is that madrigals were a kind of chamber music, designed more for the performers than an audience. A performer would be able to follow the text and yet be aware of how the other parts joined with his own to express the text. But Kermode replies that "one has only to read through the words given to any one voice in a handful of madrigals to discover the kind of nonsense each voice individually sang." Kermode refers specifically to an example cited by Fellowes to illustrate the difficulties of reconstructing a text from the music books. The example is an especially complex one from a canzonet by Morley. There is much repetition, repetition to the point of meaninglessness, and much difference among the three voices; but as Fellowes (1948, 150–52) says, Morley is especially bad about taking such liberties. Other composers repeat lines and phrases, but the result is not always nonsense. It is nevertheless a fault to those who object to the destruction of the form and proportions of the poem that is inevitable in madrigal settings. These objectors would sympathize with Tennyson, who is said to have complained that musicians made him say twice what he only wanted to say once.

But repetition of the words can increase the audibility of the text to those who happen to be outside the performers' circle. Repetition would, in fact, make it conceivable to construct a madrigal in which the words would be fairly audible to an audience. As Charles Butler wrote in 1636, "Reports [points of imitation] require Repeats: that if the Points Ditty be not apprehended at the first; yet, in the iterating thereof, it may."[5] The composer could use all the usual musical components of the madrigal and have the words understood as long as he obeyed this rule: each coherent phrase or line of the text must be stated at least once either in homophony by several voices, or by one voice in a point of imitation that does not overlap with another voice until the phrase is complete, or by one voice against other voices singing only one syllable (as with a pedal point). Polyphonic imitation could be used freely on repetitions of the phrase, and homophonic passages would still have their functions of punctuation, variety, and emphasis. Although the texts of most madrigals are relatively more audible than those of the polyphonic part-songs of Byrd or Gibbons, few obey my hypothetical rule strictly. Francis Pilkington's "Sing we, dance we on the green" (1613, no. 16) comes close because it has so much homophony, as does his "Have I found her?" (1613, no. 11).

If not many other examples come to mind it is perhaps because the musical fashion was the dominant concern of the composers who specialized in madrigals and of those who sang them. Even now, I suspect those who admire many madrigals, as I do, are first attracted to the music; the gradually understood words, or words read in scores or on record jackets, then come to illuminate the music, which in turn sometimes illuminates the words. Just as rock fans become familiar with words of songs that are unintelligible to the casual listener, so the audiences of madrigals must have come to understand the texts through sheer familiarity. And paradoxically, the musical experience of madrigals seemed to be available at least in part without the words; we must recall again the phrase "apt for viols and voices" on the title pages of so many of the madrigal books, and the practice it must have reflected. We might also consider Mark Booth's general comments (1981, 201) on the communal nature of all song that allows listeners to enjoy nonsense songs, "including art songs in languages not understood." The "affects of voice contribute some proportion" of what language puts into music, whether or not the language is understood.

Nevertheless, despite these explanations, most madrigals pose an aesthetic problem if they are to be considered vocal works aimed at a nonparticipating audience. For if the reasons for the tempo, texture, tonality, structure, mood, emotional content, and many of the details of a piece of music are dictated by a text, and that text is obscured by the very elements that are supposed to be expressive of it, how is communication of the aesthetic experience to be accomplished? This question was not lost on musicians and poets on the Continent or in England, and may have been responsible for the decline of the madrigal and the rise of the lutenist air and its descendants.

Chapter Seven
John Dowland and the Air

The problem with the madrigal as a vehicle for the singing of poetry is that the independent voice parts and frequently polyphonic texture make it difficult for a listener to hear all the words. This problem is mitigated in accompanied solo songs, especially if the singer articulates clearly and the accompaniment does not overpower him. The consort song allows both textual audibility and the musical interest of polyphony in the accompanying viol parts. The lute song or air is a close relative of the consort song, and songs may be found in arrangements for both lute and voice, and viol consort and voice. They differ mainly in the difference between the dynamic of the consort of viols and the lute. A song accompanied by a lute or lute with supporting bass viol focuses even more attention on the solo voice, for however separate and dominant the voice part in a consort song, there is always a sense in which it is only the most articulate of the five (or four, or six). In the air, solo and accompaniment are more in balance.

Like the consort song, the air includes a variety of musical types, though most are basically accompanied melody. Airs can be disguised homophonic part-songs, instrumental dance tunes, canzonets, ballets, or even madrigals; they can be consort songs with the viol parts arranged for the lute. Airs were published in a way that would allow several other options for performance as well. The model for most of the collections of airs was the first and one of the most important, John Dowland's *First Booke of Songes or Ayres* (1597). One of the most popular musical publications of the period, it was reprinted four times during Dowland's lifetime.[1] As the title page states, the songs are "of fowre partes with Tableture for the Lute: So made that all the partes together, or either of them severally may be song to the Lute, Orpherian or Viol de gambo." The songs were printed so that all parts could be read from one book by performers sitting around a table. A given song could be sung by four voices a capella; or the voices could be joined by instruments; or a single voice could sing the cantus part accompanied by the lute alone, by lute and bass viol, by the wire-stringed orpherion, by three viols, or by other possible combinations (Ward, 1977, 53–57). The commercial advantages of giving amateur musicians such a variety of performance possibilities are obvious. But in the later books, some songs are presented only in versions for one voice, lute, and bass viol, which seems to have been the preferred mode of performance for most airs. Thomas Campion amusingly writes in his preface to *Two Bookes of Ayres* (ca. 1613) that "These Ayres were for the most part framed at first for one voyce with the Lute, or Violl," but he has added more voices because "when any shall sing a Treble to an Instrument, the standers by will be offring at an inward part out of their owne nature; and, true or false, out it must, though to the perverting of the whole harmonie."

Although singing to an instrument was an old practice, and songs with lute tablatures had been published in Italy as early as 1509, the air as practiced by Dowland and his contemporaries used the lute in a new way. Dowland was a virtuoso performer on the lute and wrote many purely instrumental pieces. Ironically, the development of instrumental techniques, and the growing popularity of music for the viol, lute, and keyboard was leading music in a direction of growing independence from poetry. Yet Dowland's ability to compose idiomatically for the lute, and to write songs that were not merely tunes with improvised chords on old ground basses, or transcribed part-songs, added to the expressiveness and art of his settings.

As a solo form related to the consort song, the air is recognizably in the native tradition, not an imported exotic like the madrigal. The poetry is also close to that found in the consort song in that most of it is strophic and native; but whereas Byrd's conservative taste in poetry dominated the consort song, the verse of the air is more varied and current. Although many of the poems are anonymous, many are of good quality; and those that have been identified are by some of the better poets, including Sidney, Greville, Daniel, Jonson, Donne, and of course Thomas Campion. Other poets represented are Nicholas Breton, William Browne, Henry Chettle, Walter and Francis Davison, Thomas Lodge, Anthony Munday, George Peele, and Robert Southwell; courtiers like Sir John Davies, Sir Henry Lee, Sir Edward Dyer, and the earls of Cumberland and Essex; and even anachronisms like Wyatt and Gascoigne. Since the air is a clearer vehicle for musical presentation of poetry to an audience than the madrigal, it should not be surprising that the airs have texts of more literary substance; at least they can be longer than madrigals. The subject matter ranges from

love to religion to royal flattery, but most deal with love in a Petrarchan manner. Italian elements come into the poetry of the air more
through literary than musical channels, through imitations of Petrarchan poetry rather than direct translations of song texts.

This is not to say that there was no foreign influence on the air.
While there is nothing comparable to the Italian dominance of the
madrigal, there are at least some striking parallels between the English
air and the French *voix-de-ville* and *air de cour* (*LEA*, 5–7, Heartz,
1972). The English and French forms both tend to be homophonic
settings of strophic texts that exist in both part-song and instrumen-
tally accompanied solo versions. To cite just two pieces of evidence of
French influence, we might note that Adrian Le Roy's *Second Livre de
Guiterre, Contenant Plusieurs Chansons en forme de voix de ville* (1556) contains simple syllabic settings of strophic texts for one voice and four-
stringed *guiterne* in tablature, one of which strongly resembles Dowland's "Now O now I needs must part" (1597, no. 6). Dowland's song
was also known in instrumental versions as the "Frog Galliard," and
several of his other songs are extant as instrumental dances. Most of
the songs in Le Roy's collection are labeled with the names of dances,
galliards, pavans, or *branles*. The English also composed words to dance
tunes, so the practice itself does not derive from the French. But the
other piece of evidence is more compelling for at least some influence,
however limited. It centers on a setting of Sidney's "In a grove most
rich of shade" published in John Dowland's son Robert's anthology, *A
Musicall Banquet* (1610, no. 7). The music had been first published in
Guillaume Tessier's *Premier Livre D'Airs* as a setting for Ronsard's "Le
petit enfant amour" in 1582, when we know John Dowland was in
Paris (*LEA*, 7). That Tessier's tune fits Sidney's poem, more or less, is
apparently just a happy discovery of one of the Dowlands. But the
appearance of the music in Robert's book strongly implies that John
Dowland studied French airs in the 1580s.

Elise Jorgens finds evidence of French influence in the ways texts are
set in some airs. Her argument is detailed and complex; briefly, she
finds that many later French airs imitate the musical style of *musique
mesurée*, but without the texts in classical meters provided by Baïf and
the Académie. These airs are characterized by the same "freedom from
musical meter," smooth homophonic texture, and limited note values
as *musique mesurée*. Since stress is not important in French language or
poetic meter, this style can be used for ordinary French verse. But when
the English imitate this style, they must consider the accent of the

English texts. This they generally do, but Jorgens considers the awkwardness of Dowland's "A shepherd in a shade" (1600, no. 17) and Robert Jones's "When love on time" (1600, no. 9) to be the result of imitating French airs without proper concern for the accent (Jorgens, 1982, 106–10).

Another parallel between French airs and native English songs is that both tended toward a formal approach to setting the text. But this approach is almost inevitable in strophic songs. As we may infer from the examples cited in earlier chapters, any exaggerated response on the composer's part to the syntax of the first stanza may cause awkwardness or confusion when subsequent stanzas are sung to that music. The same conditions restrict the composer's treatment of textual details which a madrigalist would illustrate musically. So both French and English airs tend to be restrained in their use of word-painting and expressive detail.

A large number of English airs are nevertheless relatively successful as settings of poetry because many poems of the period lend themselves to musical setting. The ordinary, garden-variety Elizabethan short poem, whether or not it was written specifically for music, has several features that make setting relatively easy. First, these poems tend to have a large proportion of end-stopped lines, so that syntax matches the form of both the verse and the music. Many are in eight- or six-syllable lines, which fit comfortable musical phrases; and ten-syllable lines usually have a pause after the fourth syllable, which breaks an uncomfortably long musical phrase into two manageable ones. These poems usually have relatively clear arguments and uncomplicated syntax, and images and figurative language are usually not very dense or complex. The pervasiveness of classical rhetoric in all phases of Elizabethan letters promotes structures and arrangements of words that enhance oral communication in general, and incidentally aid in producing verse that can work effectively when sung.

Of course many of the best and most memorable poems do not fit this description. But let us examine one that does, and the song that was made from it.

> If fluds of teares could cleanse my follies past,
> And smoakes of sighes might sacrifice for sinne,
> If groning cries might salve my fault at last,
> Or endles mone, for error pardon win,
> Then would I cry, weepe, sigh, and ever mone,
> mine errors, faults, sins, follies past and gone.

I see my hopes must wither in their bud,
I see my favours are no lasting flowers,
I see that woords will breede no better good,
Then losse of time and lightening but at houres,
Thus when I see then thus I say therefore,
That favours hopes and words, can blinde no more.

This poem first appeared in Thomas Newman's unauthorized edition of Sidney's *Astrophil and Stella* (1591, sig. L4v), among what the title page calls "other rare Sonnets of divers Noblemen and Gentlemen." It is anonymous, and there is no evidence that it was prepared especially for musical setting. It is in the most common stanza form, the iambic pentameter sixain. Its subject matter is a melancholy lament that one might assume to be motivated by unrequited love; but love is not specifically mentioned, so the speaker's "faults" could be courtly and his "hopes" political. Courtier poets from Wyatt to Ralegh and Essex have written similarly ambiguous verse. Whatever the true subject, a dark mood is maintained throughout the poem, and is supported by an especially tight rhetorical structure. The "if-then" construction of the first stanza is bound up in "correlative" verse, in which the subjects of each of the first four lines are recalled in the fifth line, and the objects in the sixth, the last falling neatly in reverse order. The second stanza is similar in its recall of "favours hopes and words," but the logical structure is more inductive: the speaker lists a series of observations linked by anaphora ("I see") and draws a conclusion ("Thus . . . thus . . . therefore"). His sight counters the blinding effect that favors, hopes, and words previously had. Each stanza essentially repeats the same notion in different words, illustrating the rhetorical principle of copiousness, and specifically using the device of *expolito* or *exergasia,* a "device whereby we dwell a long time on the same point, varying the same *sententia* in different ways."[2] This tendency to accumulate rather than develop, to repeat rather than argue, is characteristic of lyric verse from Wyatt to modern popular song. The figurative language is relatively thin, and images evaporate within the line—though "flowers" in line 8 develop from the "bud" in line 7.

Dowland published a setting of this poem in his *Second Booke of Songs or Ayres* (1600, no. 11). The accompaniment, in what has been called "animated homophony," is important, but in order to focus on the fit of the words, I give only the melody (Ex. 7.1).

Example 7.1

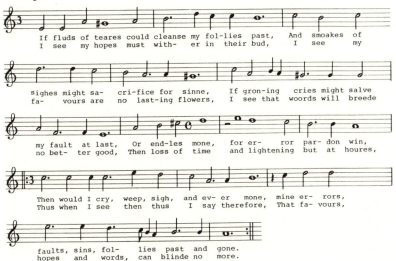

The end-stopped lines and the division of the lines into four- and six-syllable phrases make Dowland's formal setting fit both stanzas with no serious difficulties. In line 8, where the ordinary caesura would fall between the two syllables of "favours," the music allows for continuity, as it does for the slight enjambment between lines 9 and 10. Dowland's melody is beautifully structured, and the melancholy mood is reflected in the minor tonality and slow triple time. The accompaniment at "for error pardon win" contains a series of suspensions that are resolved when pardon is won (Poulton, 1982, 265). But there are restrictions on how much attention to textual detail the composer can give in the strophic setting. A madrigalist might have given a melismatic cascade of notes to illustrate the "fluds of teares," and put a rest before "sighs." But these details would not suit the corresponding words in the next stanza, "I see my hopes" and "favours." It is significant that when the madrigalist Thomas Bateson set this poem, he set it as a conservative consort song (1618, no. 12).

Most of the strophic airs of Dowland and the other composers of airs are formal in this manner. The music may be expressive of the general mood, but it is usually content to provide a melodic medium by which the poem may be clearly heard and understood. This procedure is understandable when one considers that many poems set by the lutenists were not necessarily chosen because they were technically suitable for singing. Instead, they were chosen for setting because they were popular like "Beauty sat bathing by a spring," or "When Phoebus first did Daphne love," or "Beware, faire Maides" (*LEA*, 527, 514, 602). Courtiers and others may have commissioned composers to set their verses, whether they were suitable or not. Dowland expects that the "Courtly judgement" will not judge the songs of his *First Booke* severely, "being it selfe a party," and songs like "His golden locks time hath to silver turnde" (1597, no. 18), "Times eldest sonne, olde age the heyre of ease" (1600, no. 6), "Humor say what mak'st thou heere" (1600, no. 22), and several more by Dowland and other composers are clearly occasional (*LEA*, 466–68, 478, 485–86).

Nevertheless, many strophic poems work well enough as songs. One of Dowland's great virtues is that he can write expressively within the limits of a formal approach and with verse that is not always suited in every detail to strophic setting. Graceful melodies that fit the first stanza go a long way toward covering infelicities in later stanzas; notable examples are "Sleep wayward thoughts" (1597, no. 13), "Wilt thou unkind" (1597, no. 15), "Come againe: sweet love doth now envite" (1597, no. 17), "Away with these selfe loving lads" (1597, no. 21), "Fine knacks for ladies" (1600, no. 12), "Shall I sue" (1600, no. 19), and "Say love if ever thou didst find" (1603, no. 7). A number of examples by other composers could also be cited.

A few of these poems may have been written with the possibility of singing in mind, and some others clearly were made especially for music. The latter fall into two main classes, the first of which is the contrafact, or words written to an existing tune. Dowland's books contain several songs that exist independently as instrumental dances. Elise Jorgens has argued that the question of which version came first is "largely immaterial" (1982, 129). It is for some songs, but if writing words to existing music results in strange poetical forms and meters, it is of some interest to the reader to understand this. As I noted in chapter 1, Dowland's most famous song, "Flow my teares" (1600, no. 2), or the "Lachrymae" pavan, is clearly a contrafact, since no poet would have constructed verses irregular in just the way these are without the musical model. Other dance songs, like "Now O now I needs must part" (1597, no. 6, the "Frog Galliard"), "If my complaints" (1597, no. 4, "Captaine Digorie Piper his Galliard"), "My thoughts are wingde with hopes" (1597, no. 3, "Sir John Souch his Galiard"), and "Awake sweet love" (1597, no. 19) have more normal-looking verses. "My thoughts are wingde with hopes" is in the ordinary iambic pentameter sixain. "Now O now" is in trochaics, a meter with strong musical associations deriving from Sidney; but at this time the meter could have been used without a musical model. The stanza forms of the other songs are more varied, but not extraordinary. But "Can shee excuse my wrongs" (1597, no. 5, "The Earl of Essex Galliard"), like "Flow my tears," is inconceivable as an independent poem. The first, second, fourth, and fifth stanzas are alike, but the third and sixth are different (though like each other). The first group of stanzas alternate iambic and trochaic ten-syllable lines; the third and sixth stanzas are in iambic octosyllabics, with stresses beginning the first two lines of each stanza. The trochaics are called into being by the hemiola rhythm common in the galliard (Ex. 7.2).

Example 7.2

The same rhythm that controls "Shall I call her good" and "must I praise the leaves" also controls "thou maist be abusde" and "or to bubbles which," as well as the corresponding lines in the fourth and fifth stanzas. The characteristic rhythm of the third and sixth stanzas (Ex. 7.3) is prompted by the use of a popular tune in the lute part (the tenor in the part-song version), "Will ye go walk in the woods so wild." This allusion may have something to do with the dedicatee, the earl of Essex, and his habit of retiring to the country when court affairs did not go well.[3] The point here is that the music, its rhythms, and its characteristics as a dance came first. The music is not following or expressing the text, but the reverse.

Example 7.3

Wilt thou be thus a- bus- ed still, see- ing that she will
Bet- ter a thou-sand times to dye Then for to live thus

right thee nev- er
still tor- ment- ed,

This song and most of the other dance songs are in triple time. Elise Jorgens has discussed the problem of setting English duple meter verses (iambics and trochaics) to triple meter music. Since triple time "makes its presence more strongly felt than a duple meter," the combination with duple meter verse tends to equation of verbal stress and musical duration (1982, 134, 141–43). The musical tedium that results can be broken by hemiola and other metrical shifts, as in "Now O now" (1597, no. 6). Sometimes triple time music seems to force either a distorted verbal stress, or a hemiola where the dance form does not usually require it; Jorgens (1982, 138) finds an example of this in the first phrase of "Can shee excuse" (Ex. 7.2) where the downbeat falls on "with." But, as Jorgens admits, a hemiola shift to duple time is possible, so that the singer would stress "wrongs" and "ver-." She does not say that the harmonic rhythm would support this shift: the F chord on the previous three beats does not change on "with," but the harmony moves to C on "ver-." A later passage is more questionable (Ex. 7.4):

Example 7.4

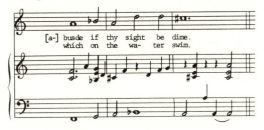

[a-] busde if thy sight be dime.
which on the wa- ter swim.

The downbeat and harmonic rhythm seem to force a stress on "thy" and "the." But the leap up to D gives some pitch stress to "sight" and "water." As a galliard, "Can shee excuse" must maintain a certain speed, which would reinforce a tendency to stress the first of a triple beat: but the setting does not make it impossible for a sensitive singer to give the proper verbal stress, and the resulting cross-rhythms add some piquancy to the song. In discussing the problems of triple time, Jorgens does not stress tempo. It would seem that the feeling of distorted stress would be greatly diminished with the smoother delivery that slower tempo would permit. For this reason, triple time would seem to be a smaller problem in a song like "If fluds of teares" (Ex. 7.1). Strong downbeats would put stresses on unimportant syllables like "And," "If," "my," "Or," and the second syllable of "sacrifice." But in performance at the tempo called for by the spirit of the text, these distorted stresses are not heard as they might be in a galliard song.

The other kind of verse written especially for singing, unlike the dance *contrafacta,* probably began with the verse instead of the music, but was conceived with the requirements of music in mind. These poems are strophic texts in which the stanzas are more consciously parallel than in the ordinary strophic poem. As we shall see, Thomas Campion is the master of this kind of poem. But the songbooks of Dowland and others also have good examples of what must have taken considerable effort and control on the part of the poet. This technical effort is sometimes so great as to overwhelm the content of the poem; but when the quality of both form and content is high, the results can make for an impressive song.

One very pleasant, if not profound, example is this anonymous poem set by Thomas Ford:

Faire sweet cruell, why doest thou flie mee,
go not, goe not, oh goe not from thy deerest,
though thou doest hasten I am nie thee,
when thou seem'st farre then am I neerest,
    Tarrie then Tarrie then Oh tarrie,
    Oh tarrie then and take me with you.

Fie, fie, sweetest here is no danger,
Flie not, flie not, oh flie not love pursues thee,
I am no foe, nor forraine stranger,
Thy scornes with fresher hope renewes me,
    Tarrie then, &c.
                                        (1607, no. 7)

There are regular iambic lines here (3–4, 9–10), but at first the poet seems liberated from meter as his speaker calls out to his fleeing sweetheart. The two stanzas run parallel in the opening exclamations and in the more regular lines, almost syllable for syllable, pause for pause. The lines are all end-stopped and all have feminine rhyme. The refrain rhyme was probably pronounced "with 'ee"; the refrain may originally have been only one line. The content is parallel as well: both stanzas urge the beloved to tarry. The second stanza is more reassuring, but the confident assertion of the fourth line matches the determination of the tenth. Released from the need to trim his notes to accommodate differences between the stanzas, Ford can exploit the drama of the situation. He sets the exclamations of the opening lines to rising notes separated by rests, and gives urgent instability to them by placing them after the main beats (Ex. 7.5). An octave leap on "seem'st farre" illustrates the text here, and expresses the "fresher hope" of the next stanza. The refrain returns to rising, offbeat exclamations on "Oh tarrie," but they take on a more pleading tone.

   Airs like Dowland's "Weepe you no more sad fountaines" (1603, no. 15) also take expressive advantage of carefully matched stanzas; in this instance, the text is especially good as a poem. In its subtle refinement of the emotions of the Petrarchan lover, it transcends convention. Its control of verbal sound makes it musical even when separated from its music; but the music is a lovely complement, and in juxtaposing the two stanzas, the music produces a phenomenon that is possible only in strophic song. After a few hearings, the listener may hear echoes of the first stanza in his memory as the second is sung, which heightens the resolution offered in the second stanza (*LEA*, 40). "Sleepe is a recon-

Example 7.5

Faire, sweet cru- ell, why doest thou flie mee, why

doest thou flie mee, go not, goe not, oh goe not from thy deerest,

ciling" corresponds to the opening line, and "look how the snowie mountaines, / heav'ns sunne doth gently waste" in the first stanza becomes "Doth not the sunne rise smiling, / When faire at ev'n he sets" in the second.

Other composers occasionally use this echo phenomenon for ironic effects. We have seen one example in Byrd's "In fields abroad" (1588, no. 22; see chapter 4). Robert Jones, in "Sweet Philomell" (1600, no. 16), characteristically uses the echo with risqué humor: the words of the first stanza, "with prick [thorn] against her breast," echo in the music when "my hands moves loves request" is sung. Jones illustrates another kind of joke that is possible in strophic song in "Thinkst thou Kate" (1605, no. 12). The stanzas embody the insensitive male attitude that a woman's "no" is really "yes"; but they are relatively innocent until they are sung. The music has a swinging, simple, triple time melody that trots the words along until the last line of each stanza. Then the first three syllables of that line are repeated on three rising sequences (Ex. 7.6):

Example 7.6

I must do [I must do] I must do as love com-mands.

"I must do" appears to express the speaker's sexual compulsion more crudely than it does when the line is completed by "as love commands" (see the *OED, do,* 16b). The same kind of bawdy joke appears in subsequent stanzas, for example: "Chiefest lesson in loves Schoole / Put it in, put it in, put it in adventure foole." ("To put in adventure" is to take a chance.)

For some strophic airs, the stanzas vary so much in meter, phrasing, and enjambment, that finding a setting to fit all stanzas would be too restricting on the composer. Rather than weaken the music with compromises, which in any case might not completely resolve all difficulties, the composers would set the first stanza as well as they could, and ignore the rest. Dowland seems to have done so in songs like "From silent night" (1612, no. 10), in which three stanzas from a much longer poem are printed in the songbook, but only the first can be comfortably sung to the music. The poem was clearly not made for singing; some early manuscripts indicate that it was written by the earl of Essex while he was in the Tower awaiting execution (*LEA,* 614). This particular song is in effect a through-composed setting of the first stanza only. Freed from the constraints of strophic setting, Dowland creates an expressive blend of lute song, consort song, and madrigal. The accompaniment consists of lute with bass and treble viols; the melody, set off by the obbligato treble viol part, has the breadth and solemnity of a consort song without its formal restraints. And several of the expressive devices associated with the madrigal appear with more frequency than they do in most strophic airs. The last feature should not be too surprising. Madrigalisms had come to affect some of the later consort songs, and Dowland had long admired some Italian composers. He once tried to get to Rome to study with Luca Marenzio; he does not seem to have made it, but in the preface to his *First Booke* (1597) he brags of his meeting with Giovanni Croce and proudly prints a letter he received from "the most famous *Luca Marenzio.*"

The text is a standard iambic pentameter sixain, but it reeks of the melancholy that had become the trademark of the man who signed himself "Jo: dolandi de Lachrimae" and who called one of his lute pieces "Semper Dowland semper dolens" (always Dowland, always grieving; Poulton, 1982, 60, 119):

> From silent night, true register of moanes,
>   From saddest Soule consumde with deepest sinnes,
>   From hart quite rent with sighes and heavie groanes,
>   My wayling Muse her wofull worke beginnes.

> And to the world brings tunes of sad despaire,
> Sounding nought else but sorrow, griefe and care.

After an opening A-major chord, the tonality is for the most part in the minor; the lines of text are all divided into shorter phrases, with rests in the voice filled in by the larger accompanying ensemble, as in consort songs; some phrases are repeated, as in madrigals. The voice drops to its lowest note (D) on "deepest sinnes," and "sinnes" is punctuated by a dissonance in the lute. The phrase "with sighes" is repeated with rests before "sighes," a madrigalist convention; and the first of several chromaticisms occurs on "wailing." The first syllable of "woeful" is repeated on a set of sequences down the chromatic scale, so that the listener first thinks the reference is to the Muse's "woe," only to realize that it is to her "woeful work" (Ex. 7.7).

Example 7.7

Here music forces the kind of enriching change of response that critics like Stephen Booth find so effective in Shakespeare's sonnets. The descending chromatic scale has the effect of making the woeful feelings more weary, more painful (Cooke, 1962, 165). Dowland uses ascending chromatics on the sequential repetition of "And to the world brings tunes," suggesting a slight optimism about the tunes; but the melody turns downward on "of sad despaire." A final slow chromatic ascent is in the approach to the concluding cadence, on "sorrow, grief and care." Dowland does not often use chromaticism like Weelkes and the Italians to modulate to remote keys, but to color the voice part and add uncertainty and pathos.

Similar effects can be found in several of Dowland's songs that are frankly through-composed. Although all the songs in the *First Booke* are strophic, six in his *Second Book* (1600) are through-composed, as are several in the later books. One is in three sections, like a madrigal (1600, nos. 6–8). These particular songs are not printed with alternate part-song versions. Especially striking is "Sorrow stay" (1600, no. 3), a song that is like the old consort song laments—and was later arranged as a consort song—but which is much more dramatic and madrigallike in its treatment of words. Before they were set to music, the words of this song may have looked like this:

> Sorrow stay, lend true repentant teares,
> to a woeful wretched wight,
> hence dispaire with thy tormenting feares:
> O doe not my poore heart affright,
> pitty, help now or never,
> mark me not to endlesse paine,
> alas I am condempned ever,
> no hope, no help, ther doth remaine,
> but downe, down, down I fall,
> and arise I never shall.

It is less promising as poetry than as an excuse for expressive music. There is no question of the music approximating the meter of the verse, because the lines are broken up by repeating words and phrases, using the rhetorical schemes of *copulatio* and *subjunctio,* along with exclamations, which give an impression of vehemency.[4] The music is full of the devices of melody and harmony that are expressive of pathos. The effect of the opening phrase is described by Deryck Cooke (1962, 70): "the first note in the melody is B flat, and it is harmonized by the chord of G minor, as the minor third; but it has hardly established itself in this character, setting the basically tragic atmosphere, when the harmony immediately changes to the chord of the dominant—D major—making it *harmonically* a minor *sixth* of D: it resolves normally moving down a semitone on to A, and the feeling of anguish is unmistakable" (Ex. 7.8):

Example 7.8

Sor- row sor- row stay,

The dramatic treatment is especially evident in the passage below (Ex. 7.9).

Example 7.9

doe not, O doe not my heart poore heart af-fright,

pit-ty, [pitty, pitty, pit-ty pitty, pitty]

The last lines of the poem are given music that is both illustrative and expressive. "But downe, down, down, down I fall" is set to a descending minor scale that is paralleled in syncopation in the bass; this line is repeated, and ends with a rising sequence on "down and arise." When this sequence is repeated, "-rise" is held for four beats on a high D, followed by a descent on "I never shall." This whole section is repeated, and the hopeful striving upward on "arise" is emphasized by having the voice hold the high D for eight beats while the lute tries to pull it down by a series of falling sequences. The final "I never shall" becomes a tragic defeat.

Dowland does not use chromaticism in this song, but between it and "From silent night" (1612, no. 10), Dowland's only peer in serious through-composed songs, John Danyel, published his *Songs* (1606). This collection contains several extended, highly expressive songs, but this one is especially remarkable (1606, nos. 13–15):

    The first part.
        Can dolefull Notes to measur'd accents set,
        Expresse unmeasur'd griefes that tyme forget?

The second part.
    No, let Chromatique tunes harsh without ground,
    Be sullayne Musique for a Tunelesse hart:
    Chromatique Tunes most lyke my passions sound,
    As if combynd to beare their falling part.

The third part.
    Uncertaine certaine turnes, of thoughts forecast,
    Bring backe the same, then dye and dying last.

This text clearly invites musical illustration, and the listener is not
disappointed. Time is forgotten when the unmeasured griefs are set to
syncopated notes, chromatic scales appear in the expected places (see
Ex. 1.3 above), and the melody falls on "their falling part." There is
much verbal repetition. Elise Jorgens (1982, 230–39) examines this
and other songs of Danyel and Dowland with the elaborate and detailed
Renaissance rhetorical treatisies in mind, and finds several suggestive
parallels between verbal and musical rhetoric. She compares Danyel
and Dowland, saying that Danyel's music does not seem to "grow from
a pervasive interpretive goal so much as from the amalgamation of
small figures of musical rhetoric, put together as they are suggested to
him more by figures of speech in the poem than by the purpose for
which the poet has used them." Dowland, on the other hand, "was
able to use the conventions of musical rhetoric to form an integrated
interpretation of the poetry he set." To illustrate Dowland's achievement, she compares Dowland's setting of "In darkenesse let mee dwell"
(1610, no. 10, examined briefly in chapter 1) with John Coprario's
setting of the same text (1606, no. 4). "The most remarkable aspect
of Dowland's genius," says Jorgens, "is that his settings are responsive
to their texts in multiple layers; not only do they interpret poetry
rhythmically and through rhetorical gesture, but on a larger scale, they
represent the whole poem in what is ultimately a purely musical
expression."

This integration of elements also includes some characteristics that
seem to derive from the Florentine Camerata of Count Bardi (see chapter 2). Some of Dowland's songs approximate the ideals of the Camerata
without showing any direct influence; but it is significant that Robert
Dowland's *A Musicall Banquet,* where John Dowland's setting of "In
darkenesse" was printed, also contains two songs from Giulio Caccini's
Nuove Musiche (1602), as well as a song from Domenico Maria Megli's
Seconde Musiche (1602). Caccini was one of the best composers influenced by the Camerata. A few of Dowland's later songs appear to be

affected by the desire of these composers to express the texts dramatically, imitating the rhythms of passionate speech, while avoiding the illustrative word-painting of the madrigalists. Passages like this in "In darknesse" seem to derive more from current Italian models than from traditional English ones (Ex. 7.10):

Example 7.10

It is significant that the accompaniment becomes more chordal at this point in order that the declamation may be more free (Spink, 1974, 42). And the rhythmic characteristic of rapid notes between two longer notes, which Jorgens (1982, 182) calls "festooning," is characteristic of Italian musical treatment of tonic accents and subsidiary syllables of Italian verse. Another passage in one of the ensemble songs from *A Pilgrimes Solace* (1612)—significantly with an Italian text, "Lasso vita mia"—looks like new monodic declamation (Ex. 7.11). But the accompaniment is in motion here and must be coordinated with the voice; the song also employs word-painting and the conceit of setting "mi fa" and other syllables to notes appropriate to the solmization syllables.

Example 7.11

Dowland's talent for incorporating the new into the more traditional led him to defend himself in the preface to the 1612 collection against accusations that what he does is "after the old manner." His accusers are "simple Cantors, or vocall singers, who though they seeme excellent in their blinde Division-making, are meerely ignorant." The reference to division-making suggests that these singers are imitating another aspect of Italian monody, florid ornamentation. Ornamented versions of some contemporary songs appear in manuscripts of this time.[5] If Dowland seems to object to them, it is probably because in some of the more extreme English examples, expressive ornamentation has descended to mere vocal display that obscures the text. The most florid passage in Dowland's works is in a song from this last book (1612, no. 8; Ex. 7.12):

Example 7.12

The subject of the text is love, but Dowland may also have intended a barb for the "Cantors" who rejected him.

Some of the younger composers around the court in the years before 1612, whether or not they were the "Cantors," were also touched by some of the new Italian influences. John Cooper, who changed his name to Coprario after a stay in Italy; Alfonso Ferrabosco the younger; Robert Johnson and Nicholas Lanier—all reveal varying degrees of attraction to the new declamatory style, and all at one time or another composed music for plays and masques. Ian Spink has asserted that the new declamatory style arose from the requirements of the native masque, with little Italian influence. It is true that most of their songs are more traditionally melodic than declamatory, and by retaining a detailed lute accompaniment as Ferrabosco and Coprario do, they do not gain the "freedom of declamation which comes with the *basso continuo* and an improvised accompaniment." Spink (1974, 42–43) says that "one gets the impression that Italianate composers such as Ferrabosco and Lanier had not so much heard the 'new music' as heard *about* it." Yet Elise Jorgens (1982, 173–89) and John Duffy (1980, 116–24, 179–98) convincingly demonstrate the presence of Italian elements in these composers' songs, and after 1628, there is no question about

Italian influence. In that year, Nicholas Lanier returned from Italy and sometime thereafter composed the first thoroughgoing recitative song—really a cantata—in English in the Italian manner, *Hero and Leander* (Emslie, 1960). But all this was in the future. The air as Dowland left it still maintained a complex set of balances between new and old, melody and declamation, and in the strophic airs, formal and expressive. Those that followed him were not as able to maintain the balances, and the music—or the poetry—tended to suffer in their songs.

Chapter Eight

Poet-Composer: Thomas Campion

The songs and other works of Thomas Campion bring together a number of strands we have been following in the preceding chapters. Campion's poems exemplify both the supple metrical technique introduced by Sidney and Spenser, and the careful construction that enhances musical setting. Campion's music exemplifies positions on the spectra of homophonic-polyphonic, French-Italian, and formal-expressive in relation to the text; it also anticipates features of the music of the next generation. As a humanist, Campion contributes to the absorption of classical themes and images by English poetry, and participates in the experimental attempts to write English verse in classical meters; he also writes original poetry in Latin. Most interestingly, he expresses himself as a theorist on many of these topics.

Yet as Campion himself writes, paraphrasing Vergil, "All doe not all things well."[1] From our perspective, Campion's *Observations in the Art of English Poesie* (1602) is a futile and belated attempt to impose classical meters on English poetry, however interesting some of the observations may be. His treatise on *A New Way of Making Fowre Parts in Counter-point* (ca. 1613) has the boldness of the amateur in ignoring older rules and approaching modern concepts of harmony and tonality, and because of its inclusion in John Playford's *Introduction to the Skill of Musick* (1660), it influenced English musicians to the end of the century; but it also has the amateur's weakness of reducing complex creative processes to an all-purpose formula.[2] Campion's own music, delightful as some of it is, shows some of this weakness in its limited range; it pales in any comparison with Byrd or Dowland.

As a maker of words for music, however, Campion is hard to beat. Most of his English lyrics were set to music, by himself and by others, and most work very well. They also read well apart from their music, which cannot be said of all song verse. For instance, the following poem is a fine example of Sidneyan verse in the incantational, rather than the dramatic, mode (Rosseter, 1601, pt. 1, no. 20):

When thou must home to shades of under ground,
and there ariv'd, a newe admired guest,
The beauteous spirits do ingirt thee round,
white Iope, blith Hellen, and the rest,
To heare the stories of thy finisht love,
from that smoothe toong whose musicke hell can move:

Then wilt thou speake of banqueting delights,
Of masks and revels which sweete youth did make,
Of Turnies and great challenges of knights,
And all these triumphes for thy beauties sake:
When thou hast told these honours done to thee,
Then tell, O tell, how thou didst murther me.

The play of vowels in "white Iope, blith Hellen," and the elevation of
the unstressed syllable "blith" after the weak stressed syllable at the
end of "Iope" produce remarkable verbal music; the sixth line also subtly elevates "smoothe" as it introduces an allusion to Orpheus. Campion's classical experiments, like Sidney's, may have helped him
develop his sensitive ear for the natural quantities of English. The first
stanza with its echoes of Propertius and its view of the classical under-
world gives way to the Elizabethan world of "masks and revels" in the
second stanza, as the lady tells of her triumphs on earth; it ends with
the speaker's shocking accusation of murder. The rhetorical emphasis
on "tell, O tell" is effective in a purely verbal reading in heightening
the impact of the last phrase. But Campion has prepared the text so
that the musical setting will enhance the total effect of the song in a
way that the words alone could not do. Since it is a strophic song, the
words of the last line are sung to the music of the sixth line (Ex. 8.1):

Example 8.1

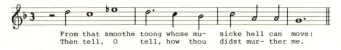

From that smoothe toong whose mu-   sicke hell can   move:
Then tell,   O   tell, how thou   didst mur- ther me.

The pitch and length of the note on "smoothe" match the elevation of
the syllable in the metrical context. The irony here is very rich: her
tongue is smooth and its music could move hell, as Orpheus did to
save his beloved; but what she will tell with that smooth tongue is
how she murdered her lover with her cruelty.

Elise Jorgens (1982, 70) observes that there is another structure, not realized in the music, in the two "When . . . then" sentences; the first of these, she says, "builds to the climactic point" in line 10, and the second brings the "riposte" of line 12. Jorgens claims that "the ironic effect of the second sentence is dependent in part upon retrospection—upon the reader's or listener's ability to recognize the parallel construction of the two sentences and to compare this short sentence with the longer one that preceded it." This structure does perhaps add yet another dimension to the irony of the last line for the silent reader, but the irony the music reveals by juxtaposing the last lines of each stanza is more powerful and, until it is heard with the music, less apparent.

Even more notable for its parallels and suitability for strophic setting is this poem (Rosseter 1601, pt. 1, no. 6):

> When to her lute Corrina sings,
> her voice revives the leaden stringes,
> and doth in highest noates appeare
> as any challeng'd eccho cleere;
> but when she doth of mourning speake,
> ev'n with her sighes the strings do breake.
>
> And as her lute doth live or die,
> Led by her passion, so must I,
> For when of pleasure she doth sing,
> My thoughts enjoy a sodaine spring,
> But if she doth of sorrow speake,
> Ev'n from my hart the strings doe breake.

The stanzas match the parallel between the lady's manipulation of her lute and her lover. The poem calls forth one of Campion's most pictorial settings. In the second line, "revives" inspires a little melismatic flourish that also suits "passion" in the second stanza. An octave leap illustrates "highest noates" that corresponds to "pleasure" in the other stanza: so also do upward leaps illustrate the "challeng'd eccho" and "sodaine spring," and minor chords "mourning" and "sorrow." In the last line of each stanza, Campion admits some rare verbal repetition (Ex. 8.2). The old madrigalist device of rests before "sighs" turns into heartbeats in the second stanza, and the breaking strings are illustrated by the descending thumps on the bass lute strings.

Both these songs were published in the volume Campion shared

Example 8.2

with Philip Rosseter, *A Booke of Ayres* (1601). All the airs in this book are solos with lute and bass viol accompaniment; there are no part-song versions. The preface to this volume, which, judging from the similar preface to *Two Books of Ayres* (ca. 1613), was probably written by Campion, is a kind of manifesto declaring what the proper aesthetic of the air should be. To begin, Campion says that an air should be like an epigram, "short and well seasoned." He warns against musical elaboration, saying that "to clogg a light song with a long Praeludium, is to corrupt the nature of it." Since airs are not polyphonic, there is no need of many rests, "unlesse it be to make a vulgar and trivial modulation seeme to the ignorant strange, and to the judiciall tedious. A naked Ayre without guide, or prop, or colour but his owne, is easily censured of everie eare, and requires so much the more invention to make it please." Songs like "I say my lady weep," set by both Dowland and Morley in their volumes of airs in 1600 (nos. 1, 5), or "Sorrow stay" (Dowland, 1600, no. 3) may be the targets of these objections. These songs, which show their consort song ancestry by retaining a good bit of semipolyphonic musical interest in their accompaniments, including preludes and rests, are safe from criticism; but Campion's point that an effective melody, a "naked Ayre," requires art to construct, just as more elaborate music does, is well taken. The statement also reflects Campion's practice, for his airs focus on the melody, the accompaniments being clearly secondary and without much independent musical interest. "But there are some," Campion continues, who "will admit no Musicke but that which is long, intricate, bated with fuge, chaind with sincopation, and where the nature of everie word is precisely exprest in the Note, like the old exploited action in the Comedies, when if they did pronounce *Memini* [I remember], they would point to the hinder part of their heads, if *Video* [I see], put their finger in their eye." This sounds more like the madrigal than Dowland's and Morley's airs, and the objection to word-painting could be applied to "When to her lute Corrina sings." But Campion admits qualifications, matters of degree, of decorum. For since "such childish observing of words is altogether ridiculous," we ought "to maintaine as well in Notes, as in action, a manly cariage, gracing no word, but that which is eminent, and emphaticall." Nevertheless, the passage is remarkably reminiscent of Vincenzo Galilei's attack on word-painting in his *Dialogo della musica antica e della moderna* (1581; Strunk, 1950, 315–19). Galilei, for instance, mocks those who, in singing this line from a sestina of Petrarch, "And with the lame ox he will be pursuing Laura," "have declaimed it to staggering, wavering, syncopated notes as though they had the hiccups." He also complains about other practices, such as setting words like "dark" to black notes. Instead of indulging in this kind of imitation, Galilei says that composers should observe how people speak under different circumstances, and imitate the tempo, pitch, and volume of their speech in the music.

Although David Greer (1967, 14) finds a few instances of Italianate declamatory passages in his later songs, Campion's humanism led him first in the direction of Baïf and the Académie rather than to Galilei and the Camerata. Campion announces in the preface to Rosseter's book that "The Lyricke Poets among the Greekes and Latines were first inventers of Ayres, tying themselves strictly to the number and value of their sillables, of which sort, you shall find here only one song in Saphicke verse; the rest are after the fascion of the time, eare-pleasing rimes without Arte." The song in question, "Come, let us sound" (no. 21), is made on the same principle as *musique mesurée*. Although Campion will write more verse in classical meters as examples for his *Observations,* he will publish no more musical settings of them. Derek Attridge (1974, 213–19, 224) remarks that Campion's setting, by strictly observing the quantity of the syllables in the notes, masks the accentual rhythm that was an important feature of sapphic verse; perhaps this effect discouraged further musical experiments in quantitative meter. For Campion's main achievement in his classical experiments was "to write quantitative verse which at the same time uses, in a fruitful way, the traditional accentual rhythms of the English language." Without simply substituting stress for quantitative length, he devises poems that "retain the traditional accentual meters" of English, but that "can also be scanned as quantitative verse." Hence the success of such quantitative poems as "Rose-cheekt Lawra," and hence also the grounds for Samuel Daniel's criticism that Campion's new verse was only normal English verse without rhyme (G. Smith, 1904, 2:356–84). Perhaps Campion, like Sidney, came to realize that rhymed English verse, if the syllables were "well weighed," could be as artful as classical imitations.

Although Campion published no more quantitative experiments after 1602, David Greer (1967, 13) notes that some of his later songs resemble *musique mesurée* in their rhythmic freedom and limited range of note values. Elise Jorgens (1982, 93–94) persuasively argues that Campion "comes progressively closer to the original attitude behind the French style, realizing that an English accentual meter cannot be accurately represented by duration, and therefore departing from the musical style of musique mesuree in an effort to adapt its philosophy to the needs of English verse." This effort "becomes generalized, and the attention to poetic meter expands to include all the formal elements of poetic composition." This results in a "tendency to give precedence in his musical settings to details of formal verse structure and the texture of the language over narrative structure or emotional content." Or in our terms, Campion's approach is more formal than expressive.

Campion's approach to the air is further illuminated in the preface to *Two Bookes of Ayres* (ca. 1613). Again airs are compared to epigrams: "Short Ayres, if they be skillfully framed, and naturally exprest, are like quicke and good Epigrammes in Poesie, many of them shewing as much artifice, and breeding as great difficultie, as a larger Poeme." The famous statement which follows needs to be seen in context: Campion has just mentioned that some like only French or Italian airs, "as if every Country had not his proper Ayre." He continues: "In these *English* Ayres, I have chiefely aymed to couple my Words and Notes lovingly together, which will be much for him to doe that hath not power over both. The light of this will best appeare to him who hath paysd our Monasyllables and Syllables combined, both of which are so loaded with Consonants, as that they will hardly keep company with swift Notes, or give the Vowell convenient liberty." English syllables must be weighed even when writing "eare-pleasing rimes." Syllables clogged with consonants take so much time to articulate, that the note, which is sounded on the vowel, may be slighted. For example, a word like "grudge" is awkward to sing to either a long or a short note. Campion will exercise his power to insure that the notes and syllables are appropriate for each other—though he is not always perfectly successful. The concern with enunciation and meter, the comparison of airs to epigrams, and the insistence on the art and value of small forms, all point to Campion's focus on detail and craftsmanship. Another quotation, this time from Campion's preface to his *Fourth Booke* (ca. 1617), is consistent with these concerns: "The Apothecaries have Bookes of Gold, whose leaves being opened are so light as that they are subject to be shaken with the least breath, yet, rightly handled, they serve both for ornament and use; such are light *Ayres.*"

The comparison with the epigram suggests some reasons for other characteristics of Campion's airs. The epigram—Campion mentions Catullus and Martial as models—was a concentrated form in a plain style, with a logical structure, and with all details contributing in some way to a single point. The point was often surprising, witty, or satirical. As Walter R. Davis says (1962, 99), "The trick of the epigram is to prepare for the ending from the start, but to hide the preparation so that the ending seems at first surprising but then immediately after seems inevitable." Expansive rhetoric, large gestures, and emotional display were not part of its decorum. So the more elaborate, emotional, and decorative music of the madrigal and serious air was perceived to be inappropriate. The melody would carry the words, which would be articulated according to their meter and form, with some restrained "gracing" for emphasis. All else, especially independent musical activity, would be distracting and indecorous.

Campion's airs are consistent in their focus on the melody and the text; but they do seem to evolve over time into a more restricted interpretation of the air as a kind of epigram. There is generally more variety in the music of the airs in Rosseter's book (1601), which contains a high proportion of Campion's most familiar songs. More of the airs in the later books have a square, formal quality that several critics have compared to hymns (Jorgens, 1982, 95). Davis notes a similar progression in Campion's masques, saying that while the theme of exchanging chaos for order remained the same, the means he used to present it "became progressively more spare." In his poems, says Davis,

Campion evolved from a disciple of Sidney, writing in a "relatively luxuriant mode," to a poet closer to Ben Jonson writing in "a spare and naturalistic mode" (Campion, 1967, xx).

These and other characteristics of Campion's songs have been explored in a number of detailed analyses of individual songs.[3] Campion's particular approaches to interpreting poetry in music may be further highlighted by an examination of some of his texts as set by other composers and by Campion himself. Campion was aware of these other settings, for in the preface to the *Fourth Booke* (ca. 1617), he writes: "Some words are in these Bookes which have beene cloathed in Musicke by others, and I am content they then served their turne: yet give mee now leave to make use of mine owne." There are at least sixteen such songs in the books of airs and madrigals and in manuscript; we can only sample them here.[4]

Only one of the songs to be examined here was published first by Campion; his settings of all the others come later, as the quotation above suggests, and may be seen as authoritative corrections of the earlier settings. "Blame not my cheeks" first appeared in Rosseter's *Book of Ayres* (1601, pt. 1, no. 14), and was set again by Robert Jones in his *Ultimum Vale* (1605, no. 9). Although we cannot see Campion's version as a "correction" of Jones's treatment of the poem, it is characteristic of his approach, as is Jones's. The poem consists of two parallel but contrasting stanzas: in the first, the lover ascribes his paleness to the needs of his "distressed" heart for "kindly heate"; in the second, he contrasts those whose warmth is in their cheeks and "outward parts" but in whose breasts "Poore Cupid sits and blowes his nailes for cold." This poem is artfully constructed to the advantage of almost any composer giving it a strophic setting. Both Campion and Jones not only repeat the music to the first stanza for the second, but also repeat the music to the first two lines of each stanza for the second two lines. Nearly half of Campion's songs repeat the first strain in this manner, extending epigrammatic economy to the musical material (Greer, 1967, 8–9). The contrast in the poem between external appearance and internal reality is enhanced by the almost line-for-line parallels between the two stanzas, for the ruddy but unfeeling suitor is described to the same music as the pale but sincere lover. Hallett Smith (1952, 284), in discussing the irony produced by the musical correspondence of the phrase "For their fat love" with "the kindly heate," "who art so cruel," and "Nurse not one spark," notes that "It might be said that

the first occurrence of the musical passage produced an effect of wist-
fulness, but when it is repeated and insisted upon, the feeling becomes
inevitably bitter" (Ex. 8.3).

Example 8.3

The kind- ly heate un-to my heart is flowne,

   Campion's music is plain and straightforward, in slow triple time,
in a minor tonality, with chordal lute accompaniment. It is not so
much the point that "The melancholy tune fits the words well but does
not illuminate them with any brilliant musical equivalents of poetic
image or description" (Lowbury, 1970, 70); rather, the music is general enough to allow the melancholy of the first stanza to turn into the
irony and bitterness of the second.
   To note a few other details of Campion's setting, the phrase "though
pale with love" in the first line seems rushed, but other words sung to
these notes (three quarters and a whole in 3/2) fit easily. One is reminded of Campion's complaint that English syllables are "so loaded
with Consonants, as that they will hardly keepe company with swift
notes" (ca. 1613, preface). Campion's music gives some emphasis,
through pitch or length, to "cheeks," "love," "heate," "cruell," and
"Quite" in the first stanza. The longer note given "by" in line 5 is
partly justified by the presence of "love" in that position in the second
stanza, and the emphasis on "cheeks" and "woe" must reconcile us to
the prominence given to "it" in line 3 (cf. Hollander, 1975, 32–33).
   Robert Jones's setting of this poem, like his other songs with words
by Campion, reflects a greater interest in the musical side of the relationship. Jones's version, like many airs, is printed with an optional
four-voice arrangement. Perhaps because of this alternative, there are
more repeated sequences and anticipations in the accompaniment of
phrases in the solo. The music is in duple time, in a major mode, and
in general gives emphasis to important words. The most striking feature of the song is the long—over seven beats—high note in the last
phrase on "forsakes," which becomes illustrative on "blows" in the second stanza. This is very effective musically, and gratifying for the singer, but it distorts the meaning of the poem: it is more appropriate for
puffing Aeolus in the corner of a map than for Cupid warming his
hands in the corner of a cold heart.

Jones published his setting of Campion's famous "There is a Garden in her face" in his 1605 volume, where it appears immediately after "Blame not my cheeks." Like that song, it has an alternate part-song version. Campion's setting, published later in his *Fourth Booke* (ca. 1617, pt. 2, no. 7), is for solo voice with lute and bass viol. Both settings are very attractive, and both convey the general mood of cheerful compliment. But in neither does the music suggest the richer significance of the imagery of the earthly paradise which John Hollander (1975, 32–33) has discovered in the poem. Again Jones stresses musical interest. The accompanying lute (or voice) part is full of imitative sequences and there is a delightful change from duple to triple meter on the fifth line. Both composers play with the tune of the street-cry "cherry-ripe" (Ex. 8.4):

Example 8.4

Cherry ripe, ripe, ripe

Jones repeats it six times in the solo part (with many repetitive imitations in the accompaniment). Although Campion repeats the words of the phrase six times as well, he uses the street cry tune only once, and there is no imitation in the accompaniment. Although Campion spends less time on the "cherry-ripe" cry than Jones, the repetition in both versions gets out of proportion: "cherry-ripe" loses its identity as a metaphor. In Jones's version especially, we forget the lady's cherry lips and are out on the streets listening to a vendor of real cherries.

Campion, in a few other instances, shows more sensitivity to the words than Jones. In the opening phrase, Jones gives the second syllable of "garden" a rather awkward pitch-accent, leaping up a third from the first syllable. Campion's setting is one of his most graceful, combining a lovely melodic arc with an easy matching of the verbal inflection (Ex. 8.5):

Example 8.5

There is a garden in her face,

Both composers are victimized somewhat by the enjambment in the
third stanza—

> Her Browes like bended bowes doe stand,
>   Threatning with piercing frownes to kill
> All that attempt with eye or hand
>   Those sacred Cherries to come nigh,

—because pauses in previous stanzas have been reflected in the music.
In the solo version by Jones the gap after "kill" is especially noticeable;
in the part-song version, however, the lower parts pick up "all" immediately after the treble finishes "kill."

In these and other resettings of his verse, Campion's versions "correct" the earlier settings by reining in the music when it threatens to
distort the sense of the poem, and by paying more attention to musical
pauses and emphases that affect the syntax or the tone of the poem.
Two final songs illustrate, in comparison to their earlier settings, a
bold and at least partly successful new departure, and a tired, unimagi-
native effort that is not saved by occasional melodic grace.

The first of these, "Thinks't thou to seduce me then," involves a
change in text as well as different music. William Corkine's version
(1610, no. 11) has three stanzas, the first two of which are close to
Campion's later text, the third entirely different. It is likely, however,
that Corkine's text (like those set by other composers) is a genuine early
version of Campion's poem. Campion may have dropped this third
stanza and substituted the two that appear with his setting (*Fourth
Booke,* ca. 1617, no. 18) because the old stanza was sententious and
abstract, if witty:

> If with wit we be deceived, our fals may be excused,
> Seeming good with flatterie grac't, is but of a few refused.
> But of all accurst are they that are by fooles abused.

The new stanzas are more concrete and enhance the dramatic sense of
the character of the singer, who is rather like some of Shakespeare's
comic heroines in her laughing, worldly-wise teasing of her unskillful
wooer:

> Ruth forgive me if I err'd from humane harts compassion,
> When I laught sometimes too much to see thy foolish fashion:
> But alas, who lesse could doe that found so good occasion?

This dramatic presentation of the speaker may account for some of the differences between Campion's and Corkine's musical treatments.

Corkine's song is pleasant, but ordinary—it is rather like some of Campion's other tunes. Like Campion, Corkine is economical: he gives the second line of each stanza the same music as the first line. His cheerful tune does not conflict with the tone of the poem—unless it could be said that it sounds too innocent for the character in Campion's version—but it does not give any noticeable emphasis to any element or otherwise enhance the effect of the poem. In comparison with Corkine's simple tune, Campion's setting seems awkward and strange. One critic was moved to say that its "irregular metres" seem "to have been dictated by musical whim rather than by attention to words" (Lowbury, 1970, 162). Looking at the printed song, perhaps humming to oneself, one might well ask why Campion gives so many single syllables two notes (a characteristic of several of the later songs), why he changes the rhythm from duple to triple so frequently, why he dwells on some syllables and hurries over others. But after singing it with the character of the speaker in mind—mocking, not always suppressing laughter—and after correcting the underlay of the words (in ELS 2:11), one begins to discover effective possibilities. In the opening phrase, laughter bubbles near the surface in the ascending eighth notes, and in the last phrase, it seems to burst out on "Parats" and "speech," and at these points in subsequent stanzas, especially the last (Ex. 8.6):

Example 8.6

Pa- rats so   can learne to prate our speech by pie- ces gleaning.
When I laught sometimes too much to see   thy fool-ish fashion.

This setting is not "dramatic" in the same way the Italian-influenced declamatory songs are; it is rather a development of the older melodic but illustrative style. "So quicke, so hot, so mad" (ca. 1617, pt. 1, no. 18) is somewhat similar.

This kind of imaginative solution did not seem available to Campion when he came to his "I must complain" after John Dowland had set it in 1603 (no. 17). The poem is not one of Campion's best efforts. He had captured its essence in two of his Latin epigrams, "In Melleam," and "Ad Cambricum," in fewer lines (Campion, 1967, 426–27, 436–37):

> I Must complain, yet doe enjoy my Love;
> She is too faire, too rich in lovely parts:
> Thence is my grief, for Nature while she strove
> With all her graces and divinest Arts
>   To form her too too beautifull of hue,
>   Shee had no leasure left to make her true.
>
> Should I agriev'd then wish shee were lesse fayre?
> That were repugnant to mine own desires:
> She is admir'd, new lovers still repayre,
> That kindles daily loves forgetfull fires.
>   Rest jealous thoughts, and thus resolve at last,
>   Shee hath more beauty then becomes the chast.
>   (*Fourth Booke*, ca. 1617, no. 17)

It is not as well constructed for musical setting as most of Campion's songs, for the third line runs strongly over into the fourth, and the fourth into the fifth. This enjambment is not matched in the second stanza. As Hollander (1975, 74) shows, Dowland solves the problem by keeping the accompaniment moving over the break between lines three and four. He keeps the break in the solo line to a bare minimum (a quarter rest) and picks up immediately the stepwise ascension (Ex. 8.7).

Example 8.7

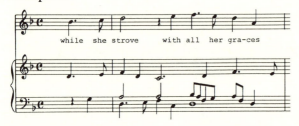

while she strove   with all her gra-ces

Since the mood of the poem alters somewhat in line 5, Dowland allows more of a definite cadence at the end of line 4; but the voice resumes after only a quarter-rest break. Other aspects of Dowland's version point to his great skill as a composer of songs, especially musically expressive songs. The accompaniment is full of fluid motion, and shows its affinity with the polyphonic accompaniments of the old consort songs. His setting of "Thence is my grief" and "Shee is admir'd" is an extended wail expressing the grief and the cause of it, utilizing

some of the ironic echo effect when the second phrase is heard sung to
the music for the first (Ex. 8.8):

Example 8.8

Thence   is   my   griefe

As this passage suggests, Dowland is not stingy with musical material:
he sets each line of the stanza to fresh music, and uses a variety of note
values ranging from an eighth to a dotted whole note. As in many airs,
the last phrase is repeated; but instead of repeating the last two lines,
as is the common practice with six-line stanzas, he repeats only the last
line, and thus avoids a break between enjambed lines. He follows the
syntax of the poem rather than the form. This separation of the last
line emphasizes its epigrammatic quality, which is further reinforced
by a change from duple to triple time. The formal division between
quatrain and couplet is subtly suggested by a shift from a quasi-poly-
phonic texture in the lute to a chordal one for both lines five and six.
In the last line (and on "enjoy" in line one) Dowland allows himself to
repeat words ("Shee had no leasure") both for musical and rhetorical
effect—they intensify, rather than detract from, the sense of the poem.
In the second stanza, the rapid repetition given to "enjoy" in the first
could be expressively used for "then wish," and the repetition of "She
hath more beauty" gives rhetorical force to the epigrammatic
conclusion.

Campion's setting, insofar as it reflects his theory of the air, illustrates what sacrifices it demands. Simplicity prevails. Most of the notes
are half notes, with a scattering of quarters, and whole notes on the
cadences; the accompaniment is plain and chordal. The duple time
music follows the poetic meter, with accented syllables falling on
downbeats. The Campion economy is there in the repetition of the
music of the first two lines for the second two lines of each stanza. The
four-square symmetry in this instance becomes rigidity, as Campion
makes no effort to mitigate the conjunction of cadence with the end of
enjambed lines. Not only are there whole-note cadences on the third

and fourth lines, but the run-on lines begin with half rests in both voice and accompaniment. The last two lines are repeated in the usual formal way despite the enjambment into line five, and despite Dowland's example. The economy of material and the lack of any strikingly expressive or imitative musical effects may be a result of theoretical restraint, but the treatment of the enjambed lines seems at best too strictly formal, and at worst a perversion of Campion's own desire to "couple my Words and Notes lovingly together." When this sort of formal overriding of syntax occurs in Byrd's songs, at least the richness of the music provides compensation. One further detail shows Campion ignoring Dowland's example in a slight but telling instance. Dowland sets the word "beautiful" in line 5 according to its natural stress, pitch, and rhythm. Campion gives an awkward pitch-stress to "ti-" by an upward leap of a sixth (Ex. 8.9):

Example 8.9 Dowland   Campion

If we could hear Campion's song without Dowland's echoing in our ears, we might find it pleasant enough, if not one of his best. The last line of each stanza is set to a gracefully descending broken curve (Ex. 8.10):

Example 8.10

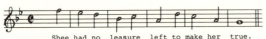

But it is a far cry from Campion's best songs—many of which are early, like "When to her lute," "It fell on a sommers day," and "Followe thy faire sunne"—and it is hard to see how it could be considered a "correction" of Dowland's.[5]

These analyses suggest that Campion was mainly concerned to provide settings that added a pleasant dimension to his poems, but would not compete with them. In some instances he is successful, holding his own with the musicians, yet giving a sensitive reading of his poem. When he is less successful, the cause seems to be a weakening of the musical imagination, or a distrust of it. Without venturing into psychoanalysis, we might at least pose the question of whether Campion restrained his music to fit his theory, or whether he cut his theory to fit his musical ability. In any event, the music of Campion's songs anticipates that of the generation of the Lawes brothers in some ways, particularly in its thinness. But Campion's verse is a rich lyric treasury that is at the same time technically more suited for music than the poems of Herrick, Carew, and others set by the later composers. That Campion could also compose music that even occasionally could come up to the quality of his verse is no mean achievement.

Chapter Nine
Coda

By 1630 the madrigal was dead; the last gasp was John Hilton's ballets, the *Airs or Fa-las* of 1627, though production had dropped sharply by 1610. Part-song singers of the mid-seventeenth century had to content themselves with catches and glees. The last book of airs with tablature for the lute was John Attey's, printed in 1622, and as early as Corkine's second book (1612), some songs were printed with only a bass line accompanying the voice. The air continued through the seventeenth century with *basso continuo* accompaniments instead of lute tablature, and with other stylistic changes. But the continuity is more evident in manuscripts than in printed books, for there is a thirty-year gap between Attey's book and John Playford's anthology, *Select Musicall Ayres, And Dialogues, for one and two Voyces, to sing to the Theorbo, Lute, or Basse Violl* (1652). In the interim were published the odd but essentially conservative *Mottects or Grave Chamber Musique* (1630) by Martin Peerson, consort songs and secular verse anthems on texts by Fulke Greville; and the baroque *Madrigals and Ayres* (1632) by Walter Porter, a student of Monteverdi, whose title page describes the songs as being "Of two, three, foure and five Voyces, with the continued Base, with Toccatos, Sinfonias and Rittornellos to them. After the manner of Consort Musique. To be performed with the Harpsechord, Lutes, Theorbos, Base Violl, two Violins, or two Viols."[1]

The air, or continuo song as this later incarnation may be called, tended to split more and more between light, tuneful songs and serious, declamatory airs. The former frequently use dancelike triple meter melodies and seem to derive from Campion, Corkine, and the composers of lighter lutenist airs, and when there is conflict between words and music, the music usually wins out. But it is thinner music. The latter differ from the serious lutenist airs in that they are much more Italianate, more like recitative than melody. The continuo style makes the declamation freer, and perhaps allows for more expressiveness in performance; but the musical richness of the more highly wrought accompaniments found in Byrd's consort songs and Dowland's airs is lost, as well as the vocal melody.

Poetry too was developing in directions that would change the possible ways it could be joined with music. As poets explored the uses of speech rhythms in verse, following Sidney and the dramatists, they found it effective to play speech patterns against lyric forms. Like the composers, the poets were expanding their own resources for more forceful expressiveness in order to move their audience. In Donne, but also in Carew and others, one finds strophic poems with varying line lengths that look like song texts, but which contain so much enjambment and metrical variation that strophic setting would be all but impossible. The content of many of these poems also makes them difficult to set to music. In the sonnet of the late sixteenth century, English poets like Sidney, but especially Shakespeare, were developing a lyric verse not for social performance but for brooding over in private. The fruits of printing, literacy, Protestant private scripture-reading, Counter-Reformation meditation, and other silent, solitary literary pursuits, as well as more traditional rhetoric and possibly Ramist logic, were poems like Shakespeare's Sonnet 124 and Donne's "The Canonization" (cf. Booth, 1981, 94–96). Multiple or shifting meanings, subtle arguments, logical development through stanzas instead of parallel reiteration—these qualities of the new poetry are not compatible with the aurally comprehensible verse that is most natural for song.

Nevertheless, some poems of Donne were set to music, and other song texts can be found to contain some "metaphysical" qualities (Walls, 1984). To some extent their success as songs depends on the degree to which the formal, metaphorical, and argumentative qualities of the metaphysical style are present. Ferrabosco's setting of Donne's "The Expiration" (1609, no. 7) is plausible, if not entirely successful, but the poem is relatively easy Donne (Duffy, 1980, 63–70). No composer dared to attempt a setting of "Lovers Infinitinesse."

So the whirligig of time brings its revenges: some of the same forces that brought poetry and music together—especially the desire for more expressive musical and poetic rhetoric—led to developments that made the union more difficult to maintain. Despite these and other difficulties, good songs would still be written during the later seventeenth century, though their musical interest might be narrower; and with Purcell would come another great composer of songs. Differences of means and differences in tastes would continue to tug song back and forth between the poets and musicians, between popular and high art, and songs would still be composed and sung. But the special quality of the relationship between the arts in the late sixteenth and early seventeenth centuries, given the volatility of the combination, is still impressive. The mastery of Byrd, the expressive richness of Weelkes, Dowland, and Danyel, the versatility of Morley, the ease and *sprezzatura* of Wilbye, Bennett, Rosseter, and Ford, the liveliness and humor of Jones, and the occasional successes of several other composers—including Campion and even Whythorne—make this body of song worthy of continual study and enjoyment.

Notes

Chapter One

1. There are a number of general studies of words and music in song not cited in this chapter but listed in the bibliography. See especially the items by Calvin Brown, V. C. Clinton-Baddeley, John Hollander, and Bruce Pattison.

2. See an important critique of Bernstein by Allan Keiler (1978).

3. From Ravenscroft, 1611, no. 20; texts in Child, 1965, no. 26, and *EMV*, 240–41; tune in Bronson, 1959-72, 1:309. In Ravenscroft, the refrains are sung by four voices and the rest by a solo with instruments. See Johnson, 1972, 30-34.

4. See the objections voiced by Kivy, 1980, 49, 60, 63; Langer, 1953, 29-31; and Zuckerkandl, 1973, 31–38; see also *New Grove*, 1980, "Expression."

Chapter Two

1. Heninger, 1974, 100. It should be noted that the harmonic series, discussed in chapter 1, is a more recent discovery. Pythagoras's discoveries are of course related to it, but are more concerned with ratios within the octave.

2. Ronsard, 1565, sig. A4; Lebèque, 1954, 111; and Reese, 1959, 382, 389.

3. LeJeune's songs appeared in *Vingtquatrieme livre d'airs et chansons . . . de plusieurs excelens autheurs* (Paris: Le Roy & Ballard, 1583). For more on the Académie, see Jorgens, 1982, 84–94; Reese, 1959, 382–87; Walker, 1946, 1948, and 1950; Walker and Lesure, 1949; and Yates, 1947. H. M. Brown, 1976, 231-32, mentions earlier German examples of music composed for Latin meters.

4. For more on the Camerata, see *New Grove;* Palisca, 1960 and 1972; Strunk, 1950, 290–301, 363–404; and Walker, 1941, 1942.

5. Thomas Tallis's tunes for Archbishop Parker's *Psalter* (ca. 1568) were labeled "meeke," "sad," "stout," "milde," etc., but these qualities referred to the supposed effect of the modes used for the tunes, which are transcribed in Boyd, 1962, 44–52, and in Tallis, 1974, 13:160–76. There was not much agreement on the effects of the modes; see Hollander, 1961, 211–12; *New Grove*, "Mode"; and Zarlino, 1983, xv.

6. See the editions of Chaucer by A. C. Baugh, F. N. Robinson, and John H. Fisher. Other heretics skeptical of the standard explanations of Chaucer's meter are I. Robinson, 1971; Southworth, 1954 and 1962; J. Stevens, 1982; and Woods, 1985.

7. Attridge, 1974, 89–100; for Roger Ascham's discussion in *The Scholemaster* (1570), see G. Smith, 1904, 1:29-33. See also Puttenham, 1936, 67-73 (see pp. xliv–liii on dating parts of the work, and lxiv–lxxiii on prosody); and Gascoigne in Smith, 1904, 1:51.

8. Alison, 1599, Psalm 41, sig. G2v, C. See also Temperley, 1:63–64, and 2:40–41, ex. 9b and 9d.

9. British Library MS Royal Appendix 58, in Dawes, 1951, no. 10. Dawes dates the manuscript earlier than John Ward, 1960, 117. Elyot, 1907, 93.

10. J. Stevens, 1961, 135–36; Ward, 1957, 175–80, esp. notes 100, 101. See H. M. Brown, 1976, 95–99 on the Italian improvisers.

11. G. Smith, 1904, 1:51, corrected from Gascoigne's *Posies* (1575), sigs. T3v–4; see Thompson, 1961, 71–75.

12. Though the service and anthem replaced the mass and motet, they do not correspond liturgically; see D. Stevens, 1966, 51–52, and Kerman, 1962b, 237–78.

13. *Injunctions Given by the Queen's Majesty* (London, 1559), no. 49, quoted by Kerman, 1962b, 281.

Chapter Three

1. Burney, 1935, 2:103. Sir John Hawkins's opinion is quoted from his marginalia by James M. Osborn in Whythorne, 1961, xv. Osborn also cites opinions by Henry Davey and Ernest Walker. See Fellowes, 1948, 34–36; Warlock, 1925, and his edition, 1927; Dent, 1968, 84; LeHuray, 1967, 188, 385-86; and Reese, 1959, 816–17.

2. The words to "Nothing is sharper then low things" were copied ca. 1590 by John Lilliat into his commonplace book, Bodleian MS Rawl. poet. 148, fol. 1. See Doughtie, 1985, 43.

3. In addition to the 1927 Warlock edition, *Three Songs* were edited by Manfred Bukofzer, 1947; "Buy new broom" is included in Warlock, 1926, 2:20-22; and twenty songs are transcribed by Jobling, 1978. "Buy new broom" is recorded by Alfred Deller on Vanguard-Bach Guild 557, and by Wilfrid Brown on Nonesuch HB–73010.

4. Whythorne, 1961, 13. I have retained Whythorne's phonetic spelling, except for the yogh and thorn; as with other quotations, I have modernized *i, j, u,* and *v.*

5. Brett (1967, 109, 136) includes a broom-seller's cry, which is mainly "Broom, broom, broom!" sung at the same pitch.

Chapter Four

1. Philip Brett has given the term "consort song" its modern definition and has done most of the major scholarship and criticism on the genre; see

both sections of the bibliography. See also Kerman, 1962a, 99–127, and Monson, 1982.

2. All consort songs mentioned in this chapter except those by Byrd can be found in Brett's anthology, 1967, which is also the source of quotations and examples 1–3 (from nos. 3 and 5).

3. National Portrait Gallery, London; the significant detail is reproduced in Brett, 1967, xx; the whole painting is shown in Poulton, 1982, between 256–57.

4. This term was coined by C. S. Lewis, 1954, 478–79, from an article by Percy Simpson (1943).

5. Kerman, "William Byrd" in *New Grove,* quoting the "Cheque-Book" of the Chapel Royal (see the edition by Edward F. Rimbault, Camden Society 3 [1872]). See also Kerman, 1962a, 99–118. Philip Brett's forthcoming book on *The Songs, Services, and Anthems of William Byrd* (Berkeley: University of California Press) should be a major contribution; in the meantime we have his 1971–72 article. See also Andrews, 1966; D. Brown, 1957; Dent, 1926; Fellowes, 1948; and Gray, 1969.

6. See Greaves (1604), Alison (1606), Ravenscroft (1609, 1611, 1614), East (1610, 1618, 1624), Leighton (1614), Amner (1615), Bateson (1618), Vautor (1619), Peerson (1620, 1630), and Pilkington (1624). Though all the songs of Gibbons (1612) have words under all the parts, Kerman, 1962a, 123–25, says that some, like Byrd's, were originally accompanied solos.

7. This work was printed on separate sheets in 1589. Brett has reconstructed the six-part work from two surviving sheets and a manuscript copy of another part in Byrd, 16:16–32.

8. Although the poet seems to consider only those vowels long by position (followed by two consonants) to be long, and although he ignores the rule that the fifth foot of the hexameter must be a dactyl, Byrd's music forces the correct scansion on the text even though Byrd must treat some vowels the poet made long as if they were short. Brett, in his note in Byrd, 16:192–93, quotes Stephen Orgel, who says that Byrd "was more concerned with the question of form than of quantity and language; and he is primarily composing hexameters, not following his text."

9. Sidney's interest in musical settings of quantitative verse is reflected in a passage in two of the *Arcadia* manuscripts; see Sidney, 1962, 389–93. For Tritonius, see H. M. Brown, 1976, 231–32.

Chapter Five

1. Obertello, 1949, 70–81; Kerman, 1962a, 44–52; Woodfill, 1953, 177–84, 229–32, 253–56, 297–301; and Slim, 1972.

2. Sidney, 1962, 479–90. Five of Sidney's versions of the Psalms (nos. 16, 28, 38, 42, and 43) are trochaic as well. Sidney's psalms were modeled after *Les CL. Pseaumes de David* (1562) by Clement Marot and Theodore Beza,

with music by Claude Goudimel; he does not appear to have used the music (Sidney, 1962, 507–8).

3. Spenser also experimented in classical meters, as can be seen in his *Letters* to Gabriel Harvey, printed in 1580; and his *Shepheardes Calender* (1579) was certainly an important step toward the new poetry. But the verse of the *Calender* was experimental and does not reflect Sidney's new way of writing iambics.

4. The extrametrical syllable is italicized in Yonge. For other examples, see Obertello, 1949, 171–74; see also Yonge, 1588, no. 14.

5. Obertello, 1949, 281; this is the octave of the sonnet Marenzio set in two parts, which were reversed by Watson.

Chapter Six

1. Fellowes, 1948, is less useful because of his inclusion of Byrd and his followers among the madrigalists; Kerman, 1962a, distinguishes between the schools, and his is the most significant single book on the subject. Individual composers are also considered in the *New Grove*—most articles are by David Brown. Less accessible but interesting is Frank Fabry's dissertation, 1964. Madrigal texts in this chapter are quoted from *EMV*.

2. The differences are crucial; see David Brown, 1969, 51.

3. See Kerman, 1962a, 166n. This song and others in the *Canzonets* of 1597 had optional lute reductions for the four lower voices. See Greer, 1966, 26–27.

4. Tovey, 1937, 5:12. See also the analyses in Fellowes, 1948, 198–202; D. Brown, 1969, 99–102; and Mellers, 1965, 47–49.

5. Butler, 1636, sig. N1; Butler's phonetic spelling is normalized. More of the passage is quoted by J. Stevens, 1958, 23.

Chapter Seven

1. Dowland's *First Booke* was reprinted in 1600, 1603, 1606, and 1613. Two airs with bandora accompaniment had been printed the year before in Barley, 1596; on this book, see *LEA*, 54–62, and Ward, 1970.

2. Erasmus, *De copia*, quoted in Sonnino, 1968, 93. On other figures of rhetoric in the air, both words and music, see Wells, 1984.

3. Poulton, 1982, 153, 226–29; see also Ward, 1977, 73–74, and *LEA*, 458. Mrs. Poulton and I disagree about the priority of music to text in this song.

4. Sonnino, 1968, 64, 174; *copulatio* allows for some words to come between the repeated words; in *subjunctio* the word is repeated immediately.

5. For example, Christ Church, Oxford, MS 439; examples from this and other manuscripts are printed in Sabol, 1978, nos. 12 and 26; see also Spink, 1971; Johnson, 1961; and Duckles, 1957.

Chapter Eight

1. From "Now winter nights enlarge" (ca. 1617, pt. 1, no. 12); Campion quotes the line from Vergil's *Eclogues* 8.63, "Non omnia possumus omnes," in the preface to *Two Bookes of Ayres* (ca. 1613). See Campion, 1967, 147, 55.

2. See Kastendieck, 1963, 175–80; the preface to Bukofzer's edition of Coprario, 1952; Campion, 1967, 32–23; and Lowbury, 171–78.

3. For example, Irwin, 1970, and Ratcliffe, 1981, both analyze "Now winter nights enlarge" (ca. 1617, pt. 1, no. 12); see also Booth, 1981, 76–96, on "I Care not for these Ladies" (Rosseter 1601, pt. 1, no. 3).

4. Not covered in the following discussion are the madrigalian settings of Jones (1607, nos. 16–17) and Vautor (1619, nos. 13–14), the part-song settings of Alison (1606, nos. 16–17), and the airs by Jones (1605, no. 17; 1609, no. 1), Pilkington (1605, no. 8), and Ferrabosco (1609, no. 8). For the last song, see Duffy, 1980, 104–6. Doughtie, 1978, discusses some of these.

5. Two other settings of this poem, both anonymous, survive in manuscript. One, Christ Church, Oxford, MS 439, p. 69, has an ornamented treble over a bass; it follows Campion's form but repeats "Shee had no leasure." A setting for voice and lute in British Library MS Add. 15117, fol. 19, also follows Campion's form but repeats in rising sequence "To frame her to to beautiful" with a descending scale on the last three words. Both have a significant break between the music for the first four and last two lines.

Chapter Nine

1. For more on these composers and their works, see *New Grove*. Spink, 1974, and Jorgens, 1982, survey and analyze the continuo songs.

Bibliography

PRIMARY SOURCES AND EDITIONS

Alison, Richard. 1599. *The Psalmes of David in Meter.* London. STC 2497.
———. 1606. *An Howres Recreation in Musicke.* London. STC 356. EM 33.
Arbeau, Thoinot (or Tabourot, Jehan). 1966. *Orchesography.* Translated by Cyril Beaumont, preface by Peter Warlock. London, 1925. Reprint. New York: Dance Horizons.
Ascham, Roger. 1967. *The Schoolmaster* (1570). Edited by Lawrence V. Ryan. Charlottesville: University Press of Virginia.
Attaingnant, Pierre. 1966. *Dixhuit basses dances* (1529). Edited by Helmut Mönkemeyer. Hofheim am Taunus: Hofmeister.
Attey, John. 1622. *The First Booke of Ayres.* London. STC 901. ELS 2:9.
Barley, William. 1596. *A New Booke of Tabliture.* London. STC 1433.
Bartlet, John. 1606. *A Booke of Ayres.* London. STC 1539. ELS 2:3.
Bateson, Thomas. 1604. *The first set of English Madrigales.* London. STC 1586. EM 21.
———. 1618. *The Second Set of Madrigales.* London. STC 1587. EM 22.
Bennet, John. 1599. *Madrigalls to Foure Voyces.* London. STC 1882. EM 23.
Brett, Philip, ed. 1967. *Consort Songs.* Musica Britannica, vol. 22. London: Stainer & Bell.
Bronson, Bertrand H., ed. 1959–72. *The Traditional Tunes of the Child Ballads.* 4 vols. Princeton: Princeton University Press.
Buck, Percy C. et al., eds. 1963. *Tudor Church Music.* 10 vols. Reprint. New York: Broude Brothers.
Byrd, William. 1588. *Psalmes, Sonets, & songs of sadnes and pietie.* London. STC 4253. EM 14.
———. 1589. *Songs of sundrie natures.* London. STC 4256. EM 15.
———. 1611. *Psalmes, Songs, and Sonnets.* London. STC 4255. EM 16.
———. 1937–50, 1962–81. *The Byrd Edition* (formerly *The Collected Works*). Edited by Edmund H. Fellowes, revised and augmented by Thurston Dart, Philip Brett et al. 20 vols. London: Stainer & Bell.
Butler, Charles. 1636. *The Principles of Musick.* London. STC 4196.
Campion, Thomas. ca. 1613. *Two Bookes of Ayres.* London. STC 4547. ELS 2d ser., vols. 1 and 2.
———. ca. 1617. *The Third and Fourth Booke of Ayres.* London. STC 4548.

ELS 2d ser., vols. 10 and 11.

————. 1967. *Works.* Edited by Walter R. Davis. Garden City, N.Y.: Doubleday.

Carlton, Richard. 1601. *Madrigals to Five voyces.* London. STC 4649. EM 27.

Case, John [?]. 1586. *The Praise of Musicke.* London.

Cavendish, Michael. 1598. *14. Ayres . . . And 8. Madrigalles.* London. STC 4878. ELS 2:7. EM 36.

Child, Francis James, ed. 1965. *The English and Scottish Popular Ballads.* 5 vols. Boston, 1882–98. Reprint. New York: Dover.

Coprario, John. 1606. *Funeral Teares.* London. STC 5679. ELS 1:17.

————. 1613. *Songs of Mourning.* London, STC 4546. ELS 1:17. Words by Thomas Campion.

————. 1952. *Rules How to Compose.* Edited by Manfred Bukofzer. Los Angeles: E. E. Gottlieb.

Corkine, William. 1610. *Ayres.* London. STC 5768. ELS 2:12.

————. 1612. *The Second Booke of Ayres.* London. STC 5769. ELS 2:13.

Cutts, John P., ed. 1959. *La Musique de Scène de la Troupe de Shakespeare.* Paris: Editions du Centre National de la Recherche Scientifique.

Danyel, John. 1606. *Songs for the Lute Viol and Voice.* London. STC 6268. ELS 2:8.

Dawes, Frank, ed. 1951. *Schott's Anthology of Early Keyboard Music.* Vol. 1. *Ten Pieces by Hugh Aston and Others.* London: Schott.

Doughtie, Edward, ed. 1970. *Lyrics from English Airs 1596–1622 (LEA).* Cambridge, Mass.: Harvard University Press.

————, ed. 1985. *Liber Lilliati.* Newark: University of Delaware Press.

Dowland, John. 1597. *The First Booke of Songes or Ayres.* London, STC 7091. ELS 1:1–2.

————. 1600. *The Second Booke of Songs or Ayres.* London. STC 7095. ELS 1st ser., vols. 5 and 6.

————. 1603. *The Third and Last Booke of Songs or Aires.* London. STC 7096. ELS 1st ser., vols. 10 and 11.

————. 1612. *A Pilgrimes Solace.* London. STC 7098. ELS 1st ser., vols. 12 and 14.

Dowland, Robert. 1610. *A Musicall Banquet.* London. STC 7099. ELS 2:20.

East, Michael. 1604. *Madrigales.* London. STC 7460. EM 29.

————. 1606. *The Second set of Madrigales.* London. STC 7461. EM 30.

————. 1610. *The Third Set of Bookes.* London. STC 7462. EM 31a.

————. 1618. *The Fourth Set of Bookes.* London. STC 7463. EM 31b.

————. 1624. *The Sixt Set of Bookes.* London. STC 7466.

Elyot, Sir Thomas. 1907. *The Boke Named the Governor* (1531). London: Dent-Everyman.

Farmer, John. 1599. *The First Set of English Madrigals.* London. STC 10697. EM 8.

Farnaby, Giles. 1598. *Canzonets to Fowre Voyces.* London. STC 10700. EM 20.

Fellowes, Edmund H., ed. 1913–24, 1956–76. *The English Madrigalists* (EM; formerly *The English Madrigal School*). Revised by Thurston Dart et al. 37 vols. London: Stainer & Bell.

————. 1920–71. *The English Lute-Songs* (ELS; formerly *The English School of Lutenist Song Writers*). Revised by Thurston Dart et al. 1st ser., 19 vols.; 2d. ser., 20 vols. London: Strainer & Bell.

————, ed. 1968. *English Madrigal Verse, 1588-1632 (EMV).* 3d ed., revised by Frederick W. Sternfeld and David Greer. Oxford: Clarendon Press.

Ferrabosco, Alfonso [the younger]. 1609. *Ayres.* London. STC 10827. ELS 2:16.

Ford, Thomas. 1607. *Musicke of Sundrie Kindes.* London. STC 11166. ELS 1:3.

Frere, W. H., and **Kennedy, W. M.,** eds. 1910. *Visitation Articles and Injunctions of the Period of the Reformation.* London: Longmans, Green.

Frost, Maurice, ed. 1953. *English and Scottish Psalm and Hymn Tunes.* London: S.P.C.K. and Oxford University Press.

Gascoigne, George. 1573. *A Hundreth Sundrie Flowres.* London. STC 11635.

————. 1575. *The Posies.* London. STC 11636.

Gibbons, Orlando. 1612. *The First Set of Madrigals and Mottets.* London. STC 11826. EM 5.

Greaves, Thomas. 1604. *Songes of sundrie kindes.* London. STC 12210. ELS 2:18. EM 36.

Hilton, John. 1627. *Ayres, or, Fa Las.* London. STC 13508.

Holborne, Antony. 1597. *The Cittharn Schoole.* London. STC 13562. EM 36.

Hume, Tobias. 1605. *The First Part of Ayres.* London. STC 13958.

————. 1607. *Captaine Humes Poeticall Musicke.* London. STC 13957.

Johnson, Robert. 1961. *Ayres, Songs and Dialogues.* Edited by Ian Spink. ELS 2:17. London: Stainer & Bell.

Jones, Robert. 1600. *The First Booke of Songes or Ayres.* London. STC 14732. ELS 2:4.

————. 1601. *The Second Booke of Songs and Ayres.* London. STC 14733. ELS 2:5.

————. 1605. *Ultimum Vale.* London. STC 14738. ELS 2:6.

————. 1607. *The First Set of Madrigals.* London. STC 14737. EM 35a.

————. 1609. *A Musicall Dreame.* London. STC 14734–5. ELS 2:14.

————. 1610. *The Muses Gardin for Delights.* London. STC 14736. ELS 2:15.

Kirbye, George. 1597. *The first set of English Madrigalls.* London. STC 15010. EM 24.

Le Huray, Peter, ed. 1965. *The Treasury of English Church Music.* Vol. 2. London: Blandford.

Levins, P. 1867. *Manipulus Vocabulorum* (1570). Edited by Henry B. Wheatley. EETS, no. 27. London.

Lichfild, Henry. 1613. *The First Set of Madrigals.* London. STC 15588. EM 17.

Marenzio, Luca. 1594. *Madrigali a Sei Voci, in Un Corpo Ridotti.* Antwerp.

————. 1966. *Ten Madrigals.* Edited by Denis Arnold. London: Oxford University Press.

————. 1967. *Sämtliche Werke.* Edited by Alfred Einstein. Publikationen Älterer Musik, vol. 4, pt. 1. Hildesheim: Georg Olms.

Mason, George, and **Earsden, John.** 1618. *The Ayres that were Sung and Played at Brougham Castle.* London. STC 17601. ELS 2:18.

Maynard, John. 1611. *The XII. Wonders of the World.* London. STC 17759. ELS 1:18.

More, Sir Thomas. 1551. *Utopia* (1516). Translated by Raphe Robinson. London.

Morley, Thomas. 1593. *Canzonets . . . To Three Voyces.* London. STC 18121. EM 1.

————. 1594. *Madrigalls to Foure Voyces.* London. STC 18127. EM 2.

————. 1595. *The First Booke of Balletts To Five Voyces.* London. STC 18116. EM 4.

————. 1595. *The First Booke of Canzonets To Two Voyces.* London. STC 18119. EM 1.

————. 1597. *Canzonets . . . Celected out of the best and approved Italian Authors.* London. STC 18126.

————. 1597. *Canzonets . . . To Five and Sixe Voices.* London. STC 18126. EM 3.

————. 1597. *A Plaine and Easie Introduction to Practical Musicke.* London. STC 18133.

————. 1598. *Madrigals to five voyces. Celected out of the best approved Italian Authors.* London. STC 18129.

————. 1600. *The First Booke of Ayres.* London. STC 18115.5. ELS 1:16.

————. 1601. *Madrigales The Triumphes of Oriana.* London. STC 18130. EM 32.

Mundy, John. 1594. *Songs And Psalmes.* London. STC 18284. EM 35b.

Nashe, Thomas. 1958. *Works.* Edited by R. B. McKerrow, revised by F. P. Wilson. 5 vols. Oxford: Blackwell.

One and Fiftie Psalmes of David in English metre in *The Forme of Prayers and Ministrations . . . at Geneva.* 1557 (1556 for 1557). Geneva. STC 16561.

Peerson, Martin. 1620. *Private Musicke.* London. STC 19553.

————. 1630. *Mottects or Grave Chamber Musique.* London. STC 19552.

Pepys, Samuel. 1974. *The Diary of Samuel Pepys.* Edited by Robert Latham and William Matthews. 11 vols. London: Bell & Sons.

Pilkington, Francis. 1605. *The First Booke of Songs or Ayres.* London. STC 19922. ELS 1:7 and 15.

————. 1613. *The First Set of Madrigals and Pastorals.* London. STC 19923. EM 25.

————. 1624. *The Second Set of Madrigals, and Pastorals.* London. STC 19924. EM 26.

Puttenham, George. 1936. *The Arte of English Poesie.* Edited by Gladys Doidge Willcock and Alice Walker. Cambridge: Cambridge University Press.

Ravenscroft, Thomas. 1609. *Deuteromelia.* London. STC 20757.

————. 1609. *Pammelia.* London. STC 20759.

————. 1611. *Melismata.* London. STC 20758.

————. 1614. *A Briefe Discourse.* London. STC 20756.

Rollins, Hyder E., ed. 1924. *A Handful of Pleasant Delights.* Cambridge, Mass.: Harvard University Press.

————, ed. 1927. *The Paradise of Dainty Devices (1576–1606).* Cambridge, Mass.: Harvard University Press.

————, ed. 1931. *The Phoenix Nest.* Cambridge, Mass.: Harvard University Press.

————, ed. 1931. *A Poetical Rhapsody.* 2 vols. Cambridge, Mass.: Harvard University Press.

————, ed. 1935. *England's Helicon.* 2 vols. Cambridge, Mass.: Harvard University Press.

————, ed. 1965. *Tottel's Miscellany.* Rev. ed. 2 vols. Cambridge, Mass.: Harvard University Press.

Ronsard, Pierre. 1565. *Abbrege de l'Art Pöetique François.* Paris.

Rosseter, Philip, and Campion, Thomas. 1601. *A Booke of Ayres.* London. STC 21332. ELS 1:4, 8–9, 13.

Sabol, Andrew J., ed. 1978. *Four Hundred Songs and Dances from the Stuart Masque.* Providence: Brown University Press.

Sidney, Sir Philip. 1962. *Poems.* Edited by William A. Ringler, Jr. Oxford: Clarendon Press.

————. 1973. *Miscellaneous Prose.* Edited by Katherine Duncan-Jones and Jan van Dorsten. Oxford: Clarendon Press.

Slim, Colin, ed. 1972. *A Gift of Madrigals and Motets.* 2 vols. Chicago: University of Chicago Press.

Smith, G. Gregory, ed. 1904. *Elizabethan Critical Essays.* 2 vols. Oxford: Clarendon Press.

Spink, Ian, ed. 1971. *English Songs 1620–1660.* Musica Britannica, vol. 33. London: Stainer & Bell.

Sternfeld, Frederick W., ed. 1964. *Songs from Shakespeare's Tragedies.* London: Oxford University Press.

Stevens, Denis, ed. 1954. *The Mulliner Book* (1951). Rev. ed. Musica Britannica, vol. 1. London: Stainer & Bell.

Stevens, John, ed. 1962. *Music at the Court of Henry VIII.* Musica Britannica, vol. 18. London: Stainer & Bell.

Strunk, Oliver, ed. 1950. *Source Readings in Music History.* New York: W. W. Norton.

Surrey, Henry Howard, earl of. 1920. *Poems.* Edited by Frederick M. Padelford. Seattle: University of Washington Press.

Tallis, Thomas. 1974. *English Sacred Music.* Edited by Leonard Ellinwood, revised by Paul Doe. Early English Church Music, vol. 13. London: Stainer & Bell.

Tomkins, Thomas. 1622. *Songs Of 3. 4. 5. and 6. parts.* London. STC 24099. EM 18.

Vautor, Thomas. 1619. *The First Set: Beeing Songs of divers Ayres.* London. STC 24624. EM 34.

Virgili, Lavinio, ed. 1952. *Madrigalisti Italiani.* Rome: De Santis.

Ward, John. 1613. *The First Set of English Madrigals.* London. STC 25023. EM 19.

Warlock, Peter, ed. 1926. *Elizabethan Songs . . . for one voice . . . and four stringed instruments.* 3 vols. London: Oxford University Press.

Watson, Thomas. 1590. *The first sett, Of Italian Madrigalls Englished.* London. STC 25119.

Weelkes, Thomas. 1597. *Madrigals to 3. 4. 5. & 6. voyces.* London. STC 25205. EM 9.

———. 1598. *Ballets and Madrigals To five voyces.* London. STC 25203. EM 10.

———. 1600. *Madrigals of 5. and 6. parts.* London. STC 25206. EM 11–12.

———. 1608. *Ayeres Or Phantasticke Spirites.* London. STC 25202. EM 13.

Whythorne, Thomas. 1571. *Songes, for three, fower, and five voyces.* London. STC 25584.

———. 1927. *Oxford Choral Songs from the Old Masters,* nos. 354-65. Edited by Peter Warlock. London: Oxford University Press.

———. 1947. *Three Songs.* Edited by Manfred Bukofzer. New York: Music Press.

———. 1961. *Autobiography.* Edited by James M. Osborn. Oxford: Clarendon Press.

Wilbye, John. 1598. *The First Set of English Madrigals.* London. STC 25619. EM 6.

———. 1609. *The Second Set of Madrigales.* London. STC 25619a. EM 7.

Wyatt, Sir Thomas. 1975. *Collected Poems.* Edited by Joost Daalder. London: Oxford University Press.

Yonge, Nicholas. 1588. *Musica Transalpina.* London. STC 26094.

———. 1597. *Musica Transalpina. The Second Booke of Madrigalles.* London. STC 26095.

Youll, Henry. 1608. *Canzonets.* London. STC 26105. EM 28.

Zarlino, Gioseffo. 1983. *On the Modes.* Edited by Claude Palisca. New Haven: Yale University Press.

SECONDARY SOURCES

Alpers, Paul, ed. 1967. *Elizabethan Poetry.* New York: Oxford University Press.

Amis, Kingsley, ed. 1978. *The New Oxford Book of English Light Verse.* New York: Oxford University Press.

Andrews, H. K. 1966. *The Technique of Byrd's Vocal Polyphony.* London: Oxford University Press.

Arnold, Denis. 1965. *Marenzio.* London: Oxford University Press.

Attridge, Derek. 1974. *Well-Weighed Syllables.* Cambridge: Cambridge University Press.

————. 1982. *The Rhythms of English Poetry.* London: Longmans.

Auden, W. H., ed. 1938. *The Oxford Book of Light Verse.* London: Oxford University Press.

Auden, W. H., Greenberg, Noah, and **Kallman, Chester,** eds. 1970. *An Elizabethan Song Book.* Garden City, N.Y.: Doubleday Anchor, 1955. Reprint. New York: W. W. Norton.

Beardsley, Monroe c. 1972. "Verse and Music." In *Versification: Major Language Types,* edited by W. K. Wimsatt, 238–52. New York: Modern Language Association and New York University Press.

Bergeron, David M. 1972. *Twentieth-Century Criticism of English Masques, Pageants and Entertainments: 1588–1642.* San Antonio: Trinity University Press.

Bernstein, Leonard. 1976. *The Unanswered Question.* Cambridge, Mass.: Harvard University Press.

Booth, Mark. 1981. *The Experience of Songs.* New Haven: Yale University Press.

Bowden, William R. 1951. *The English Dramatic Lyric, 1603–1642.* New Haven: Yale University Press.

Boyd, Morrison C. 1962. *Elizabethan Music and Musical Criticism* (1940). Rev. ed. Philadelphia: University of Pennsylvania Press.

Brett, Philip. 1961–62. "The English Consort Song, 1570–1625." *Proceedings of the Royal Musical Association* 88:73–88.

————. 1964. "Edward Paston (1550–1630): a Norfolk Gentleman and his Musical Collection." *Transactions of the Cambridge Bibliographical Society* 4:51–69.

————. 1971–72. "Word-Setting in the Songs of Byrd." *Proceedings of the Royal Musical Association* 98:47–64.

————. 1972. "The Two Musical Personalities of Thomas Weelkes." *Music and Letters* 53:369–76.

————. 1979. "Words and Music in the English Renaissance: A Reconsideration." Paper read at December meeting of the Modern Language Association of America.

Bronson, Bertrand H. 1967. "Literature and Music." In *Relations of Literary Study,* edited by James Thorpe, 127–50. New York: Modern Language Association.

———. 1969. *The Ballad as Song.* Berkeley: University of California Press.

Brown, Calvin S. 1948. *Music and Literature.* Athens: University of Georgia Press.

Brown, David. 1957. "William Byrd's 1588 Volume." *Music and Letters* 38:371–77.

———. 1969. *Thomas Weelkes.* London: Faber & Faber.

———. 1974. *Wilbye.* London: Oxford University Press.

Brown, Howard M. 1964. "The Genesis of Style: The Parisian Chanson 1500–1530." In *Chanson and Madrigal 1480–1530,* edited by James Haar, 1–50. Cambridge, Mass.: Harvard University Press.

———. 1976. *Music in the Renaissance.* Englewood Cliffs, N.J.: Prentice Hall.

Bukofzer, Manfred. 1942. "Speculative Thinking in Mediaeval Music." *Speculum* 17:165–80.

Burney, Charles. 1935. *A General History of Music* (1789). Edited by Frank Mercer. 2 vols. New York: Harcourt, Brace.

Chater, James. 1981. *Luca Marenzio and the Italian Madrigal.* 2 vols. Ann Arbor: UMI Research Press.

Clinton-Baddeley, V. C. 1941. *Words for Music.* Cambridge: Cambridge University Press.

Clynes, Manfred, and Nettheim, Nigel. 1982. "The Living Quality of Music: Neurobiologic Patterns of Communicating Feeling." In *Music, Mind, and Brain: The Neuropsychology of Music,* edited by Manfred Clynes. New York: Plenum Press.

Coker, Wilson. 1972. *Music and Meaning.* New York: Free Press.

Cooke, Deryck. 1962. *The Language of Music* (1959). Reprint. London: Oxford University Press.

Cooper, Grosvenor, and Meyer, Leonard B. 1960. *The Rhythmic Structure of Music.* Chicago: University of Chicago Press.

Dart, Thurston, and Brett, Philip. 1960. "Songs by William Byrd in Manuscripts at Harvard." *Harvard Library Bulletin* 14:343–65.

Davis, Walter R. 1962. "Melodic and Poetic Structure: the Example of Campion and Dowland." *Criticism* 4:89–107.

Day, Cyrus L., and Murrie, Eleanore B. 1940. *English Song Books 1651–1702: A Bibliography.* London: Oxford University Press for the Bibliographical Society.

Dent, Edward J. 1926. "William Byrd and the Madrigal." In *Festschrift für Johannes Wolf,* 24–30. Berlin.

———. 1968. "The Sixteenth Century Madrigal." In *The Age of Humanism 1540–1630,* edited by Gerald Abraham, New Oxford History of Music, 4:33–95. London: Oxford University Press.

Dobson, E. J. 1957. *English Pronunciation 1500–1700*. 2 vols. Oxford: Clarendon Press.

Doughtie, Edward. 1965. "Words for Music: Simplicity and Complexity in the Elizabethan Air." *Rice University Studies* 51:1–12.

———. 1978. "Sibling Rivalry: Music vs. Poetry in Campion and Others." *Criticism* 20:1–16.

Duckles, Vincent. 1957. "Florid Embellishment In English Song of the Late Sixteenth and Early Seventeenth Centuries." *Annales Musicologiques* 5:329–45.

———. 1966. "The English Musical Elegy of the Late Renaissance." In *Aspects of Medieval and Renaissance Music,* edited by Jan LaRue, 134–53. New York: W. W. Norton.

Duffy, John. 1980. *The Songs and Motets of Alfonso Ferrabosco, the Younger.* Ann Arbor: UMI Research Press.

Einstein, Alfred. 1944. "The Elizabethan Madrigal and 'Musica Transalpina.'" *Music and Letters* 25:66–77.

———. 1949. *The Italian Madrigal* Translated by A. H. Krappe et al. 3 vols. Princeton: Princeton University Press.

Emslie, McDonald. 1960. "Nicholas Lanier's Innovations in English Song." *Music and Letters* 41:13–27.

Fabry, Frank J. 1964. "The Poetry of the Secular Polyphonic Vocal Forms in England (1588–1627)." Ph.D. diss., University of Texas.

———. 1970. "Sidney's Verse Adaptations to Two Sixteenth-Century Italian Art Songs." *Renaissance Quarterly* 23:237–55.

———. 1973. "Sidney's Poetry and Italian Song-Form." *English Literary Renaissance* 3:232–48.

Fellowes, Edmund H. 1948. *The English Madrigal Composers* (1921). Rev. ed. London: Oxford University Press.

Fowler, David. 1968. *A Literary History of the Popular Ballad.* Durham, N. C.: Duke University Press.

Garside, Charles, Jr. 1966. *Zwingli and the Arts.* New Haven: Yale University Press.

———. 1979. "The Origins of Calvin's Theology of Music: 1536-1543." *Transactions of the American Philosophical Society* 69, no. 2:22–29.

Gray, Walter. 1969. "Some Aspects of Word Treatment in the Music of William Byrd." *Musical Quarterly* 55:45–64.

Greer, David. 1966. "The Lute Songs of Thomas Morley." *Lute Society Journal* 8:25–37.

———. 1967. "Campion the Musician." *Lute Society Journal* 9:7-16.

———. 1967–68. "The Part-Songs of the English Lutenists." *Proceedings of the Royal Musical Association* 94:97–110.

Hartman, Charles O. 1975. "The Criticism of Song." *Centennial Review* 19:96–107.

Hawkins, Sir John. 1963. *General History of the Science and Practice of Music*

(1776). Reprint. 2 vols. New York: Dover.

Heartz, Daniel. 1972. *"Voix de ville:* Between Humanist Ideals and Musical Realities." In *Words and Music,* edited by Laurence Berman, 115–35. Cambridge, Mass.: Harvard University Department of Music.

Heninger, S. K., Jr. 1974. *Touches of Sweet Harmony: Pythagorean Cosmology and Renaissance Poetics.* San Marino, Calif.: Huntington Library.

Hollander, John. 1970. *The Untuning of the Sky.* Princeton: Princeton University Press, 1961. Reprint. New York: W. W. Norton.

———. 1974. "Music and Poetry" and "Song." In *Princeton Encyclopedia of Poetry and Poetics,* edited by Alex Preminger et al. 2d ed. Princeton: Princeton University Press.

———. 1975. *Vision and Resonance.* New York: Oxford University Press.

Hunter, G. K. 1970. "Drab and Golden Lyrics of the Renaissance." *Forms of Lyric,* edited by Reuben Brower, 1–18. English Institute Papers. New York: Columbia University Press.

Ing, Catherine. 1968. *Elizabethan Lyrics* (1951). Reprint. London: Chatto & Windus.

Ingram, R. W. 1960. "Words and Music." In *Elizabethan Poetry,* 130–49. Stratford-upon-Avon Studies, no. 2. London: Edward Arnold.

Irwin, John T. 1970. "Thomas Campion and the Musical Emblem." *Studies in English Literature* 10:121–41.

Jobling, Joan. 1978. "A Critical Study and Partial Transcription of the Two Published Collections of Thomas Whythorne." Ph.D. diss., University of Sheffield.

Johnson, Paula. 1972. *Form and Transformation in Music and Poetry of the English Renaissance.* New Haven: Yale University Press.

Jorgens, Elise Bickford. 1982. *The Well-Tun'd Word: Musical Interpretations of English Poetry 1597–1651.* Minneapolis: University of Minnesota Press.

Kastendieck, Miles M. 1963. *England's Musical Poet, Thomas Campion.* New York: Oxford University Press, 1938. Reprint. New York: Russell & Russell.

Keiler, Allan R. 1978. "Bernstein's *The Unanswered Question* and the Problem of Musical Competence." *Musical Quarterly* 44:195–222.

———. 1981. "Two Views of Musical Semiotics." In *The Sign in Music and Literature,* edited by Wendy Steiner, 138–68. Austin: University of Texas Press.

Kerman, Joseph. 1962a. *The Elizabethan Madrigal.* New York: American Musicological Society.

———. 1962b. "The Elizabethan Motet: A Study of Texts for Music." *Studies in the Renaissance* 9:237–78.

Kermode, Frank. 1949. Review of *Music and Poetry of the English Renaissance,* by Bruce Pattison. *Review of English Studies* 25:265–69.

Kivy, Peter. 1980. *The Corded Shell.* Princeton: Princeton University Press.

Kökeritz, Helge. 1953. *Shakespeare's Pronunciation*. New Haven: Yale University Press.

Langer, Susanne. 1951. *Philosophy in a New Key* (1942). 2d. ed. New York: New American Library.

———. 1953. *Feeling and Form*. New York: Scribner's.

Lebèque, Raymond. 1954. "Ronsard et la Musique." In *Musique et Poesie au XVIᵉ Siècle*, 105–19. Paris: Centre Nationale de la Recherche Scientifique.

Le Huray, Peter. 1967. *Music and the Reformation in England 1549–1660*. New York: Oxford University Press.

Lewis, C. S. 1954. *English Literature in the Sixteenth Century*. Oxford: Clarendon Press.

Long, John H. 1955–71. *Shakespeare's Use of Music*. 3 vols. Gainesville: University of Florida Press.

———. 1967. "Music for a Song in 'Damon and Pithias.'" *Music and Letters* 48:246–50.

———, ed. 1968. *Music in English Renaissance Drama*. Lexington: University of Kentucky Press.

Lowbury, Edward, Salter, Timothy, and Young, Alison. 1970. *Thomas Campion: Poet, Composer, Physician*. New York: Barnes & Noble.

Lowinsky, Edward. 1960. "Early Scores in Manuscript." *JAMS* 13:126-71.

McCoy, Richard C. 1979. *Sir Philip Sidney: Rebellion in Arcadia*. New Brunswick: Rutgers University Press.

Mace, Dean T. 1969. "Pietro Bembo and the Literary Origins of the Italian Madrigal." *Musical Quarterly* 55:65–86.

Manifold, J. S. 1956. *Music in English Drama: From Shakespeare to Purcell*. London: Rockliff.

Mazzaro, Jerome. 1970. *Transformations in the Renaissance English Lyric*. Ithaca: Cornell University Press.

Mellers, Wilfrid. 1965. *Harmonious Meeting*. London: Dobson.

Meyer, Leonard B. 1956. *Emotion and Meaning in Music*. Chicago: University of Chicago Press.

Monson, Craig. 1982. *Voices and Viols in England, 1600–1650*. Studies in Musicology, no. 55. Ann Arbor: UMI Research Press.

The New Grove Dictionary of Music and Musicians. 1980. Edited by Stanley Sadie. 20 vols. London: Macmillan.

Obertello, Alfredo. 1949. *Madrigali Italiani in Inghilterra*. Milan: Bompiani.

———. 1955. "Tecnica e Stile dei Traduttori Elisabettiani dei Madrigali Italiani." *Paideia* 10:3-20.

Ong, Walter J. 1958. *Ramus, Method, and the Decay of Dialogue*. Cambridge, Mass.: Harvard University Press.

Orgel, Stephen. 1965. *The Jonsonian Masque*. Cambridge, Mass.: Harvard University Press.

Orlov, Henry. 1981. "Toward a Semiotics of Music." In *The Sign in Music and Literature,* edited by Wendy Steiner, 131–37. Austin: University of Texas Press.

Palisca, Claude. 1960. *Girolamo Mei: Letters on Ancient and Modern Music to Vencenzo Galilei and Giovanni Bardi.* New York: American Institute of Musicology.

————. 1972. "The 'Camerata Fiorentina': A Reappraisal." *Studi musicali* 1:203–36.

Palmer, Rupert S., Jr. 1969. *Thomas Whythorne's Speech. Anglistica* vol. 16.

Pattison, Bruce. 1970. *Music and Poetry of the English Renaissance* (1948). 2d ed. London: Methuen.

Poulton, Diana. 1982. *John Dowland* (1972). 2d ed. London: Faber & Faber.

Ratcliffe, Stephen. 1981. *Campion: On Song.* London: Routledge & Kegan Paul.

Raynor, Henry. 1958a. "Framed to the Life of the Words." *Music Review* 19:261–71.

————. 1958b. "Words for Music." *Monthly Musical Record* 88:174–82.

Reese, Gustave. 1959. *Music in the Renaissance* (1954). 2d ed. New York: W. W. Norton.

Richardson, David A. 1978. "The Golden Mean in Campion's Airs." *Comparative Literature* 30:108–32.

Robinson, Ian. 1971. *Chaucer's Prosody.* Cambridge: Cambridge University Press.

Rudenstine, Neil L. 1967. *Sidney's Poetic Development.* Cambridge, Mass.: Harvard University Press.

Samson, Patricia. 1963. "Words for Music." *Southern Review* (Australia) 1:46–52.

Sanders, Ernest H. 1973. "Polyphony and Secular Monophony: Ninth Century-*c.* 1300." In *Music from the Middle Ages to the Renaissance,* edited by Frederick W. Sternfeld, 89–143. New York: Praeger.

Scher, Steven. 1982. "Literature and Music." In *Interrelations of Literature,* edited by Jean-Pierre Barricelli and Joseph Gibaldi. New York: Modern Language Association.

Seng, Peter J. 1967. *The Vocal Songs in the Plays of Shakespeare.* Cambridge, Mass.: Harvard University Press.

Shapiro, Michael. 1977. *Children of the Revels.* New York: Columbia University Press.

Shore, David R. 1981. "The *Autobiography* of Thomas Whythorne: An Early Elizabethan Context for Poetry." *Renaissance and Reformation,* n.s., 5, no. 2:72–86.

Simpson, Claude M. 1966. *The British Broadside Ballad and its Music.* New Brunswick: Rutgers University Press.

Simpson, Percy. 1943. "The Rhyming of Stressed with Unstressed Syllables in Elizabethan Verse." *Modern Language Review* 38:127–29.

Smith, Barbara Herrnstein. 1968. *Poetic Closure*. Chicago: University of Chicago Press.

Smith, Hallett. 1946. "English Metrical Psalms in the Sixteenth Century and their Literary Significance." *Huntington Library Quarterly* 9:265–66.

—————. 1952. *Elizabethan Poetry*. Cambridge, Mass.: Harvard University Press.

Smith, Michael. 1974. "English Translations and Imitations of Italian Madrigal Verse." *Journal of European Studies* 4:164–77.

Sonnino, Lee A. 1968. *A Handbook to Sixteenth Century Rhetoric*. London: Routledge & Kegan Paul.

Southworth, J. G. 1954. *Verses of Cadence*. Oxford: Blackwell.

—————. 1962. *The Prosody of Chaucer and His Followers*. Oxford: Blackwell.

Spiegel, Glenn S. 1980. "Perfecting English Meter: Sixteenth-Century Criticism and Practice." *JEGP* 79:192–209.

Spink, Ian. 1960. "English Cavalier Songs, 1620–1660." *Proceedings of the Royal Musical Association* 86:61–78.

—————. 1974. *English Song: Dowland to Purcell*. London: Batsford.

Stein, Jack M. 1971. *Poem and Music in the German Lied*. Cambridge, Mass.: Harvard University Press.

Steiner, George. 1975. *After Babel*. New York: Oxford University Press.

Stevens, Denis. 1952. *The Mulliner Book: A Commentary*. London: Stainer & Bell.

—————. 1966. *Tudor Church Music* (1961). 2d ed. New York: W. W. Norton.

Stevens, John. 1958. "The Elizabethan Madrigal: 'Perfect Marriage' or 'Uneasy Flirtation.'" *Essays and Studies* 11:17–37.

—————. 1961. *Music and Poetry in the Early Tudor Court*. London: Methuen.

—————. 1966. "Shakespeare and the Music of the Elizabethan Stage." In *Shakespeare in Music*, edited by Phyllis Hartnoll, 3–48. New York: St. Martins.

—————. 1982. *The Old Sound and the New: An Inaugural Lecture*. Cambridge: Cambridge University Press.

Temperley, Nicholas. 1979. *The Music of the English Parish Church*. 2 vols. Cambridge: Cambridge University Press.

Thompson, John. 1961. *The Founding of English Metre*. New York: Columbia University Press.

Tippet, Michael. 1970. "Conclusion." In *A History of Song*, (1960), edited by Denis Stevens, 461–66. 2d ed. New York: W. W. Norton.

Toft, Robert. 1984. "Musicke a Sister to Poetrie: Rhetorical Artifice in the Passionate Airs of John Dowland." *Early Music* 12:173–99.

Tovey, Donald. 1937. *Essays in Musical Analysis*. 6 vols. London: Oxford University Press.

Valéry, Paul. 1943. *Tel Quel*. Paris: Gallimard.

Walker, D. P. 1941–42. "Musical Humanism in the 16th and Early 17th Centuries." *Music Review* 2:1–13, 111–21, 220–27, 288–308; 3:55–71.

————. 1946. "The Aims of Baïf's *Académie de Poésie et de Musique.*" *Musica Disciplina* 1:91–100.

————. 1948. "The Influence of *Musique Mesurée à L'Antique,* Particularly on the *Airs de Cour* of the Early Seventeenth Century." *Musica Disciplina* 2:141–63.

————. 1950. "Some Aspects and Problems of *Musique Mesurée à L'Antique.*" *Musica Disciplina* 4:163–86.

————, and **Lesure, François.** 1949. "Claude Le Jeune and *Musique Mesurée.*" *Musica Disciplina* 3:151–70.

Walls, Peter. 1984. "'Music and Sweet Poetry'? Verse for English Lute Song and Continuo Song." *Music and Letters* 65:237–54.

Ward, John M. 1957. "Music for *A Handfull of pleasant delites.*" *JAMS* 10:175–80.

————. 1960. "The Lute Music of MS Royal Appendix 58." *JAMS* 13:117–25.

————. 1966. "*Joan qd John* and Other Fragments at Western Reserve University." In *Aspects of Medieval and Renaissance Music,* edited by Jan LaRue, 832–55. New York: W. W. Norton.

————. 1970. "Barley's Songs Without Words." *Lute Society Journal* 12:5–22.

————. 1977. "A Dowland Miscellany." *Journal of the Lute Society of America* 10.

Warlock, Peter. 1925. *Thomas Whythorne, An Unknown Elizabethan Composer.* London: Oxford University Press.

Weiner, Seth. 1981. "Renaissance Prosodic Thought as a Branch of 'Musica Speculativa.'" Ph.D. diss., Princeton University.

Wells, Robin Headlam. 1984. "The Ladder of Love: Verbal and Musical Rhetoric in the Elizabethan Lute-song." *Early Music* 12:173–99.

Winn, James A. 1981. *Unsuspected Eloquence.* New Haven: Yale University Press.

Winters, Yvor. 1939. "The 16th Century Lyric in England." *Poetry* 53:258–72, 320–35; 54:35–51.

Woodfill, Walter L. 1953. *Musicians in English Society from Elizabeth to Charles I.* Princeton: Princeton University Press.

Woods, Susanne. 1985. *Natural Emphasis: English Versification From Chaucer to Dryden.* San Marino, Calif.: Huntington Library.

Yates, Frances A. 1947. *French Academies of the Sixteenth Century.* London: Warburg Institute.

Zuckerkandl, Victor. 1956. *Sound and Symbol.* Translated by Willard Trask. Bollingen Series, vol. 44, pt. 1. New York: Pantheon.

————. 1973. *Man the Musician.* Translated by Norbert Guterman. Bollingen Series, vol. 44, pt. 2. Princeton: Princeton University Press.

Index